ROUTLEDGE LIBRARY EDITIONS: WW2

Volume 36

US WARTIME AID TO BRITAIN 1940–1946

US WARTIME AID TO BRITAIN
1940–1946

ALAN P. DOBSON

Routledge
Taylor & Francis Group

LONDON AND NEW YORK

First published in 1986 by Croom Helm Ltd

This edition first published in 2022
by Routledge
2 Park Square, Milton Park, Abingdon, Oxon OX14 4RN

and by Routledge
605 Third Avenue, New York, NY 10158

Routledge is an imprint of the Taylor & Francis Group, an informa business

© 1986 Alan P. Dobson

All rights reserved. No part of this book may be reprinted or reproduced or utilised in any form or by any electronic, mechanical, or other means, now known or hereafter invented, including photocopying and recording, or in any information storage or retrieval system, without permission in writing from the publishers.

Trademark notice: Product or corporate names may be trademarks or registered trademarks, and are used only for identification and explanation without intent to infringe.

British Library Cataloguing in Publication Data
A catalogue record for this book is available from the British Library

ISBN: 978-1-03-201217-9 (Set)
ISBN: 978-1-00-319367-8 (Set) (ebk)
ISBN: 978-1-03-202978-8 (Volume 36) (hbk)
ISBN: 978-1-03-202981-8 (Volume 36) (pbk)
ISBN: 978-1-00-318611-3 (Volume 36) (ebk)

DOI: 10.4324/9781003186113

Publisher's Note
The publisher has gone to great lengths to ensure the quality of this reprint but points out that some imperfections in the original copies may be apparent.

Disclaimer
The publisher has made every effort to trace copyright holders and would welcome correspondence from those they have been unable to trace.

US Wartime Aid to Britain 1940-1946

Alan P. Dobson

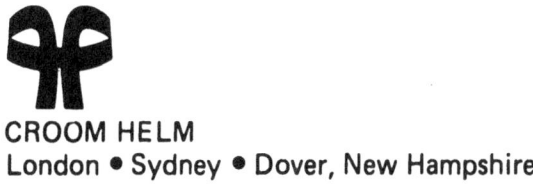
CROOM HELM
London • Sydney • Dover, New Hampshire

©1986 Alan P. Dobson
Croom Helm Ltd, Provident House, Burrell Row,
Beckenham, Kent BR3 1AT
Croom Helm Australia Pty Ltd, Suite 4, 6th Floor,
64-76 Kippax Street, Surry Hills, NSW 2010, Australia

British Library Cataloguing in Publication Data

Dobson, Alan P.
   U.S. wartime aid to Britain 1940-1946.
   1. Lend-lease operations (1941-1945)
   2. Great Britain – Economic policy – 1918-1945
   3. Great Britain – Economic policy – 1945-
   I. Title
   940.53'1   D753.2.G7

ISBN 0-7099-0893-8

Printed and bound in Great Britain by Mackays of Chatham Ltd, Kent

CONTENTS

Acknowledgements

	INTRODUCTION	1
1.	THE SUPPLY PROBLEM AND ITS SOLUTION	14
2.	TRADE TALKS AND LEND-LEASE CONSIDERATION	35
3.	THE ATLANTIC CHARTER AND LEND LEASE	62
4.	THE WHEAT TALKS AND THE MUTUAL AID AGREEMENT	93
5.	RESERVES EXPORTS AND RECIPROCAL AID	126
6.	LEND-LEASE TAKE-OUTS AND EXPORT RESTRICTIONS	159
7.	STAGE II LEND-LEASE AND THE QUEBEC CONFERENCE	185
8.	CONCLUSION	216
	SOURCES AND SELECT BIBLIOGRAPHY	229
	INDEX	234

I DEDICATE THIS BOOK

TO MY PARENTS

Acknowledgements

This book developed out of part of my doctoral thesis which I began in 1973; along the way from then until now I have received financial assistance for my research from the following, all of whom, or which, I most gratefully thank: the Social Science Research Council (as it was known in the early 1970s) for a two year scholarship for my doctoral research; the Durham University Graduate Society and Department of Politics, both of which provided help and part-time employment for me; U.C. Swansea and its fieldwork and research fund; and finally, the British Academy which granted me £1,500 in 1981 enabling me to research archives in the US.

I would also like to thank Dr. David Manning (Durham), Professor Peter Calvert (Soton.), Professor W. H. Greenleaf (Swansea), and Professor Warren Kimball (Rutgers) for supporting me in my academic career both in intellectual and practical matters. Most of all, however, I shall always be indebted to Charles Reynolds of the Department of Politics in Durham; he first encouraged me to consider pursuing an academic career, and then later supervised my doctoral thesis. I taught myself to be a historian, but he helped to show me what history is.

Although the book was a long time incubating, in the end I wrote it in just over six months. I was greatly encouraged during that period by my friend Steve Short, who read the manuscript and corrected my punctuation, grammar and syntax. I envy his ability to express himself in the written medium of English, and I am deeply grateful for all the help he gave me. One of the more amusing errors he corrected was my claim that Ambassador Winant 'sent a garbled version of the Cabinet to Washington'!!

Once the manuscript was completed it was typed out by Pat Yates who has worked incredibly hard to meet deadlines, and always did so with a will and with good humour; my thanks go to her also.

Finally, I would like to thank my wife Bev. for tolerating my moods, and Becky and Jessie for being patient, reasonably quiet, and for not touching Daddy's papers while he was writing his story.

As for the story itself, it is not really 'mine', I just found it in the various archives I worked in, nevertheless, I do of course take full responsibility for how it appears here.

INTRODUCTION

'With your relations eat and drink,
but do no business.'
An old Levantine proverb.[1]

Britain and the US had engaged in normal business relations ever since 1783, with only occasional interruptions in the nineteenth century because of international and civil wars. In the twentieth century war had a different effect from what had gone before. It brought the two countries together as allies, which resulted in increased economic activity, cooperation and interdependence, but in the Second World War it also fostered the idea of a family relationship. Two of the most impressive achievements of the Second World War were the integration of Anglo-American efforts and the time and resources the two allies devoted to wartime and postwar economic affairs. The number and scope of the topics which fall into the latter category is staggering. They range from aviation rights to long-term meat contracts, from the International Monetary Fund to the international sale of wheat, from the abortive International Trade Organisation to Lend-Lease and the vast array of economic issues which it subsumed.

Lend-Lease was the linchpin of the Anglo-American economic relationship during the war. According to the most authoritative estimate Britain received $27 billion-worth of Lend-Lease aid from the US, without cash payments, and Britain in her turn provided America with $6 billion-worth of Reverse Lend-Lease[2]. This was at a time when the official exchange rate was four dollars to the pound, when twelve Shredded Wheat cost just over three pence (8d.) and petrol just under ten pence (1s.11d.) per gallon[3]. Ironically, although there were economic disputes before the Second World War, it was during this period, when the two countries were most intimately allied, and the idea of a family relationship between the two English speaking

Introduction

countries was at its height, that the old Levantine proverb became most pertinent.

The war years witnessed an intensification of the economic problems which had existed prior to the war, and the emergence of a broad spectrum of new and intractable ones. They were not differences between strangers which might flare up at a chance encounter and then gradually dissolve and die by neglect. The difficulties were continually focused in the minds of members of each administration by the sustained contact, cooperation and discussion required by the fight against the Axis, and by their hopes for the reconstitution of the international economy. The demands of total war, the dire circumstances of Britain in 1940 and hopes for the future forced Britain and the US to ignore the admonition of the old Levantine proverb and establish a close economic relationship that paralleled their growing political, military and familial ties.

Lend-Lease in many ways was the most successful point of contact in the Anglo-American economic special relationship, but it also generated some of the most bitter disputes. The arguments which arose had wide ranging implications and were both symptomatic and illustrative of more general conflicts between British and American economic interests. Thus the story of American wartime aid to Britain through Lend-Lease has a rather broader scope than one might first imagine. It involves the story of how both countries jostled for positions they believed would be beneficial for them in the postwar world economy, as well as an account of the political decisions made concerning the close wartime interaction of the two national economies. In order to understand the ferocity with which the British and Americans bargained and argued with each other during the life of Lend-Lease, it is firstly necessary to explain the existence in 1939 of broad areas of Anglo-American economic conflict, and some of the implications the outbreak of war had for their economic relations.

From the repeal of the Corn Laws in 1846 to the introduction of the Ottawa system of Imperial Preference in 1932, Britain was the exemplar of free trade. For much of this time British industry led the world and Britain prospered under a trade doctrine which insisted on free and open access to raw materials and markets. One of the consequences of this was that British economic prosperity became heavily dependent upon international trade, and even

Introduction

when it became clear that many of her industries had become vulnerable to foreign competition successive British governments were reluctant to upset the free-trade system from which they had so clearly benefited in the past. It was not until the end of the 1920s that a political coalition began to emerge which seriously challenged the efficacy of untrammelled *laissez-faire* . In the light of a substantial decline in Britain's share of the world export market from around fourteen per cent to under eleven per cent during the period 1913 to 1929 [4], and because of the onset of the Depression, Britain moved towards protectionism. The government decided to take defensive measures and to try to sustain Britain's level of trade by consolidating links with the Commonwealth and Empire. At Ottawa in 1932 a system of intra-imperial tariff preference was established[5]. This was the first instance of substantial peacetime protectionism since 1846. The dominant political forces which grew up in support of Imperial Preference constituted a rather unholy alliance of imperialists such as Leopold Amery and Beaverbrook, members of the Labour Party who wanted to insulate Britain from the worst vagaries of the capitalist international economy and, later, a growing band of pragmatists. The pragmatists saw imperial economic relations as a means of encouraging postwar trade and as a possible alternative to cooperation with the US if American policies turned out to be unacceptable. Imperial economic arrangements and the political factions associated with them had a major impact upon Anglo-American economic relations during the war.

Britain's departure from the canons of international free trade would not have had such an impact upon Anglo-American relations if it had not been for Cordell Hull. The US had practised a policy of protectionism throughout her history. In 1930 the Hawley-Smoot Act raised American tariffs to new heights. Thus it would have been rather difficult for the US to complain of British protectionism had it not been for the arrival of Hull as President Roosevelt's Secretary of State. Hull was strongly convinced of the benefits of free trade and this became one of the cornerstones of State Department policy. Hull vehemently attacked Britain's preferential tariff system, which placed higher charges on US imports into Britain than on those from empire sources, not only because it was protectionist, but more importantly because it was discriminatory and might set an influential

Introduction

precedent for other countries. Hull believed such an eventuality would seriously damage American interests, for he saw international free trade as an antidote to war and as a means to universal prosperity, as well as enabling the US to export excess agricultural and manufactured goods.

The problem of agricultural surpluses was a long-standing one and Hull was joined by Henry Wallace, Roosevelt's first term Secretary of Agriculture and later Vice President, in his hopes for solving the problem through increased exports, though as we shall see Wallace and his successor at the Department of Agriculture, Claude Wickard, were more concerned with expanding exports than with any doctrinal commitment to *laissez-faire*. On the industrial side, once the magnitude of the explosive increase in America's industrial capacity was grasped, support for Hull's free trade ideas mounted, both within the government and in the business community, as a means to facilitate the export of excess American production. Britain was widely seen as the main obstacle to a freer international economy because of her imperial trade arrangements (and later her sterling controls) because of the major role she played in the international economy and because of the example she set others. It seemed to Hull and his followers that at the very point in history that America needed to abandon her protectionist policies and enter world export markets in a really big way Britain was turning away from free trade, was busy erecting barriers and controls, and setting a precedent other countries would probably follow.

In 1934 Hull began the task of trying to turn the protectionist tide by successfully guiding the Reciprocal Trade Agreements Act through Congress which enabled the executive branch of government to reduce existing tariffs by up to fifty per cent for reciprocal benefits from other countries. In 1938 the act bore fruit with Britain in the form of the Anglo-American Trade Agreement[6], but the advantages so gained by Hull were short lived. Once war broke out the war exemption clause was invoked and Britain began to intensify controls over her economy.

The inter-war story of Anglo-American monetary and financial relations was just as full, if not fuller, of differences and recriminations. Britain became increasingly aware after the First World War of her relative decline as an industrial power. Particularly, by comparison with the US, her natural

Introduction

resources, and even her manufacturing base, seemed slender. Understandably, the British resented both their loss of economic supremacy and the rise of the US, and perhaps this was most acutely felt, and most obvious, in the field of finance. It did not go unnoticed in London that while Britain emerged from the Great War saddled with debts to the US, her Johnny-come-lately ally had undergone a transformation during the war from debtor nation to the world's leading creditor. In the US the attitude towards the Great War was rather different. There soon grew up a school of highly influential revisionist historians who argued that Britain and France had duped the US into fighting and paying for a war on their behalf, and had then created an unjust peace at Versailles[7]. They had torn President Wilson's principles to shreds, imposed punitive reparations on Germany and ensured, as Keynes had so brilliantly explained[8], that economic chaos would ensue. When America tried to salvage something from the economic mess in Europe by encouraging lending to Germany and by revising her reparations obligations through the Dawes and Young plans, in 1924 and 1929 respectively, the European response seemed to be yet another slap in the face. Europe and Britain began to move down the road of protectionism and economic discrimination, and later defaulted on their war debts to the US. A direct consequence of this was the Debt Default Act of 1934, sponsored by the arch-isolationist Hiram Johnson, which prohibited America from extending loans to, or buying bonds from, defaulters. There was also a widespread determination not to become involved again in European dynastic squabbles. The Neutrality Law, passed in 1935, proscribed arms sales to belligerents and forbade the use of American shipping in the trade of war supplies. By 1939 there was little sympathy in America for the cost Britain had had to pay in human and economic terms during the Great War [9].

Another aspect of the monetary and financial side of the economic relationship between the US and Britain was the growth of the idea of responsibly controlled capitalism within the Roosevelt Administration. Hull, in many ways was the odd one out in Washington with his commitment to free trade. A much more prevalent attitude was a mild form of domestic and international *dirigisme* , with the former, spiced with no small element of economic nationalism, taking precedence over the latter. This was only too apparent at the London Economic

Introduction

Conference in 1933 when Roosevelt torpedoed British attempts to stabilise the international money markets by announcing that: 'The sound internal economic system of a nation is a greater factor in its well-being than the price of its currency'[10]. He refused to allow the US to become a party to the stabilisation plan. The Roosevelt Administration turned away from international cooperation to concentrate on reorganising the US domestic economy in the conviction that recovery would have to come there first. Hull's internationalism was understandably affronted by this and the incident gave an early indication of different attitudes within Roosevelt's Government, which were to complicate life greatly for the British during the war.

One of the leading exponents of responsible controls for capitalism was Henry Morgenthau, who was appointed Secretary of the US Treasury on 17 November 1933. Morgenthau, and his senior advisers such as Harry Dexter White, Bell, Foley, Bernstein and Oscar Cox, were all committed to the idea of government controls to ensure that capitalists did not behave irresponsibly in the future and cause a repeat of the Depression. As the years passed Morgenthau and White realised that America's domestic economic stability also depended upon the stability of the international monetary system. The Treasury Secretary became convinced that financial and monetary power had to be taken away from Wall Street, and more particularly from the 'City' in London, and placed in the responsible hands of Henry Morgenthau and his colleagues. This necessarily involved a paramount position for the dollar, which was to be the medium through which control was to be exercised, and a concomitant reduction in the role of sterling to the extent that it, and by implication the British Government, would be highly constrained in the type of monetary policies they could pursue. Morgenthau was not anti-British, indeed he was one of the leading advocates of aid to Britain, but he was opposed to British international monetary and financial policies and he was determined to place the US and the dollar firmly in the driving seat in this area.

Neither the State Department nor the US Treasury wanted Britain to be so strong economically that she could act contrary to American economic interests, but it was difficult to strike a balance between economic unviability and British economic independence from the US. This problem was

Introduction

compounded by a clash of tactics resulting from the different emphases the departments placed upon free trade and the control of the international monetary system. The Treasury wanted severe restrictions on the level of British gold and dollar reserves to ensure a controlling voice for America and the dollar in the international monetary sphere; the State Department believed that if Britain was starved of reserves to the extent desired by the Treasury then this would undermine Britain's ability to adopt free trade policies after the war, thus invalidating all the hard work done by the State Department to pressurise Britain into committing herself to postwar policies of economic de-control. The results of all this were attacks on two fronts upon what the British perceived to be their economic interests. This two-pronged attack, and the triangular relationship between London, the State Department and the US Treasury, supplies some of the main themes for this story, though of course to suggest that there were only two centres of policy making in Washington is an over-simplification.

A number of people concerned with economic policy-making had different reasons and goals from those which motivated Hull and Morgenthau. Some simply wanted to promote American economic interests and paid little heed to the international consequences - Wallace and Wickard, for example, in the 1941-42 Wheat Talks. There was also a large amount of Anglophobia in Washington, much of it emanating from Capitol Hill, but it was also present in the Roosevelt Administration and when combined with economic nationalism had some impact upon relations with Britain. Notable instances of men with this kind of disposition include Leo Crowley, the Foreign Economic Administrator 1943-45, Adolf Berle and Breckinridge Long of the State Department, and H. L. Whitney of the Foreign Economic Administration (FEA) who played an important part in the operation of restrictions over British commercial exports imposed under the auspices of Lend-Lease. On many occasions such views were counter-balanced by Anglophiles such as Acheson and Stettinius in the State Department, and Bernhard Knollenberg and Charles Denby in the FEA, but as the war progressed hard-liners on policy towards the British began to gain the upper hand.

While London was at one of the apices of the triangle which included the State Department and the US Treasury, this should not be taken to mean that a unanimous view on economic policy prevailed in His

Introduction

Majesty's Government. A wide variety of views existed which developed and changed as the war progressed: however, the British Government was more successful than the American containing such views within the formal decision-making process. The majority of ministers in London agreed in principle with American views concerning freer trade and international agreement to stabilise monetary exchange rates, and wished to open up access to raw materials, international communications and investment opportunities in an orderly way. They believed that such policies, pursued in cooperation with the US, would promote Britain's interests. The difference between this group, which might be aptly described as liberal pragmatists, and the Americans was the means of achieving this common goal. As the war progressed, and Britain's economic position deteriorated, there was increasing concern over Britain's ability to compete with the US immediately the war ended. The solution was seen in terms of a transitional period for Britain and various safeguards for her in the international agreements which were under wartime discussion with America. For example, in the talks which resulted in the establishment of the International Monetary Fund (IMF), one of the main goals of the British Cabinet and Maynard Keynes was to secure more flexibility than the Americans wanted for exchange rate adjustments in the immediate postwar period.

The large group which made up the category which I have called liberal pragmatists had differences of attitude within itself towards the Americans. The Board of Trade, the Economic Section of the War Cabinet Secretariat, and Lord Cherwell - who was Churchill's close friend - along with 'S Branch' which he had helped to set up and which advised the Prime Minister on economic and scientific matters were well disposed, on the whole, towards Hull and free trade. At the same time they disliked Morgenthau's policies, which weakened Britain's finances and reduced her ability to undertake free trade at the end of the war. Sir Frederick Leith-Ross of the Ministry of Economic Warfare and Richard Law of the Foreign Office, who became very important in economic policy-making in the latter part of the war, were highly pro-American, though this is not to say that they lost sight of British interests. Nigel Ronald, FO Counsellor and adviser on economic matters, was less sanguine about American policies. Successive Chancellors of the Exchequer Kingsley Wood, Sir John

Introduction

Anderson and Hugh Dalton were even more sceptical and suspicious. The first, as a party stalwart, had the additional concern that if the government made too many concessions, particularly on Imperial Preference, this would have a divisive effect upon the Conservative Party.

Outside the group of pragmatists the strongest opposition to American economic policies came from imperialists such as Leopold Amery, Lord Cranborne and Beaverbrook, and from the Labour Party which had its own ideas about domestic economic dirigisme. In the early part of the war Arthur Greenwood, Minister Without Portfolio was the most effective Labour Party opponent of American policies. Both the left and the imperialists suspected American motives and wanted to insulate Britain from US economic influences as far as possible, though as we shall see for rather different reasons.

One final opponent of America's economic goals needs to be mentioned: the Minister of Agriculture and Fisheries, R. S. Hudson. Britain was the world's main purchaser of agricultural produce. Wheat was her largest single import item. America was the world's main surplus producer of food. The obvious thing to do was to bring the two together and, indeed, for many years Britain was a major customer of the US. In the inter-war years, however, an idea had grown up in Britain that for strategic reasons she should try to diminish her dependence upon foreign food supplies by encouraging home production. Needless to say, this idea became even more popular with the onset of the Second World War. In addition to increased home production, Imperial Preference, which shifted British purchases away from the US to the Dominions, and wartime controls to conserve dollars also reduced British imports of American agricultural products. These factors taken together sowed the seed of a serious dispute between the two countries. The Wheat Negotiations, 1941-42, which were the first wartime attempt to deal explicitly with this problem, turned Hudson violently against US economic policies and his opposition was to have major consequences. While he remained Minister of Agriculture, no Conservative led government could take his opposition to American policies lightly, because of the electoral dependence of the party upon rural and farming interests for which Hudson was the main political representative.

Clearly, then, while Britain and the US entered into a collaborative venture in the Second World War

Introduction

unprecedented in history, at the same time there was great potential for argument and conflict in the economic sphere. On trade, monetary, raw material and agricultural policies there were serious and substantial differences between the two nations. The simple fact was that with Germany out of the equation of international economic relations Britain and the US were the two great economic rivals of the world, or at least so it seemed in the 1940s. Conflict was going to be difficult to avoid, particularly since the wartime collaboration occurred at a time when Britain was in economic retreat and America was on the verge of advancing into the world economy. The war accelerated both those trends. Among a great many other things the war was about the clash of the economic new and the economic old; the economic defensive versus the economic aggressive.

The main worry and preoccupation of the British Government during the war, strategic matters apart, was the prospect of a huge adverse balance of payments after the war. We shall have occasion to consider why this was so later, but for the moment suffice it to say that unless this fact is constantly borne in mind it is not possible to understand the actions and policies of British ministers and officials. When Britain ran out of money towards the end of 1940 Lend-Lease, devised to solve Britain's supply problem, also clouded the balance-of-payments issue, putting it into a kind of suspended animation for the duration of the war, though as we shall see, not putting British minds at rest concerning Britain's lack of reserves and her future prospects. There were no cash payments involved in Lend-Lease, hence the suspension of the balance of payments problem, but there was an equivalent of what the law of contract calls consideration. Firstly, in September 1941, the British agreed that the level of British commercial exports should be at the irreducible minimum necessary for the successful prosecution of the war[11]. Secondly, in February 1942, the State Department extracted a commitment, albeit a rather equivocal one, from Britain in the Mutual Aid Agreement to cooperate with the US in the creation of an open, free-trade, world economy[12]. The British agreed with great reluctance to this. They already doubted the ability of the British economy to withstand the icy blast of economic competition from the US after the war. Things, however, were about to get much worse.

Introduction

After the US entered the war the British thought that the harsh terms controlling Britain's commercial export trade, and American pressure tactics such as those used in the Lend-Lease Consideration Talks, which led to the Mutual Aid Agreement, could no longer be justified and should be abandoned. These hopes were strengthened by the talk of pooling resources for the war effort and equality of sacrifice, but London was to be rudely disappointed. Lend-Lease was soon used by Morgenthau, later aided and abetted by Crowley and his FEA, to limit the accumulation of gold and dollar reserves by Britain and to intensify the restrictions on her export trade. These policies not only weakened Britain's general economic position, they also diminished the likelihood of Britain being able to carry out the commitment to freer trade she had given the State Department. This, in its turn, revived the antagonism between Hull and his acolytes on the one hand and London on the other.
    The British argued that the Lend-Lease Agreement should be construed in a broad way to compensate Britain for her wartime sacrifices for the common good and to allow her to build up sufficient reserves to provide her with an adequate base for the eventual return to a peacetime economy. The US Treasury and the FEA disagreed. Part of the problem was the different contributions the two countries made to the war effort. Britain thought her lone stand from 1940 to December 1941, her liquidation of overseas assets and her loss of export markets should all be taken into account. Furthermore, until D-day Britain and the Commonwealth had more men under arms than the US, and throughout the war the UK was more highly mobilised for war production. The relative economic cost of the war to Britain was also much higher and more damaging than it was in the US; indeed, the US flourished economically during the war years. Morgenthau and Crowley saw things in a rather different perspective. They were sensitive to congressional criticisms and saw the larger gross American economic contribution to the war effort as more salient than the economic burdens Britain had had to undertake and her losses of blood, sweat and tears. The crucial factor was that Britain and the US were long standing rivals in the economic field and there was a natural disposition on both sides not to recognise the cogency of the arguments of the other, though Morgenthau did become more helpful to

Introduction

Britain after the IMF conference at Bretton Woods in 1944, which appeared to achieve many of his goals in the international monetary field. Britain and the US might have embarked upon a joint military and economic venture, but they still had their own economic interests to nurture. In the pages which follow I have tried to trace the story of the politics of Anglo-American economic cooperation and conflict within the context of Lend-Lease. This introduction is a series of generalisations about the main problems which emerged and the positions which were held by various groups and individuals in London and Washington, which will be amplified in the main body of the book. During the period of the narrative, those positions, and the reasoning behind them, developed and changed. Such detail can only be assimilated properly as the historical account unfolds; nevertheless, an overview is useful and I hope this introduction has indicated one.

NOTES

1. Taken from, Lord Hankey, *Diplomacy by Conference*, (Ernest Benn, London, 1946), p.151.
2. R.G.D. Allen, 'Mutual Aid Between the US and the British Empire', *Journal of the Royal Statistical Society*, **109** (1946), p.245.
3. 'The Way We Were', *1945 Daily Mail Pictorial History of Our Times*, **1** (Phoebus Publishing Company, 1975), pp.64-65: N.B. the precise dollar/sterling exchange rate was 4.03:1.
4. S. Pollard, *The Development of the British Economy 1914-1967* (Edward Arnold, London, 1973), p.188.
5. For a fuller account of British inter-war imperial economic policy see: I.M. Drumond, *Imperial Economic Policy 1917-1939* (Allen and Unwin, London, 1974).
6. Cmd.5882, 'Anglo-American Trade Agreement', 1938.
7. W.I. Cohen, *The American Revisionists - The Lessons of Intervention in World War I* (University of Chicago Press, 1967).
8. J.M. Keynes, *The Economic Consequences of the Peace* (Macmillan, London, 1920).
9. A.A. Offner, *The Origins of the Second World War: American Foreign Policy and World Politics 1917-1941* (Praeger, New York, 1976).
10. Quoted from H.B. Hinton, *Cordell Hull* (Hurst and Blackett, London, 1941), p.158.

Introduction

11. Cmd.6311, 'The Export White Paper', 10 Sept. 1941.
12. For the text of the Consideration, or The Mutual Aid Agreement as it was formally called, see: <u>A Decade of American Foreign Policy, Basic Documents 1941-49</u> (US Government Printing Office, Washington, 1950); and Cmd.6341, 'Principles Applying to Mutual Aid', 23 Feb. 1942.

Chapter One

THE SUPPLY PROBLEM AND ITS SOLUTION

On 7 December 1940, one year to the day before the Japanese attack on Pearl Harbor and America's entry into the war, Churchill wrote to Roosevelt, 'The moment approaches when we shall no longer be able to pay cash for shipping and other supplies'[1]. Fifteen months of war were about to bankrupt Britain.

There were three crucial problems concerning Britain's supply programme during 1939 and 1940. Firstly, Britain had been woefully unprepared for war; she could only offer four army divisions to France in September, 1939. Even the RAF, on which many of Britain's rearmament efforts had been expended, had only half as many bombers as the Luftwaffe[2]. Britain urgently needed supplies of arms and material, and as the months of war passed it became clear that the problem was not solely one of a lack of preparedness, but also of a general inability on the part of the economy to meet Britain's war requirements. Secondly, the British Government knew that German U-boat attacks upon shipping, bringing food, raw materials and equipment to the UK, would hinder Britain's war production, threaten the British people with severe privation and might possibly do worse. Thirdly, while supplies from the US, including destroyers, were seen as a potential solution to the first two problems, the American Neutrality Law constituted an obstacle which would have to be surmounted before the agricultural and industrial capacity of the US could be fully drawn upon by Britain.

President Roosevelt and Secretary of State Hull, knowing that France and Britain would need American assistance against Germany, wanted to amend the Neutrality Law: as early as May 1939, they had begun a campaign in Washington to change

The Supply Problem and its Solution

isolationist sentiment and repeal the embargo on arms sales to belligerents; however, Isolationists in Congress, led by Senator Borah of Idaho, refused to be moved. Hull and Roosevelt were angry, but as the Vice President, John Nance Garner, commented to the President in a crucial meeting with Borah in mid July, '"Well, Captain, we may as well face the facts. You haven't got the votes, and that's all there is to it"'[3]. Four months later the story was different. The German blitzkrieg in Poland and a new initiative by Roosevelt changed the balance of Congress. Roosevelt offered the Isolationists a deal: the administration would support proposals to exclude all American shipping from the war zones in exchange for an amendment to the Neutrality Law, which would allow cash-and-carry arms sales to belligerents. This was far from being an even-handed proposal from Germany's point of view, for it clearly discriminated in favour of Britain and France since they had the naval power and the merchant shipping which would allow them to take advantage of this law. Despite the obvious way the proposal favoured France and Britain, both houses of Congress accepted it by large majorities in early November. Public opinion had shifted since July and the situation in Europe was more critical; nevertheless, the rump of the Isolationists was angry. One of their leaders, the Republican senator Arthur Vandenberg, entered in his diary, 'In the name of "democracy" we have taken the first step, once more, into Europe's "power politics"...What "suckers" our emotions make of us'[4]. The President had got his way but the Isolationists might prevent him from consolidating and carrying public opinion with him in his attempts to help France and Britain. He did not want to be a victim of the kind of national disillusionment that had occurred after President Wilson had taken America into the First World War, and he was determined to build his bridges more carefully. This meant moving cautiously down the road which first led to 'all aid short of war' and only then, if perhaps inevitably, to war itself.

During the winter of 1939/40 some $50 million of arms were bought from the US by France and Britain and as the flow of supplies from America increased the problem of paying cash for them became more acute. The British Government tried to overcome its dollar shortage in two ways. Firstly, during the first twelve months of the war, the government took a succession of measures to bring

The Supply Problem and its Solution

sterling, imports and exports under stricter control[5]. Dollars were conserved for essential purchases by prohibiting certain imports from the US and by switching from the US to other sources of supply for others, though in some cases these sources were more expensive, but the overriding consideration was that they could be bought for sterling or soft currencies. The second tactic was an export drive to earn more dollars.

British economic controls and the intensification of discrimination deprived many American agricultural producers of their markets, and Britain's export drive led to increased tension in third markets between British and American manufacturers: this was particularly so in Latin America. These developments aroused anti-British sentiment in a number of influential groups in the US, some of which were not normally Anglophobic and the President of the Board of Trade, Oliver Stanley, was soon receiving complaints from Washington. Cordell Hull, although he had pressed for the cash-and-carry policy, was unwilling to accept that it was economically and militarily necessary for the British government to control its dollar expenditures in every way it could in order to optimise their usefulness to the war effort. His immediate reaction to the intensification of Britain's economic controls was to speak out strongly against them on behalf of American exporters. On 22 January he protested to Stanley that,

> there is a steadily increasing feeling in this country that American and other interests are being severely injured by discriminations and unnecessary restrictions, the effects of which will extend into peacetime, perhaps permanently, to the detriment of American interests;[6]

The spectre of a world economy closed to American exports and investment, and denying America raw materials, manifested itself vividly in Hull's mind. Rather interestingly, Hull's vision of an ideal world economy was diametrically opposed to the view held by many politicians of the left, and expounded most notably by Lenin in 'Imperialism, The Highest Stage of Capitalism'[7]. Hull believed free-trade and an open world economy dove-tailed with peace and did not (as Lenin had argued) result in aggravated

The Supply Problem and its Solution

competition leading to war. He also believed that it was economic autarky, discrimination and controls [whether of the Soviet, Nazi, or any other variety] which led to war, and the Second World War seemed very much to him to confirm these views[8].

The Americans continued to express concern in the months that followed and they made a series of representations to the British at various official levels[9]. The British, unfortunately, were too preoccupied with war matters to deal effectively with the trade crisis brewing with the US. Oliver Stanley was disturbed by the complaints, but he found it difficult to see what positive action he could take to placate the Americans given the war situation. Some members of the British Government hoped that the American farm lobby would pressurise Roosevelt and Congress into emasculating the Johnson Act, thus enabling American farm produce to be shipped to Britain on credit and de-fusing most of the tension in Anglo-American trade relations. These hopes were never fulfilled because of Roosevelt's fear of giving the Isolationists more ammunition with which to attack the administration and with which to turn public opinion against it. As the trade situation continued to deteriorate the State Department Executive Committee on Commercial Policy (ECCP) gave more thought to the problem of US exports to Britain. The situation of American agricultural surpluses was becoming acute but, as Henry Grady (Chairman of the ECCP) noted, the problems involved were substantial and not simply attributable to British waywardness[10]. Grady acknowledged that the international shortage of dollars was not only the fault of foreigners; American policies were also partly to blame, and he suggested a number of ways the US might remedy the situation. While Grady sought to put the trade issue in perspective, which involved spreading the burden of responsibility for America's agricultural surplus problem, he also felt obliged to hand a strong letter of complaint to the British Embassy, on 4 May, because of mounting criticism in the US of British economic policies. Herbert Feis, an Anglophile and the State Department's adviser on international economic policy, expressed reservations about the implied threat in the last sentence of the note, but it was sent off unaltered. It ran as follows:

The Supply Problem and its Solution

> In view of the sharp curtailment of American exports to the United Kingdom and the British colonies of products included in the trade agreement [i.e. 1938 Anglo-American Trade Agreement], and the depreciation of British currency, the maintenance of the trade agreement is becoming increasingly more difficult.[11]

Throughout the summer and autumn problems persisted. The Americans were cautious about starting any talks or taking any actions that might prove politically embarrassing during 1940. It was an election year and Roosevelt was standing for an unprecedented third term of office. Clearly, talks which brought Britain's new trade controls to public attention might result in a bad press for the administration, nevertheless, the hopes of Grady and his ECCP for moves on the trade front were not entirely disappointed. Both Henry Morgenthau and Roosevelt raised with Sir Frederick Phillips the possibility of forcing out more British exports to the US to relieve Britain's dollar shortage. Phillips was the senior British Treasury representative in Washington from 1940 until his death in 1943, and he played an important role in many of the Anglo-American economic talks which took place during that period. Phillips relayed the thoughts of Morgenthau and the President to London, where they were eagerly taken up by the new President of the Board of Trade, Oliver Lyttleton. He instructed D'Arcy Cooper of the British delegation in Washington to explore with the Americans the possibility of a supplement to the 1938 trade agreement,

> which would make their market more accessible to United Kingdom exporters, and offset some of the disadvantages which they suffer in consequence of the rise of costs in this country.[12]

This suggestion, that the British and Americans should review their trade relations, was passed on to Grady on 30 October. It was well timed, because a couple of days later Hull made his dissatisfaction with existing British trade policies abundantly clear when he lectured members of the British delegation in Washington[13]. On 12 December Harry Hawkins, one of Hull's leading disciples and

The Supply Problem and its Solution

head of the Division of Commercial Policy and Agreements, reported to Hull that the department's Trade Agreements Committee unanimously favoured positive action on the British suggestion for a supplement to the trade agreement of 1938[14]. Four days later Hull forwarded that recommendation to the President, who appended his familiar 'OK' to it and returned it[15]. The scene was set for an attempt to solve Anglo-American trade problems.

While the Board of Trade was trying to overcome the difficulties involved in trade relations with the US, Britain's supply situation continued to worsen. Roosevelt was well aware of this, but re-election considerations and fears of what the Isolationists might do limited his scope for action. In June 1940 he broadened the political base of his administration by bringing in Frank Knox as Secretary of the Navy and the notorious war-hawk Henry Stimson as Secretary of War. Both were Republicans and the appointments were clearly made with an eye to combating the spread of anti-Rooseveltian and pro-Isolationist sentiment in the Republican Party. At the same time that Roosevelt was strengthening his hand against the Isolationists, France collapsed and Britain was left alone, ill-armed and ill-prepared, to face Germany, which raised new questions about extending aid to Britain. Was it aid for a lost cause? If so, why antagonise Germany needlessly by giving help to Britain? Would it not be more prudent to keep the equipment for American forces for the defence of the continental US?

The defeat of France and the loss of the British Army's equipment at Dunkirk in May 1940 compounded Britain's supply problem. Industry was increasingly turned over to war production with the results that the nation's export earning capacity was ineluctably reduced while imports continued, depleting her gold and dollar reserves apace. As Edward Stettinius put it in his history of Lend-Lease the British, 'needed their factories and their raw materials to manufacture bombs for export over Germany, not peacetime goods to sell to friendly nations'[16]. Britain could not sustain enough export production both to pay for vital raw materials and equipment from abroad and simultaneously to reserve enough industrial capacity for the level of production necessary for prosecuting the war against Germany and Italy. The india-rubber island, as Angus Calder has called

The Supply Problem and its Solution

wartime Britain, was stretched in innumerable ways to meet the demands of the war, but the economic logic of 1940/41 dictated that the tension between the need for exports and the need for war production would snap it in two unless outside aid was forthcoming[17].

On 10 May 1940 Churchill took over from Chamberlain as Prime Minister and formed the National Government. Almost immediately pleas started to flow across the Atlantic for statements of support from Roosevelt, for supplies, for munitions and above all for destroyers. British and allied shipping losses were mounting alarmingly; they were to exceed 3.5 million tons in 1940 and over 4.3 million tons in 1941. Destroyers were the key weapon for fighting the U-boat menace to merchant shipping bringing supplies to Britain.

Churchill's pleas presented the President with a new difficulty. Not only did Roosevelt have to calculate the possible political repercussions of aid to Britain, and whether it would and could be used effectively by her to stop the advance of Germany, but he now also had to contemplate extending aid on a non-commercial basis. On the 15 May Churchill, for the first time as Prime Minister, wrote to Roosevelt describing some of Britain's supply problems and requirements. Most importantly for the long-term, he stated, 'We shall go on paying dollars for as long as we can, but I should like to feel reasonably sure that when we can pay no more, you will give us the stuff all the same'[18]. Roosevelt was not very responsive to Churchill's initial pleas. France was still in the fight, though only just, and officials in Washington continued to hope that Hitler could be stopped on the continent of Europe. Such chimerical hopes disappeared as May and the Germans advanced. Churchill repeated his requests for aid on 18 and 20 May, on 1 June and again, with some desperation, on 15 June[19]. The fall of France was imminent and the US Ambassador in London, Joseph Kennedy, was reporting pessimistically to Washington (as the British knew full well because they had cracked the State Department codes) about Britain's chances of survival and about her will to resist. Churchill was well aware that Roosevelt was now calculating the benefits for America from extending aid to Britain against the odds on Britain surviving, against depriving US forces of much needed material and against the danger of needlessly antagonising

The Supply Problem and its Solution

Germany if aid failed to prevent Britain's defeat or capitulation. Churchill used the only thing Britain had left which featured prominently in American minds when they thought about the defence of the US.

> Although the present government and I personally would never fail to send the fleet across the Atlantic if resistance was beaten down here, a point may be reached in the struggle where the present ministers no longer have control of affairs and when very easy terms could be obtained for the British islands by their becoming a vassal state of the Hitler empire[20].

Churchill pointed out that the British Navy combined with those of Italy, Japan and France, and in conjunction with Germany's industrial capacity, would pose a vital threat to the US. The Prime Minister made it plain that America's best option was to give Britain aid now, to stengthen Britain and Churchill's government, and prevent the emergence of a Quisling-type regime in London. Britain only had 68 destroyers fit for service, both to protect her shipping lanes against 55 German and 100 Italian submarines and to fend off the expected cross-channel invasion. 'We must ask therefore', wrote Churchill, 'as a matter of life or death to be reinforced with...destroyers'. Roosevelt, for the time being, did not act. A month and a half passed before Churchill pressed Roosevelt once again for destroyers. At the end of July he urged Lord Lothian, the British Ambassador in Washington, to press the British case and on 31 July he made a personal appeal to the President[21]. On 1 August Lothian took the opportunity of a meeting with Stimson and Knox to plead for the transfer of destroyers to the UK and met with a favourable response. Harold Ickes, Secretary of the Interior, Morgenthau and now, Roosevelt himself, favoured positive action on the British request for destroyers. The President appears to have been influenced in his decision by more favourable reports about Britain's chances of survival. The Battle of Britain was still raging, but the achievements of the RAF warranted cautious optimism. On 2 August the US Cabinet agreed in principle to the transfer of destroyers. At the same time it

The Supply Problem and its Solution

recognised that Congress might prove recalcitrant and would require a *quid pro quo* which could be clearly seen as such. With Britain already short of dollars cash-payment seemed to be out of the question and some other form of payment would have to be sought. A more immediate issue, however, was the procedure by which the destroyers were to be transferred to the Royal Navy.

If Congress was to be approached for authorisation for the transfer, as Roosevelt at first thought it would have to be, then the Isolationists might delay matters until it was too late to help Britain. At this point Britain found a good friend in the form of Dean Acheson, who was temporarily out of government service. He had resigned from the Treasury in November 1933 but was to re-enter government employment on 1 February 1941 when he became an Assistant Secretary of State. During the second week of August Acheson, along with B. V. Cohen, T. D. Thatcher (formerly a New York district judge and Solicitor General in the Hoover Administration) and George Rublee, drew up a document of legal considerations. It stated that Roosevelt had the authority, without congressional permission, to transfer destroyers to the UK providing the Chief of Naval Operations stated that they were not necessary for the defence of the US. Their paper was published in the New York Times on Sunday 11 August. Public reaction and, after some nudging from Acheson, the opinion of the Attorney General, R.H. Jackson, were both favourable. It only remained for the President to be persuaded. Acheson set to work again and brought pressure to bear circuitously via Lothian, Lord Athlone (the Governor General of Canada) and the Canadian Prime Minister, McKenzie King[22]. On 13 August Roosevelt informed Churchill that he thought that it was possible for him to accede to the request for an immediate supply of destroyers for Britain[23].

Ambassador Lothian now began to discuss terms, and during the following three weeks some hard bargaining took place. The Americans wanted a pledge from the British Government that in the event of a German victory the British fleet would be sent overseas for the defence of the empire. They also wanted a handsome quid pro quo which would deflect any domestic criticism of the destroyers deal. The British were reluctant to give the pledge that the Americans requested because it would publicly countenance the possibility of defeat: this was

The Supply Problem and its Solution

undesirable from the point of view of domestic morale. On the 'payment' issue the British eventually agreed to lease bases in the Caribbean and Newfoundland to the US for 99 years. This type of exchange had been mooted on a number of occasions in the past; however, the British were not happy about a straight swop of bases for destroyers. It was felt in London that it might set as a precedent for harsh bargains in the future. As Churchill later put it in his memoirs, 'There was of course no comparison between the intrinsic value of these antiquated and inefficient craft and the immense permanent [sic] strategic security offered the United States by the enjoyment of the island bases'[24]. The British agreed to transfer the bases to America but they wanted to give them, as opposed to exchanging them, for the destroyers. Two independent but simultaneous transactions would take place which would detract from the commercial character of the deal and emphasise the close mutual interests of Britain and the US. Unfortunately, Roosevelt's political circumstances would not allow this: he needed to emphasise the businesslike nature of the deal so in the end a compromise was struck. Some bases were presented as a free gift, others specifically for the destroyers. There was also a compromise concerning the requests for a public statement that the fleet would be dispatched to various parts of the Empire if Britain was defeated. Churchill confirmed in writing that such was the policy of his government but this was not bruited about in London[25].

The agreement was finally signed on 2 September 1940. In Washington it was presented as a single quid-pro-quo business agreement, which greatly benefited the US. In London the emphasis was placed on the parallel transactions of Britain giving some bases voluntarily to the US and the US handing over destroyers, for which she got some others. The deal was a turning point in the supply relationship between the two countries. No matter how good the bargain was for the US this could not disguise the facts that the agreement was one which could only have been reached between close friends and that it was not a straightforward commercial arrangement. It pointed the way for Lend-Lease. The Isolationists saw it very much in terms of Roosevelt getting off what little was left of the fence, and they were right. America no longer even had the formal appearance of being neutral.

The Supply Problem and its Solution

The destroyers deal was an important victory over the Isolationists and strengthened Britain's defences without her having to pay precious dollars. This was just as well because by the autumn of 1940 Britain was rapidly approaching bankruptcy. During the summer of 1940 the British Government had hoped that it could continue the cash-and-carry programme well into 1941. In August re-assessments drastically altered the picture and it looked as if Britain would run out of dollars by the end of the year. The increase in British orders placed in America after the fall of France and an understandable desire on the part of American businessmen for advance payments were the main causes of the rapid deterioration of Britain's dollar position.

Sir Frederick Phillips was sent to Washington and given the job of trying to find a solution to Britain's American supply problem. His task was not an easy one. In August the US Cabinet turned down the idea of a dollar loan. Members of the administration were worried about congressional and public reactions to such a proposal, particularly as it would require the repeal of the Johnson Act. They also wanted to avoid the kind of mess which had followed the First World War because of war debts[26]. In July Morgenthau had advised Phillips that Britain should sell off her overseas assets and this line was repeatedly taken by the Americans during the following eight months. Just prior to the presidential election Lothian reported to London that Britain was expected to sell all her assets in Latin America and the US, but this in fact never happened. Some of the assets simply could not be speedily liquidated and in the case of others even the Americans acknowledged that their market value was so depressed because of Britain's wartime predicament that it would have been inequitable for her to sell them. Substantial sales did take place, some £70 million of overseas assets from August 1940 to March 1941, but they were insufficient to fill the gap between Britain's dollar holdings and her supply needs. Oliver Lyttleton suggested that non-economic concessions to the US, something along the lines of the destroyers deal, might be considered, or, if it could be arranged, a dollar loan repayable in goods over a five year period. The latter suggestion was not looked on favourably by the British Treasury, which was already concerned about the prospect for Britain's postwar balance of

The Supply Problem and its Solution

payments, and unrequited exports would obviously not help matters. Continued American pressure for the sale of overseas assets caused additional concern because the sale of investments would reduce dividend payments and exacerbate any postwar balance of payments problem.

On 7 December Churchill wrote one of the most momentous of his war letters to the US President:

> The moment approaches when we shall no longer be able to pay cash for shipping and other supplies. While we will do our utmost..., I believe that you will agree it would be wrong in principle and mutually disadvantageous if..., Great Britain were to be divested of all saleable assets....Such a course would not be in the moral or economic interests of either of our countries.[27]

According to R.E. Sherwood[28] Roosevelt brooded over Churchill's letter for some days but, as he had firmly tucked another presidential election victory under his belt in November, he now felt politically secure enough to come forward with a radical initiative. Ten days after the Prime Minister had despatched his letter appealing for assistance the President spoke publicly about his idea for abolishing 'the silly, foolish, old dollar sign'. At the end of the month in a 'fireside chat', Roosevelt talked about the need for long-term aid for Britain and of America becoming the arsenal for the democracies[29]. This was the beginning of the story of Lend-Lease.

While members of the US Treasury prepared the Lend-Lease Bill, and while Congress duly debated on it, Britain grimly held on against Hitler and Mussolini. Churchill's 7 December appeal for aid greatly benefited Britain in the long term by solving her wartime supply problem, but it did little to alleviate the immediate dollar shortage, and furthermore, members of the Roosevelt Administration paid little heed to Churchill's arguments about asset stripping. The Americans continued to press Britain to sell assets and assume new liabilities. Morgenthau suggested that a temporary solution to Britain's hard currency shortage would be unilaterally to take over £200 million of French gold held in Canada. The British, no doubt bearing in mind their sinking of the French

The Supply Problem and its Solution

Fleet at Mers-el-Kebir in July and the susceptibilities of the Quebec French, thought that these were considerations of such political weight that they did not take Morgenthau's advice.

The next move by the Americans concerned £42 million of gold at Capetown which had been earmarked for the British Government. The account of the 'South African gold incident' in the official British history is somewhat misleading. Its author writes that after Phillips had explained the difficulties concerning the suggestion that Britain should take over French gold in Canada:

> The matter thereupon went to the President who, accepting the difficulty of taking the French gold at the moment, startled the British authorities by arranging for a United States warship to call at Capetown for all the gold that could be mustered there. This was not an offer; it was a statement of the President's decision and of action taken.[30]

It has since been explained that the Americans did not take such liberties. In fact, it was Phillips who first mentioned the possibility that America might acquire British gold in South Africa in a conversation with Morgenthau on 19 December, upon this unauthorised suggestion the Americans acted with indecent haste[31]. The US Treasury was not content with simply re-earmarking the gold: it wanted physical possession of it and by 23 December this idea had worked its way up to the President, who readily concurred with the Treasury view, and informed Phillips of his decision to send the *USS Louisville* to Capetown where it would pick up the gold. Unfortunately as Phillips had kept Whitehall oblivious of the preliminary goings-on, when the news came through of Roosevelt's decision the distress felt there was more acute than it need have been.

The most furious member of the British Government was Max Beaverbrook. On 26 December he gave vent to his feelings in a memorandum to Churchill:

> It would appear that the United States are demanding our South African gold and proposing to carry it away.

The Supply Problem and its Solution

> That is a decision I would resist very strongly and seek to destroy with every means in my power. Our financial relations with the Americans have been so loosely handled that it is necessary, now and forthwith to take up a firm policy and to push it in the face of obstacles and even to the extent of rupture.[32]

It is true that Beaverbrook was not a temperate man but in his position as Minister for Aircraft Production, which he had held since August 1940, he was well aware of Britain's dependence upon American supplies and so for him to protest in the manner he did shows just how seriously he took the problem of economic relations with the US.

Churchill noted Beaverbrook's comments. He would not, of course, countenance the possibility of a breach with the Americans, however, he was very angry. In an early draft of a letter to Roosevelt he referred to the 'sheriff collecting the last assets of an helpless debtor'. By 2 January, when the PM did finally send a letter concerning the South African gold, he had been somewhat mollified by Roosevelt's broadcast on 29 December in which he announced his commitment to the long-term supply of Britain. The British Embassy in Washington had also done its best to tone down Churchill's language. The relevant part of the final draft read:

> I agree with your proposal to stave off our difficulties by sending a warship to Cape Town to collect the gold at our disposal there amounting, I believe, to about 30 million sterling. I ought to let you know that this transaction will almost certainly become known to the world with varying reactions.[33]

On 6 January 1941 the British Cabinet was notified by America that the gold had arrived safely in the US. To many members of the government in London the episode was not only an example of American high-handedness; it also made America seem avaricious, particularly as US gold holdings topped $22 billion (a very large proportion of the world's monetary gold) whereas Britain's entire reserves now totalled less than half a billion dollars.

The reaction in Washington to the appearance of 42 million of British gold was to question whether

The Supply Problem and its Solution

Britain was as penurious as Phillips and others so often claimed. Henry Morgenthau, however, had few illusions about Britain's position. During the period November 1940 to March 1941 he was Britain's constant friend and a strong advocate of financial help. At the end of December 1940 Morgenthau and Roosevelt were aware that in the months before Lend-Lease came into operation there was clearly going to be an interim finance crisis caused by a shortfall of about $225 million for Britain's supply requirements. On 3 January Morgenthau's staff drew up a plan for emergency credit assistance to be extended to Britain through the government's Reconstruction Finance Corporation (RFC), which was under the authority of the Secretary of Commerce Jesse Jones, a Texas businessman. On 8 January Morgenthau urged Roosevelt to approve the plan, and he did[34]. In the days that followed Morgenthau and Phillips cobbled together various provisions and procedures, not without difficulty and argument, which eventually allowed Britain to place orders at the rate of $35 million a week in the US. Britain's interim supply problem was thus solved, but only at the cost of accumulating additional liabilities. The terms of the RFC loan, which were not finalised until July, were harsh in terms of the collateral Britain had to give[35].

The idea that Britain should post collateral was also frequently mooted in relation to Lend-Lease right up to the passage of the act in March 1941. Even the US Treasury, in the person of Harry Dexter White, made demands for collateral though it was mainly the State Department that made the running on this. Hull had difficulty in understanding how the British Empire could become so short of money so quickly and was unhappy that the British had not carried out Morgenthau's requests that they should sell all their assets in the Western Hemisphere. He calculated the British still had foreign holdings to the value of $18 billion and he repeatedly suggested that some of this should be offered as collateral for Lend-Lease.

Roosevelt tried to explain to Hull that the value of Britain's assets was probably only half the Secretary's estimate and that many of Britain's holdings could not be liquidated in a way which would benefit the US and be fair to the UK. The President expressed his concern over Britain's financial plight and mentioned to Hull the possibility of a $1 billion loan being raised via

The Supply Problem and its Solution

Jones' RFC[36]. Roosevelt's views failed to deter Hull from pressing the British to put more money up front. On 11 January in conversation with Phillips he urged the posting of up to $2 billion for Lend-Lease:

> this action would go further to disarm critics and to keep this whole movement on a favorable basis than anything else that might be said or done. But I made no impression...so far as I could see.[37]

Apart from the RFC loan nothing ever materialised out of these pressures for collateral, but one final demand for the sale of assets could not be resisted.

In the run-up to the introduction of the Lend-Lease Bill in Congress Morgenthau asked the British to sell something big to sweeten congressional opinion. Britain had already sold off considerable amounts of easily liquidated assets and the flow of sales had depressed the market; consequently, when Britain was more or less obliged to sell the Courtaulds owned Viscose Corporation of America to meet Morgenthau's request, only approximately one third of its market value was realised. Once again the British felt hard-done-by and their suspicions and resentments towards America in their economic relations began to intensify.

The Lend-Lease Bill went before Congress in early January, and contrary to a long-held view it did not originate in the minds of Edward Foley, General Counsel in the US Treasury, and his assistant Oscar Cox. In a memorandum written at the time of Cox's death in 1966, Stephen J. Spingarn, without actually naming anyone, though the detail he gives suggests he was one of the authors, claims that two Treasury lawyers under orders from Foley worked out the Lend-Lease Bill and that,

> it was "stolen from a statute passed some 6 or 7 months earlier (in June 1940) authorizing the Secretaries of War and Navy to manufacture, purchase and repair war materials for the American Republics. The two Treasury lawyers involved naturally remembered the recent statute when they got the assignment late one afternoon in late Dec. 1940 or early January 1941 to draft a bill to carry out the President's proposals. It was an

The Supply Problem and its Solution

elementary legislative drafting job of about two hours or so that night for them to take the 1940 law, blow all the restrictions out of it and then turn it into a bill which, with only minor revisions by the reviewing authorities, became the bill introduced as the Lend-Lease bill in both houses of Congress on January 10, 1941.[38]

There was quite a struggle to get the Lend-Lease Bill through Congress. It was eventually passed with substantial majorities in both houses, the voting was 260 for to 165 against and 60 for to 31 against in the House and in the Senate respectively, but strong opposition was evident and the fact that the act would have to be renewed every year meant that the administration could not afford to ignore the political situation on Capitol Hill. A further difficulty arose four days after the bill became law. On 15 March Harold Smith, the Director of the Budget, while testifying before the House Appropriations Committee, stated that none of the $7 billion for Lend-Lease would be used to pay for materials contracted for before 11 March, that the UK had sufficient dollars to meet her existing obligations and that any remaining British assets in the US could be given as security for defence equipment supplied under Lend-Lease[39]. These statements restricted the administration's freedom of action more tightly than the actual provisions themselves of the Lend-Lease Act. Smith clearly did not think that the sale of the Viscose Corporation had sufficiently sweetened congressional opinion. Over the following months Morgenthau did ease the situation for the British by getting the American service departments to take over some of Britain's pre-Lend-Lease contracts[40], nevertheless, the British were not sanguine about having to scrape the barrel, as they put it, before they could benefit from American aid.

By mid-March 1941 the three key supply problems which had confronted Britain in 1940 were well in hand. Britain's war production and the swelling tide of supplies crossing the Atlantic, first by virtue of cash-and-carry and then by Lend-Lease, were soon to make up for the lack of Britain's war preparedness. The Atlantic supply route was kept open with the help of the fifty destroyers from the US, though shipping lanes remained vulnerable and

The Supply Problem and its Solution

were a real headache until March 1943, when long-range air surveillance turned the Battle of the Atlantic decisively in favour of Britain and the US. By July 1943 more allied shipping was being built than sunk. The stance of America during 1940 changed dramatically and by the end of the year Roosevelt had committed his administration to a policy of 'all aid short of war' for Britain.

It remained to be seen what price Britain would have to pay for American help. The war had already cost Britain dearly. Export markets and its gold and dollar reserves were all but gone and a considerable proportion of overseas assets had been sold. Sterling debts were rapidly accumulating in North Africa, and the US had been acting in a manner that many ministers in London thought was inappropriately grasping. The cash-and-carry policy had swallowed Britain's gold and dollar reserves and caused additional dollar liabilities. America had taken possession of Britain's last nest-egg of gold in South Africa and had struck a hard bargain in the destroyers deal. Pressure to sell assets, most notably the sale of the Viscose Corporation, aroused fears in London that the US had at least one eye upon gaining some commercial advantage from the war at Britain's expense. Finally, Lend-Lease allowed an even greater conversion to war production in Britain than would otherwise have been possible, and it accelerated Britain's wartime move away from a market economy. Both these factors were to be important in the coming years and were to complicate the economic relations between the two countries.

It was thus with some apprehension that British negotiators began to work with their American counterparts in the spring and early summer of 1941 on the two most pressing, and as we shall see ultimately inter-related, economic issues - the Supplementary Trade Talks and the Lend-Lease Consideration Negotiations.

NOTES

1. W. F. Kimball, Churchill and Roosevelt: The Complete Correspondence, 3 Vols. (Princeton University Press, New Jersey, 1984), Vol.I, p.108, Churchill to Roosevelt, 7 Dec. 1940.
2. L. Hart, History of the Second World War (Pan, London, 1973), p.18.
3. Quoted from J. E. Wilz, From Isolation to War (Routledge and Kegan Paul, London, 1969), p.72.

The Supply Problem and its Solution

4. A. H. Vandenberg Jr. and J. A. Morris, *The Private Papers of Senator A. H. Vandenberg* (Houghton Mifflin, Boston, 1952), p.3.

5. Restrictions were imposed under the authority of the 'Import, Export and Customs Defence Act, 1939', and by SR and O (1940) No.708 and No.1732, 12 May and 27 Sept. respectively.

6. Hull memo. 'Representations to the British Government on Effects of Import Controls on American Business and Agriculture', 22 Jan. 1940, National Archives Washington, State Department 641-116/2578 (hereafter only decimal file numbers are given for State Dept. references).

7. V. I. Lenin, *Imperialism, the Highest Stage of Capitalism*, Selected Works Vol.I (Progress Publishers, Moscow, 1967).

8. C. Hull, *The Memoirs of Cordell Hull*, 2 Vols. (Hodder and Stoughton, London 1948), Vol.I, p.81.

9. See: Moffatt memo. 25 Jan. 1940, 841.711/3027, Welles memo. 9 Feb. 1940, 641.116/2603, and memo. of conversation, between Hull and Ambassador Lothian, 20 March 1940, 611.4131/2487a.

10. Grady to Hull, 14 May 1940, 611.0031/749½.

11. Grady to British Embassy, 25 April 1940, and note by Feis, 2 May 1940, both at 611.4131/2487a.

12. British Embassy to Grady, 30 Oct. 1940, enclosing letter of instruction to D'Arcy Cooper, 611.4131/2547.

13. Memo. of conversation between Hull, Butler, Chalkley, Cooper and Stirling, 2 Nov. 1940, 611.4131/2519.

14. Hawkins to Hull, 12 Dec. 1940, 611.4131/2524.

15. Hull to Roosevelt, 16 Dec. 1940, 611.4131/2523.

16. E. Stettinius, *Lend-Lease, Weapon for Victory* (Macmillan, New York, 1944), p.246.

17. A. Calder, *The People's War* (Cape, London, 1971).

18. Kimball, *Correspondence*, Vol.I, p.37, Churchill to Roosevelt, 15 May 1940.

19. Ibid, pp.39, 40, 41, 49-51.

20. Ibid, pp.49-51, Churchill to Roosevelt, 15 June 1940.

21. Ibid, pp.56-57, Churchill to Roosevelt, 31 July 1940.

22. D. Acheson, *Morning and Noon* (Houghton Mifflin, Boston, 1965), pp.222-224.

23. Kimball, *Correspondence*, Vol.I, pp.58-9, Roosevelt to Churchill, 13 Aug. 1940.

24. W. S. Churchill, *History of the Second World War: Their Finest Hour* (Cassell, London, 1948), p.357.

25. For further detail see: J. E. Wilz, *From Isolation to War* (Routledge Kegan and Paul, London 1969), and J. R. M. Butler, *Lord Lothian* (Macmillan, London, 1960).

26. H. A. Notter, et al, *Postwar Foreign Policy Preparation, 1939-45* (Department of State Publication 3580, Washington, 1950), pp.37-8.

27. Kimball, *Correspondence*, Vol.I, p.108, Churchill to Roosevelt, 7 Dec. 1940.

28. R. E. Sherwood, *Roosevelt and Hopkins, An Intimate History* (Harper, New York, 1948), p.224.

29. S. I. Rosenman, *The Public Papers and Addresses of Franklin Delano Roosevelt*, 13 Vols. (Harper, New York, 1938-51), Vol.9, 149 and 643.

30. R. S. Sayers, *History of The Second World War, UK Civil Series, Financial Policy* (HMSO and Longmans Green, London, 1956), p.384.

31. W. F. Kimball, 'Beggar My Neighbor: America and the British Interim Finance Crisis 1940-41.' *Journal of Economic History 29* (Dec. 1969) pp.190-194, quoting source F. D. Roosevelt Library, H. Morgenthau Diary (hereafter H.M. Diary) 341 pp.190-94, memo. Cochran to Young, 19 Dec. 1940.

32. A. J. P. Taylor, *Beaverbrook*, (Hamish Hamilton, London, 1972), pp.439-440.

33. Kimball, *Correspondence*, Vol.I, pp.120 and 123-24, editorial comment and Churchill to Roosevelt, 2 Jan. 1940.

34. H.M. Diary 346, pp.8-23, 8 Jan. 1941.

35. Washington to Foreign Office (FO), 18 July 1941, Public Record Office, FO371/28802, W8780/37/49 (hereafter only PRO reference and departmental piece numbers will be given).

36. Roosevelt to Hull, 11 Jan. 1941, 841.24/1387.

37. See: memo. of conversation between Hull and Phillips, 11 Jan.1941, 841.24/440; and Hull, *Memoirs*, Vol.II, pp.923-924.

38. Spingarn memo. 29 Oct. 1966, H. S. Truman Library, S. J. Spingarn Papers, folder: Correspondence re the Lend-Lease Act of 1941.

39. H. M. Diary, 405, pp.49-50, 4 June 1941.

The Supply Problem and its Solution

40. On 18 March 1941 the following conversation took place between Morgenthau and Purvis, head of the British Purchasing Mission in Washington. Purvis: 'I take it...that you are [not] in any way unsympathetic to the idea of new contracts coming under Lend-Lease Bill later if - I mean, when the Appropriations Bill comes through that it would be retroactive'. Morgenthau: 'I'm entirely sympathetic with the idea; I'm the instigator of it'.

Morgenthau was true to his word and fought hard to get relief for the British on their pre-Lend-Lease contracts. During 1942, however, this issue became entangled with the broader question of the level of gold and dollar reserves that the US should help Britain to maintain and Morgenthau's attitude towards this was far less helpful, as we shall see in Chapter 5.

Chapter Two

TRADE TALKS AND LEND-LEASE CONSIDERATION

Churchill described Lend-Lease as a 'most unsordid act'. It was undoubtedly magnanimous in conception, though from time to time it was to prove less so in execution. Lend-Lease was unique in that it committed the US to supplying Britain before any price had been negotiated. Even Hull's attempts to get Britain to pledge collateral prior to receiving aid had failed. The views of the US Treasury prevailed instead and they allowed the Lend-Lease Bill to become law on the basis of the President being given wide discretion when determining re-payment.

> 3(b) the terms and conditions upon which any such foreign Government receives any aid authorized under Sub-section (a) shall be those which the President deems satisfactory, and the benefit to the United States may be payment or repayment in kind or property, or any other direct or indirect benefit which the President deems satisfactory.[1]

The Secretary of the Treasury had been politically more adventurous than the Secretary of State over the Lend-Lease Bill but once it was law and Congress had appropriated $7 billion for the aid programme matters changed. When it came to making proposals for Lend-Lease Consideration it was Hull who was politically adventurous and Morgenthau who was business-like and cautious. The different views of the two departments and the problem of allocating jurisdiction over the consideration issue, all of which we shall be looking at shortly, delayed formal talks with the British until 12 June. In the meantime negotiations were taking place on a supplement to the 1938 Anglo-American Trade Agreement. They were eventually superseded by

Trade Talks and Lend-Lease Consideration

various negotiations which arose out of Lend-Lease, but while they lasted they were seen as important and they raised the matter of Britain's postwar economic policy, which was later to become the central issue in the Consideration Talks.

On 23 December 1940 the head of the British trade negotiating team in Washington, J. A. Stirling of the Ministry of Economic Warfare, outlined the objectives of the Supplementary Trade Talks to his opposite number, Harry Hawkins, as follows,

> reductions of United States duties with a quid pro quo consisting of a wartime guarantee regarding British imports of American agricultural products and reductions of the margins of British Imperial duty preferences.[2]

From this apparently anodyne statement of intent serious problems immediately arose. Hawkins thought the maximum tariff reduction of fifty per cent allowed under the Reciprocal Trade Agreement Act would not be sufficiently compensated for by a fifty per cent reduction of British preferences. Following Hull's convictions about the evils of discrimination, Hawkins wanted the abolition of Imperial Preference. A second problem was how to compensate parties to the Ottawa Agreements for their loss of preferential access to British markets. Neither Stirling nor ministers in London could see how they could meet the requests made by Hawkins, particularly under wartime circumstances, and as a consequence, in the months that followed progress was negligible. By May it seemed unlikely that Stirling would be able to offer a satisfactory amount of relief to American exporters in the form of a supplementary trade agreement; however this was no longer a serious problem because Lend-Lease had started to finance American exports to Britain. While Lend-Lease effectively circumvented the wartime obstacles Britain had placed in the path of American exports, the question of a British quid pro quo for US tariff reductions still had to be resolved. Hawkins came forward with the idea of a deferred quid pro quo. He suggested that if Britain could not abandon Imperial Preference and exchange controls now she could at least commit herself to doing so at the end of the war[3].

Stirling passed this idea on to London where the response was unfavourable. Even the Board of Trade, which was well disposed to a liberal economic

Trade Talks and Lend-Lease Consideration

order, was unable to accept the proposal: R. J. Shackle sent two amendments to the British proposals, on its behalf, which Lord Halifax and Stirling had presented to the Americans. Halifax had become UK Ambassador in Washington after the untimely death of Lord Lothian in December 1940. The amendments stated that Britain 'could not afford to surrender the advantages accorded to their exports of metal goods in Dominion markets', and that the UK Government 'must in candour make it clear that they may be compelled because of scarcity of Exchange to maintain restrictions upon imports of tobacco and other American goods after the war'[4]. When Stirling informed Hawkins of the amendments, the American conceded that Britain should have some transitional safeguards for her economy, but he thought that the way the Board of Trade had expressed itself was unacceptable and that if Hull found out then all hell would be let loose. Stirling wrote to London that he thought the additions to Britain's extant proposals would have a 'deplorable effect' in Washington[5]. The Board of Trade remained essentially unmoved. 'We do not wish to insist upon proposed additions..., but we must be fully assured, before being committed to formal negotiations, that these reservations are accepted in principle by the United States'[6].

Attitudes in Britain were becoming increasingly defensive. The idea of abandoning economic controls without a clear picture of postwar conditions, and particularly of American postwar economic policy, was widely seen in London as highly dangerous. While Hull was busy propagating the idea of a liberal world economy, notably in a major speech for the inauguration of the National Foreign Trade Week (which we shall look at in detail shortly) Leopold Amery, head of the India and Burma Office, was drafting a vitriolic letter to the British Foreign Secretary Eden which was diametrically opposed to Hull's views. This was the beginning of a long campaign waged by Amery during the war to mobilise a defence against what he saw as the dangerous economic demands made of Britain by the US. Amery, who believed that the Empire, and imperial economic relations, were highly beneficial for Britain, drew Eden's attention to the dangers of abandoning Imperial Preference, because the return of a Republican administration would probably revive protectionism in the US. He described Hull as an anachronism and expressed his fear that the US Secretary of State might drag Britain into

Trade Talks and Lend-Lease Consideration

disastrous economic commitments which could not be kept and which would thus lead to bitter mutual recriminations. Amery's letter was widely circulated in government departments and it was replied to a week later by Eden[7].

> I confess I am alarmed, not so much by Mr. Hull's conservative ideas about the Most-Favoured-Nation Clause [a principle whereby the most favourable import arrangement on a commodity made with x is then universally applied i.e. this is another name for non-discrimination], as by the absence of any indication that the American Administration recognise the infinite harm done to international economic security and stability by what Keynes calls the "unbalanced creditor position of the U.S.A."'[8]

The fact that Eden was critical of American economic policy carried weight, especially as he was more aware than most of the dangers of upsetting the Americans. Others within the government, such as Kingsley Wood, Arthur Greenwood, the head of the Dominions Office Viscount Cranborne and the Colonial Secretary Lord Moyne, evinced varying degrees of support for Amery's viewpoint, though his vigorous attack on Hull's views simply reinforced rather than created concern about the State Department's economic policies.

It was clear that the trade talks needed new direction if they were to continue. On 16 May Halifax suggested to Hull that the Dominions should be brought into the talks so that they could discuss compensation directly with the Americans for any loss of preferences which might result from the Anglo-American negotiations. Hull agreed[9]. This was welcomed in London because it switched the emphasis to trade-offs of preferences for tariffs and away from the American idea of a deferred quid pro quo and because it provided a temporary breathing space for the British to take stock of things.

May had witnessed a number of developments which gave London cause for concern. J. M. Keynes, who was attached to the British Treasury during the war, went to Washington in May to try to get some financial relief for contracts Britain had undertaken prior to Lend-Lease. Keynes was intellectually mercurial, rather arrogant, witty and

Trade Talks and Lend-Lease Consideration

sometimes handicapped in his diplomatic career by his academic honesty. While in Washington he candidly told Hawkins and others that Britain would probably have to continue with a wide range of economic controls after the war. These statements, and the lack of progress in the trade talks, irritated and frustrated members of the State Department. Hawkins began to realise that the Supplementary Trade Talks were unlikely to be a successful vehicle for promoting a liberal world economic order unless more leverage could be applied to the British. At the very moment that the trade talks looked as if they might disappoint the State Department more positive progress began to occur on Lend-Lease Consideration, which provided Hull and his acolytes with a second line of attack.

By the end of May the British knew that consideration would soon have to be discussed with the Americans and they were also aware that part of the consideration might take the form of a British declaration on postwar economic policy. The British Government was not averse to a general declaration of intent but it would have wanted to enter a series of caveats if specific policies had been mentioned. Two letters, jointly from the Treasury and the Board of Trade to Stirling and Phillips, disclosed how the British Government was thinking in early June. The gist of the two letters was the same; one of them, after stating that the government was looking to a gradual postwar relaxation of controls, continued,

> We do not know what our postwar exchange and import licensing policy will be, and we must avoid in the discussions on trade policy making any statements which can be quoted as pledges or which can tie our hands. We feel that it would be a mistake to enter into any discussions with the Americans about the techniques of Payments Agreements and their possible adaptation to post-war conditions, we should think it unwise to indicate now that it will be our aim not to discriminate as regards imports between countries except as a result of our being heavily indebted to particular countries[10].

We must now explore how the British Government's position on postwar economic policy fared in the Consideration Talks. Early American thoughts on consideration were concentrated on

Trade Talks and Lend-Lease Consideration

repayment in the form of goods and services. Oscar Cox, who was in the US Treasury but was about to leave it to become General Counsel of the Lend-Lease Administration, minuted on 8 March that the American public might think they were being taken for a ride by the British unless there was some substantial repayment for Lend-Lease. Cox was something of an Anglophile, but, as Frank Lee of the British Treasury commented later in the war, he was not a strong character and he had a tendency to sacrifice principles (for this read British interests) to political expediency[11]. Cox acknowledged that consideration might not be called for at all, but if it was then British investments in American armaments firms, interests in Bolivian tin, rare books and an extra copy of the Magna Carta might be taken in recompense. A few days later the list of British goodies was expanded to include everything from raw materials and aviation rights to joint British and American sovereignty over Hong Kong[12]. When the President signed the Lend-Lease Bill on 11 March Cox was already on his second draft of the Consideration Agreement[13]. Two days later Roosevelt gave the Treasury authority to negotiate a quid pro quo with the British along lines that the President had already informally discussed with Morgenthau. After the preparatory work done by Cox, Morgenthau was able to respond quickly: to the letter of thanks to the President for his new brief he attached a copy of the draft Consideration Agreement. He also sent Hull a copy at the same time[14].

The Treasury's draft was a commercial repayment agreement couched in broad terms. It stipulated that articles not used up were to be returned, that non-agricultural commodities used up were to be compensated for in similar kind, and that an equivalent dollar value was to be returned in tin, rubber, jute and other imperial products for Lend-Lease agricultural commodities, information and defence materials. Alternatively, any other materials acceptable to the President could be called for or, by subsequent agreement, any direct or indirect benefit agreed to by the President could be accepted. The determination of value was to be left to the President and no transfer of Lend-Lease goods to third parties was to be allowed without presidential approval.

On 14 March, after further discussion between Morgenthau, the President and his close assistant Harry Hopkins (who was effectively in charge of

Trade Talks and Lend-Lease Consideration

Lend-Lease, though its official head was General J. H. Burns), some alterations to the draft were made but they did not alter its overall character. On 2 April Foley, the Treasury's General Counsel, sent the revised proposals to Morgenthau. Until now the Treasury had been firmly in the driving seat but Foley, with some prescience, recognised that problems could easily arise with the State Department once diplomatic negotiations were started. In a note which accompanied the re-draft Foley suggested that the Secretary, 'ascertain...whether or not Treasury, or State, is to take the Agreement up with the British'[15]. The President had asked the Treasury to liaise with the State Department, and despite Roosevelt's order of 13 March which gave Morgenthau the authority to draft and negotiate a quid pro quo a delicate jurisdictional problem clearly still existed.

The draft that Morgenthau sent to the State Department on 14 March sparked off a different line of thought on consideration. Hull gave Assistant Secretary of State Adolf A. Berle the job of formulating the State Department's views. Berle was an unfortunate choice from the British point of view because his pet hate was Britain's latter-day mercantilism. Unlike Hull, however, he was not doctrinally committed to free-trade; in its stead he wanted to extend a version of the New Deal to the international economy in a way which would further American commercial interests and expand American power: British imperialism and the international economic system Britain controlled both posed obstacles to Berle's ambitions. In the draft consideration agreement he wanted to make a start at removing those obstacles.

Berle's judgement on the Treasury draft was, 'It is a meaningless agreement because you cannot collect on it'. He began work on a new version, '...really slanting it not towards repayment but towards economic cooperation after the war'[16]. Military items used up in the war effort were to be regarded as contributions to the peace of the world and their cost written off. Items which survived were to be returned and Britain should accept some obligation for Lend-Lease in reverse. Britain should permit the US to participate in any British cartel arrangements governing tin, rubber, jute and chemicals; she was to enter the freest possible trade arrangements with the US, peg the Ottawa preferences and enter negotiations for their reduction in a manner compatible with the public interests of the US and the UK[17].

This first draft of Berle's exemplified the attitude pervading the State Department. There still existed strong feelings there about both the sad fate which had befallen President Wilson's ideals at Paris in 1919 and the economic chaos of the inter-war years, which was attributed partly to the failure of internationalism and partly to the combined effect of reparations and war debts. It was with the fear of uncollectable and disruptive debts (which among other things could prevent Britain from adopting liberal economic policies) in mind that Berle and others who later took up the consideration problem advocated an agreement which was astonishingly generous in not demanding any substantial repayments in cash, goods or services. On the other hand, the conviction that the Consideration Agreement should be used to promote an open world economy faced Britain with political and economic costs which the government was not sure it could afford.

By the latter part of April 1941 two different documents on consideration existed which meant that the question about jurisdiction between the State Department and the Treasury was no longer simply academic. During the three week period before 16 May Roosevelt changed his mind about which department was to have authority over the Consideration Agreement. Roosevelt came to the conclusion that the quid pro quo should not be primarily in the form of a cash repayment. The Treasury thus lost its main jurisdictional claim and the President's exclusion of large cash repayments meant that wider policy matters, which were more within the State Department's preserve would have to be discussed with the British. Hopkins gave confirmation of this to Keynes on 21 May when he explained that the President had given the consideration job to the State Department, 'on the grounds it raises political rather than financial issues'[18]. In the letter which gave Hull authority over the Consideration Agreement Roosevelt wrote, 'Although I presume the agreement will not provide primarily for a return to us of cash, I think, nevertheless, you should consult with Secretary Morgenthau in regard to the broad provisions of the agreement'[19]. The President notified Morgenthau of his decision and the latter accepted it with apparent good grace - though as we

Trade Talks and Lend-Lease Consideration

shall see he was not entirely happy about the matter[20].

Hull and his colleagues were delighted with the new brief. By May 1941 they had strong grounds for wanting to take charge of the Consideration Agreement. State Department attempts to get Britain to commit itself to liberal postwar economic policies were being thwarted in the Supplementary Trade Talks and Lend-Lease Consideration presented an obvious opportunity to retrieve the situation.

The momentum of postwar economic-policy formulation was mounting rapidly in Hull's department. Notwithstanding the setback in the Supplementary Trade Agreement Talks, Berle was busy reaffirming the State Department's commitment to freer trade in the text of a major speech that he was preparing for Hull. The speech was scheduled for 18 May at the inauguration of the National Foreign Trade Week. It consisted of five principles: extreme nationalism must not be allowed to express itself in excessive trade restrictions, non-discrimination must be the rule not the exception in international commercial relations, raw material supplies must be available to all nations without discrimination, international agreements regulating the supply of commodities must fully protect the interests of the consuming countries and international finance must aid essential enterprises and the development of the recipient countries, and permit repayment of investments through the processes of trade [21]. State Department colours were thus nailed to the mast in a very positive way at the start of the Anglo-American talks on consideration.

Hull put Assistant Secretary of State Dean Acheson in charge of the Consideration Agreement and of liaising with the Treasury. The job by right should have gone to Berle, but at the time Acheson, as he explained in his memoirs, was about the only person in the State Department with whom Morgenthau would talk because he sided with the Treasury in its bitter dispute with Hull to freeze Japanese assets in the US [22]. Acheson was one of the most industrious and competent men Hull had at his disposal. Roosevelt had indicated that he wanted progress with the British on the Consideration Agreement before his first Lend-Lease Report to Congress on 10 June and Acheson dutifully moved quickly. On 21 May he presided over a meeting which drew up a new draft along the lines previously pursued by Berle. The proposals now stated that articles returned discharged any repayment obligation; that there was to be no charge for articles used for the purpose for which they had been supplied; that the President could off-set any benefits received from Britain against Lend-Lease agricultural supplies and any balance remaining at the end of the war was to be written off so as not to burden the British; and finally, that the British were to fall in line with the State Department's vision of the postwar world economy. By the end of the month Hull had approved the new draft [23].

The gist of Acheson's proposals were informally passed on to the British and, on the whole, they were well received. Keynes noted that part of the draft could conflict with the Ottawa Agreements, 'but State Department officials were aware of our probable unavoidable dependence on exchange control and licensing after the war, and will agree to a declaration in a form which would not involve us in a lack of candour'[24]. He was soon to be disabused of this belief. Even though the impression in London was that the declaration would be anodyne in character there were doubts expressed about the prudence of forging ahead with the Consideration Talks. Nigel B. Ronald, Counsellor in the Foreign Office with special reference to economic and postwar affairs, thought 'it would appear expedient to play for time in the expectation that if America came into the war we should get much better terms than we could hope for now!'[25].

The US Treasury also had reservations about Acheson's draft. On the morning of 4 June a lengthy discussion took place in the Treasury between the Secretary, the economist Jacob Viner (who was a longstanding adviser to Morgenthau) and senior departmental staff, including Bell, Foley and Harry White. Bell explained that the Treasury draft Consideration Agreement had been fairly tight and commercial whereas the State Department had drawn up a document which fell into two parts and between two stools. It tried to specify a quid pro quo in the first three sections and it attempted to sketch a blueprint for the postwar international economy in the fourth section: on both counts it failed. White and Viner took particular exception to the postwar economic declaration partly because of its inadequacy and partly because Roosevelt had only given the State Department authority to draw up a quid pro quo: he had not given it a blank cheque to draw up the ground rules for the postwar

Trade Talks and Lend-Lease Consideration

international economy which was a realm in which the Treasury could legitimately claim to have a say. The general view of the meeting was that the draft was muddled. It was an hermaphrodite: it had failed to be either enough of one thing or the other. The quid pro quo was insufficient to make it a business agreement and the blueprint was not fully worked out. It did not go far enough in its demands upon Britain and it raised questions of high policy which needed to be sorted out by Hull, Morgenthau and Roosevelt. They concluded that matters would be less complicated if the two parts of Acheson's draft were split up and embodied in separate agreements.

Morgenthau was not as sanguine about making an issue of the State Department draft as were his advisers. It became obvious during the course of the meeting that Morgenthau was peeved about the way the Consideration Agreement had been handled. His dislike of Hull, and his previous problems with the State Department, were biliously regurgitated. 'Mr. Hull has twenty odd trade treaties' mocked Morgenthau, 'and where has it got us?' At one point Morgenthau became petulant claiming he would no longer be the President's 'whipping boy' on foreign affairs and threatening to abandon the whole question of consideration. A timely intervention by White prevented this; he suggested that Acheson and Bell should get together to try to sort things out and Morgnethau, calming down, agreed[26].

In the afternoon discussions were renewed, this time with Acheson present. He explained that his department had shifted away from the idea of a repayment document because it believed that it was unwise to lay obligations upon Britain which would drain her reserves. The main operating clause was now the fourth one which Acheson said required the British to be, 'willing to go quite a way toward either cracking now or laying the foundation for cracking the Ottawa agreements and the various restrictive monopolistic agreements and practices which they had had'[27]. In response to some of the points which Viner, White and Foley repeated from the morning session Acheson said that there was some support in the State Department for a wider approach on the postwar declaration but he believed that it was better to get a narrow legalistic agreement to which the British could be held and that although there was a danger in this because future conditions were indeterminable he did not think that matters could be left till the end of hostilities. Foley pointed out that this was all very well but that

Trade Talks and Lend-Lease Consideration

they did not really know what the President wanted. As this point sank in Acheson agreed to countenance the idea of splitting his document into two separate agreements, as the Treasury officials had wanted to do in the morning session, and prepare them for presentation to the President in order to elicit his views. Once the meeting had agreed to this those present then decided it would be necessary to propose an Anglo-American commission to coordinate the quid pro quo agreement and the postwar declaration, and to develop postwar economic policies in more detail. With this apparently acceptable compromise between Acheson and the Treasury team the meeting broke up with some degree of optimism[28].

During the next four days two problems emerged. Firstly, once the postwar declaration was hived off from the quid pro quo document it then demanded very little of the British. Oscar Cox in a note to Hopkins remarked that exemptions from repayments for the British, except for non-military supplies, might be politically dangerous and it would be better to have a more open-ended agreement so that more concrete reimbursements could be called for if necessary[29]. The second problem concerned repayment for military items used up in the war. The State Department stuck to its original position (that their cost should be written off) but Morgenthau, while professing not to be against the idea in principle, refused to recommend it to the President. He thought serious political implications were involved and a decision should be left entirely to Roosevelt. On the 9 June it was clear that a joint statement from the Treasury and the State Department could not be presented to the President. Morgenthau was now thoroughly browned off with the Consideration Agreement and concluded that the State Department 'can do anything they want with it'[30].

On 9 June Hopkins and Acheson saw the President to discuss the consideration issue. Roosevelt had some sympathy with the views of the Treasury. Hopkins recorded that, 'The President thinks that the supplies which are destroyed in the war should be included in the agreement. He is anxious, however, that the whole agreement be one in which the ultimate payments can really be made'[31]. The President wanted something substantial from the British but rejected the idea of a recorded debt. This eventually led the State Department to reintegrate the postwar declaration into the

Trade Talks and Lend-Lease Consideration

Consideration Agreement as the only acceptable means of acquiring tangible benefits for the US; however, for the time being, matters remained fluid. Roosevelt mentioned a number of things which it would have been politically imprudent to disclose publicly, such as British collaboration in establishing an international police force and a customs union in the West Indies. Acheson put it to the President that he did not like talking about the consideration he wanted and he did not like the consideration he could talk about. Roosevelt agreed, but nevertheless asked Acheson to try his hand at a new draft[32].

The consultations with Roosevelt on 9 June established, albeit rather vaguely, the basis for talks with the British. Roosevelt's deadline for 10 June had been met and he could tell Congress that progress was being made on Lend-Lease Consideration. The first formal exchange took place between Undersecretary of State Sumner Welles and Halifax on 12 June, but Acheson had kept Keynes informally in the picture and on 10 June Halifax was able to report to the Chancellor of the Exchequer, Kingsley Wood, and the Prime Minister about the latest American ideas on consideration. Lend-Lease articles were to be categorised as expended, returnable, military and non-military. Payment, in terms of some kind of reverse Lend-Lease and an exchange of information and inventions, was only to be made for the last category. Halifax added that nothing had been said about payment by delivery of British raw materials, but it looked as if political commitments on postwar trade policy were going to be asked for and there was a proposal that a joint Anglo-American commission be set up to sort out economic policies[33].

Halifax's summary arrived in London at the same time that Amery's warnings about American economic policies, which had been prompted by the Supplementary Trade Talks, were being digested by ministers. Kingsley Wood, worried about the financial angle, wrote to Eden, 'I agree [with Amery] that our object must be not to commit ourselves more than we can help as to what our policy will be after the war'[34]. Wood's mood of caution was evident in a telegram, approved by Churchill, which was sent to Halifax and Keynes explaining the government's attitude to the proposals mooted by Acheson. Churchill and Wood wanted to avoid both dollar liabilities and any specific postwar commitments. Wood was also against the idea of an Anglo-American commission because, as he explained to Eden later in the month, he was frightened it would immediately raise difficult issues such as Imperial Preference[35].

On 20 June Keynes explained to Acheson his government's position, though without fully disclosing the reasoning behind it. He ended by reporting that, 'consideration for the articles transferred should be found in military and political considerations and in the field of broad economic collaboration'[36]. British views about commitments to economic collaboration were somewhat different from those in the State Department, but unwittingly the British had nudged the State Department back towards the idea of incorporating a statement about postwar economic policies in the Consideration Agreement. They had done this in two ways: firstly by rejecting the idea of an Anglo-American commission, which had been put forward as an alternative means of dealing with postwar economic policies, and secondly by excluding commitments to any form of repayment, which meant that without a declaration of postwar intent the Consideration Agreement would lack consideration. The main question now was exactly what would the declaration contain.

In late June arrangements were made for Halifax and Keynes to meet with the President on 8 July to discuss the consideration problem. A number of ideas had been bandied about by State Department officials since the meeting on 20 June and the ever cautious Chancellor of the Exchequer was worried by them. He wrote to Churchill on 28 June, 'We clearly cannot give Keynes permission to broach these ideas when he sees the President on Tuesday'[37]. Keynes was ordered instead to listen passively, unless it became necessary to reject the possibility of Britain accepting any dollar liabilities[38]. The substance of the proposals the President made at the meeting was generous. Section one paragraph three later ran that there was to be no cash account, and that nor were any goods or assets to be called for which would burden the British in any way. According to the British account of the meeting the President expressed a strong desire for a general agreement and said that he did not see any urgency for detailed provisions. This was partly because he was not clear what form such provisions should take and partly because the ideas he did have, which were the same as he had related to Acheson on 9 June, might not be acceptable to public opinion.

Trade Talks and Lend-Lease Consideration

Roosevelt added that he did not evisage any future demands for reciprocal Lend-Lease and that he was not in favour of making fine distinctions between war and non-war-materials[39]. The British had feared that a separate non-war-material category might have led to demands for repayment in kind or in similar kind. The heart of the consideration Keynes later wrote lay in section two.

> President shall be entitled to ask for deliveries in kind or property or for direct or indirect benefits under all or any of the following heads as may be agreed in detail hereafter, subject to I(3) above.
> a)   Defence of the United States.
> b)   Maintenance of the future peace of the world.
> c)   Post-war relief and reconstruction.
> d)   Post-war trade and economic policy.[40]

The President suggested that Keynes should undertake further talks on the above basis with Acheson and draw up a new draft. Keynes readily agreed for he now believed a satisfactory agreement was in sight. He told Acheson afterwards about what had transpired and promised that he would return to discuss matters once he had received new instructions from London[41].

Keynes and Halifax described the meeting with the President to Kingsley Wood in optimistic terms. They were encouraged by what the President had said, and in particular by his statement that there was no need for detailed provisions in the agreement. Keynes did suspect, however, that Acheson would press for further elucidation as regards sub-headings 'a' to 'd', and he asked Wood for permission to do this[42]. Kingsley Wood refused. The attitude in the Treasury was concisely expressed with suitably dry humour in a note exchanged between two senior officials, David Waley and Richard N. Hopkins. 'If President himself is anxious to go slowly, surely it is not the right policy for us to try to go fast'[43]. Kingsley Wood and Churchill ordered Keynes not to enter detailed discussions. He was to restrict himself to a declaration of common purpose , and to section one paragraph three of the proposals Roosevelt had discussed on 8 July, followed by something along the lines of, 'the

Trade Talks and Lend-Lease Consideration

British Government will be happy to discuss with the United States Government in due course further measures of co-operation over a wider sphere'. Further than this Keynes was not to go and he, 'should not put forward other proposals even in a tentative form'[44]. Kinglsey Wood thought this matter was so important that he sent another telegram personally to Keynes to explain the Treasury's position more fully.

> The proposals regarding defence of the United States and post-war trade and economic policy have most far-reaching implications and involve commitments into which we should not wish to enter lightly or without the fullest understanding of the exact interpretation likely to be placed on them, whether by the present or by some future Administration. We warmly agree with the President that attempts to define such matters at this stage might lead to great difficulties and we hope you will be able in your discussion with Acheson to confine him to the general questions which the President seems to have in mind...especially now that the President has himself given such a clear lead that he does not at present wish for definitions[45].

Kingsley Wood had always been cautious in his dealings with the US and in early July that disposition was strongly reinforced by developments in the Supplementary Trade Talks. The entry of the Dominions into the discussions had relieved the pressure on Britain momentarily but by July the situation had become tense. Repeated statements by Keynes, such as the following to Hawkins in early July, only increased the State Department resolve to pursue its goal of a liberal world economy while Britain was vulnerable to American pressures.

> In a short discussion with Hawkins, Keynes said in asking us to undertake not to make our purchases from any country dependent upon its purchases from us or on the exchange position, Americans might be asking us to do the impossible so long as they remained a creditor country, maintained an export balance, and did not lend abroad[46].

Trade Talks and Lend-Lease Consideration

Hawkins remained unpersuaded and told Keynes that the economic controls he had in mind would not be acceptable to Hull or to American businessmen. On 4 July Halifax reported that, 'a situation of some delicacy' existed in the Supplementary Trade Talks. Hawkins wanted to negotiate reductions in tariffs and in imperial tariff preferences, and to retain the 1938 agreement otherwise intact. This would mean that at the end of the war Britain would not be able to discriminate against US imports covered by the trade agreement. Halifax commented,

> Keynes and Phillips advise me that despite the admitted goodwill of the State Department, the propositions put forward by the latter are dangerous. Any return to pre-war conditions, particularly as regards trade between the United States and the United Kingdom, is impossible. There is no chance that our balance of payments will permit it.[47]

Stirling and Keynes, for their part, could not get Hawkins to agree to controls which would safeguard Britain's transition to a peacetime economy even with a nullification clause which either party could activate if it believed the general intent of the agreement was being breached. Nevertheless, Halifax thought something along those lines should still be pursued, combined with an attempt to explain Britain's economic plight to the Americans. Kingsley Wood, Duncan (who had recently returned as head of the Board of Trade) and Eden agreed with Halifax, though they now doubted whether their goals could be achieved within the trade talks. As the reply to Halifax put it, 'The immediate problem is to find a means of permitting the present negotiations to continue and if possible produce useful results without prejudice to the general problem'[48]. The trade talks did continue in a desultory fashion for months without agreement being reached and we shall have occasion to refer to them again briefly, but the main focus of Anglo-American economic discussions was about to move decisively elsewhere. The reply to Halifax of 16 July concluded rather ominously, 'You will doubtless bear in mind that similar considerations and difficulties may arise out of "consideration" discussions'[49].

On 15 July Keynes renewed talks with Acheson on the Consideration Agreement. The draft he presented

Trade Talks and Lend-Lease Consideration

embodied the proposals that Roosevelt had discussed on 8 July and, as instructed by the Prime Minister and Kingsley Wood, Keynes added nothing further apart from an indication that Britain was prepared to talk about economic collaboration at an unspecified date in the future. The British had grasped the opportunity presented in the talks with Roosevelt to keep the agreement general and to avoid commitments to immediate talks which would have inevitably led to questions of postwar economic policy, but they had gone too far for Acheson. His immediate reaction to the British draft was to point out that it excused Britain from any liabilities in the form of goods, assets or any other type of specific obligation. Keynes agreed but indicated that the President and the Prime Minister appeared to favour such verbose vacuity. Acheson insisted that the US Government would not accept such a one-sided agreement and that the State Department in particular would oppose it in no uncertain terms; with that the meeting came to a rather inauspicious end[50].

Acheson was clearly unhappy during the meeting, and later, in conversation with Redvers Opie, Second Secretary at the British Embassy, he described Keynes as a bad envoy and as having put conclusions into Roosevelt's mouth. By this Acheson was not referring to the general nature of the British draft so much as to the way the British had taken license from their talks with the President to give only a vague commitment to discussions on economic collaboration. Acheson said to Opie that Roosevelt 'blew up' when he heard about this and in a memorandum for the State Department expressed himself, 'very bluntly on the show of reluctance' to enter talks shown in the British draft[51]. When we look at this memorandum we shall see that Acheson was exaggerating. This is understandable because the issue at stake was seen as crucial by members of the State Department, and Acheson wanted the British to believe that they had the full support of the President. In fact the President's support was more passive than the State Department would have liked.

The British Government's reluctance to commit itself to talks and evidence of its thinking in the Supplementary Trade Talks now led the State Department to revert to the idea of incorporating specific provisions for postwar economic policy in the Consideration Agreement. Early State Department drafts had included rather narrow, legalistic provisions which required Britain to abandon, or at

Trade Talks and Lend-Lease Consideration

least begin to abandon, Imperial Preference but at the meeting with Treasury officials on 4 June Acheson had agreed to separate what they called the quid pro quo from the economic policy commitments on the understanding that a joint Anglo-American commission would be established to formulate postwar economic policies. In other words, providing some framework was created in which Britain could be moved towards the abolition of Imperial Preference and other forms of economic controls, Acheson and his colleagues would be content. By 17 July the British had not only rejected the commission but they were also circumspect about the very idea of talks on future economic collaboration. The goal which the State Department had always sought in the Consideration Talks was thus now in jeopardy and this was the main reason why Acheson and his colleagues fell back on the idea of including specific references to future economic policies in the Consideration Agreement. In addition to this both Berle and Hawkins now believed it was essential to take a strong line with the British.

On 17 July Berle minuted in his diary that a first class battle was going on over Lend-Lease; he followed this on 23 July with the comment that, 'most amazing negotiations going on between Acheson and Keynes', and he continued that the position, 'is that the British do not propose to pay anything, anywhere at any time..., in post-war economic arrangements we shall jolly well have to take care of ourselves'[52]. Undersecretary Welles was also alerted to the problem. On the same day that Acheson talked with Keynes he sent Welles a note describing the British proposals as too vague and he mentioned the possibility that Welles might talk about them with Roosevelt[53]. Three days later the President had decided that he was not happy with developments. He wrote to Acheson on 18 July that the British draft, 'is so vague I do not understand it myself'[54]. This was a bit unfair given what he had said to Halifax and Keynes on 8 July, furthermore the rough outline of a re-draft he enclosed for Acheson's guidance was neither very specific nor clear, neither does it appear as 'hot' and 'blunt' as Acheson later described it to Opie. The UK was to return material the President thought might be useful, and due allowances would be made for the restoration of normal economic relations and for British capacity to purchase US goods. In consideration for Lend-Lease the US was to give due weight to the value of information received from

Trade Talks and Lend-Lease Consideration

Britain and the British Government was to continue discussions with the US, 'covering measures of aid and of cooperation over a wider sphere'[55].

The State Department acted decisively despite the lack of a clear lead from the President. Members of the department interpreted Roosevelt's memorandum to Acheson very broadly and included in their re-draft a strong article which would have committed Britain to liberal postwar economic policies. Significantly, Roosevelt was only informed about the new draft over the telephone, before it was put to the British[56]. He approved it for negotiating, but it is very doubtful if he realised exactly what demands the document contained. In the next chapter we shall see he was not prepared wholeheartedly to support similar demands at the Atlantic Conference, and while the rather different context might explain this we shall also see that his support for detailed provisions continued to be lukewarm throughout the Consideration Talks. Some months later a memorandum by Hull to the President gave the impression that the State Department had simply fulfilled Roosevelt's wishes in the new draft.

> Its purport was to carry out your instructions that decision regarding the quid pro quo was to be deferred to a final settlement and that it should then be framed within certain broad principles relating to world peace and international economic relations. These principles were stated in Article VII.[57].

In fact Acheson and his colleagues had taken liberties with Roosevelt's memorandum of 18 July. They were determined to include the kind of detailed commitments that Roosevelt had told Halifax and Keynes were not necessary. Hawkins in particular was adamant. Keynes' talk of postwar controls and the difficulties Hawkins had encountered in the Supplementary Trade Talks convinced him that the influence of Keynes and of those of similar ilk had to be countered otherwise there would be a danger of a disastrous trade war between the US and Britain. In a retrospective memorandum of 4 August Hawkins went into a lengthy description of the economic difficulties confronting the US because of Britain. Sixteen pages on, Hawkins proposed a way of getting Britain to adopt policies amenable to the US, 'The appropriate instrument for crystallizing and, if

Trade Talks and Lend-Lease Consideration

possible, settling the issue presented is the lend-lease agreement'[58].

On 28 July Acheson and Keynes met again. The new American draft was presented and was by no means wholly objectionable, but problems arose over the key article, number seven.

> VII The terms and conditions upon which the United Kingdom receives defence aid from the United States of America and the benefits to be received by the United States of America in return therefor, as finally determined, shall be such as not to burden commerce between the two countries but to promote mutually advantageous economic relations between them and the betterment of world wide economic relations, they shall provide against discrimination in either the United States of America or the United Kingdom against the importation of any produce originating in the other country; and they shall provide for the formulation of measures for the achievement of these ends[59].

Keynes wanted to reach an agreement but, nevertheless, he vehemently objected to this article. According to Acheson,

> he burst into a speech such as only he could make. The British could not 'make such a commitment in good faith'; 'it would require an imperial conference'; 'it saddled upon the future an iron-clad formula from the Nineteenth-Century'; 'it contemplated the...hopeless task of returning to a gold standard'; and so on[60].

Keynes later apologised for cavilling at the word 'discrimination', but the damage was done[61]. Acheson coldly explained that the intent of article seven was that at the end of the war, after Britain had received vast quantities of aid, she was simply to be prohibited from taking whatever trade measures she liked against the US. He went on to admit that technical language had been used which prohibited Imperial Preference and possibly import and export exchange controls. Keynes subsequently reported to London that Acheson's ideas on discrimination were

Trade Talks and Lend-Lease Consideration

technical whereas the President had had nothing so specific in mind[62]. Before the meeting ended Keynes cooled down and promised Acheson that he would try to explain the American position to the British Government in London, to which he was due to return the following day. Before parting Keynes warned Acheson that assessment of the draft in London might take some time[63].

Halifax and Keynes had been optimistic after their talk with Roosevelt on 8 July; they were now disappointed by the turn of events. Halifax told the Foreign Office that in his opinion the Americans were determined to get some assurances regarding British postwar economic policies, but as article seven stood he thought it was too specific and that it could prove highly embarrassing. He did not recommend acceptance of the new American draft though he was eager for Britain to commit herself to liberal economic policies in a general way.

The problems of discrimination and economic controls were proving to be ubiquitous, and American attitudes about them had hardened. On 1 August Hawkins wrote to Acheson that Keynes must be made to realise that US public opinion would not accept British discriminatory policies. He thought Keynes' approach was too academic and oblivious of political realities. Three days later Hawkins circulated his lengthy memorandum about the problems British economic policies posed for the US and he also raised the matter of discrimination in the American Cabinet[64]. Such were the 'economic consequences of Mr. Keynes' as one historian has put it[65].

Keynes was aware of the growing hostility to British evasiveness in Washington and he was frightened of the situation deteriorating. He wanted the British Government to be as forthcoming as possible but he was not prepared to accept article seven as it stood. He put forward a re-formulation of the second part of the article for Kingsley Wood.

> they shall provide for joint and agreed action by the U.S. and the U.K., each working within the limits of their governing economic conditions, directed to the progressive attainment of a balanced international economy which would render unnecessary policies of discrimination and other impediments to the freedom of trade.[66]

Trade Talks and Lend-Lease Consideration

The Chancellor of the Exchequer liked this. He and Keynes wanted safeguards against two possible eventualities. Firstly, the imposition on Britain of a unilateral obligation to reduce or to abolish preferential tariffs and commercial and exchange controls. If such commitments were unavoidable then they should be tied to commensurate US concessions on tariffs. The inclusion of the phrase 'agreed and joint action' was to emphasise the reciprocity of the obligations. Secondly, Keynes and Wood were acutely aware of Britain's vulnerability to the vagaries that they expected in the postwar international economy, and consequently any commitments had to be conditional upon economic conditions prevailing then.

By August 1941 the first climax of the differences in the Anglo-American economic alliance was rapidly approaching. For nearly nine months British and American negotiators had haggled over economic policies and speculated about the future. At the end of July matters were coming to a head. Keynes and Wood hoped that their reformulation of article seven of the US draft agreement of 28 July would allow agreement to be made, but before matters could proceed further Churchill, Roosevelt and their advisers at the Atlantic Conference pre-empted them and took up the question of future economic policy themselves. The manner in which Churchill and Roosevelt eventually agreed on the economic clause of the Atlantic Charter, and the substance of it, had a major bearing upon the character of subsequent Anglo-American economic discussions and policies.

NOTES

1. 'The Lend-Lease Act', Section 3. 55 Stat. (Part 1) 31 (1941).
2. Memo. of conversation between Stirling, Hawkins, Cooper, Fuqua, 23 Dec. 1940, 611.4131/2541.
3. See Dominions Office to Southern Rhodesia 31 May 1941, A4191/2354/45, FO371/26252.
4. Shackle to Stirling, 9 May 1941, A3435/2354/45, FO371/26251.
5. Stirling to Board of Trade, 11 May 1941, A3495/2354/45, FO371/26251.
6. Board of Trade to Stirling, A3565/2354/45, FO371/26251.
7. Amery to Eden, 30 May 1941, W6669/37/49, FO 371/28799.
8. Eden to Amery, 6 June 1941, W6669/37/49, FO 371/28799.

Trade Talks and Lend-Lease Consideration

9. Halifax to Hull and his reply, 16 and 21 May 1941, 611.4131/2560. See also Halifax to FO, 23 May 1941, A3895/235/45 and Dominions Office to New Zealand, South Africa and Australia, 31 May 1941, A4191/2354/45, FO371/26252.
10. Treasury and Board of Trade to Phillips and Stirling, 5 and 9 June 1941, W6315/37/49, FO371/28799.
11. Frank Lee, Treasury Delegation in Washington to F.E. Harmer, Treasury, 6 Dec.1944, Public Record Office T160/1375/F17942/010/6 (hereinafter only P.R.O. reference will be given).
12. Cox memoranda, 8 and 14 March 1941, F.D. Roosevelt Library, Cox Papers, box 78, folder: Aid to Britain, Vol.VI.
13. Lend-Lease Consideration, second draft, 11 March 1941, ibid.
14. Roosevelt to Morgenthau and his reply 13 and 14 March 1941, F. D. Roosevelt Library, Roosevelt PSF, box 100, and Hopkins Papers, box 305, folder: Background to Lend-Lease.
15. Foley to Morgenthau, 2 April 1941, Roosevelt PSF, box 49, folder: G.B. Transfer of Defence Articles.
16. Berle Diary, 14 March and 15 April 1941, F.D. Roosevelt Library, Berle Papers, box 212.
17. Ibid.
18. Keynes to Teasury 21 May 1941, T160/1105/F17 660/02/1.
19. Roosevelt to Hull, 16 May 1941, 841.24/603
20. Morgenthau to Roosevelt, 20 May 1941, Roosevelt PSF, box 100.
21. Berle Diary, 13 May 1941, Berle Papers, box 212. Text of the speech at Halifax to Eden, 9 June 1941, A4395/3795/45, F0371/26264.
22. D. Acheson, *Present At The Creation* (W. W. Norton Company, New York, 1969), p.23.
23. Acheson to Berle, Hawkins, Feis et al, 21 May 1941 and memo. 22 May 1941. Not everyone in the department agreed with the new draft. James Dunn, one of the European specialists, thought the quid pro quo should be kept separate from economic policies which the department wanted to press upon the British, Dunn to Acheson 22 May 1941, nevertheless by the end of May Hull had approved the draft. All sources at 841.24/603.2.
24. Keynes to London, 25 May 1941, T160/1105/F17660/02/1.
25. Ronald to Waley, 30 May 1941. The FO was upset with the Americans because after suggesting

that Britain pay part of the construction costs for the bases exchanged for American destroyers, the Americans had said the British could not use the bases whereas certain Latin American countries could. Ibid.

26. H.M. Diary, 404, pp.235-247, 4 June 1941.
27. Ibid., pp.269-333.
28. Ibid.
29. Cox to Hopkins, 6 June 1941, Hopkins Papers, box 325, folder: Lend-Lease Operation III.
30. H.M. Diary, 406, p.163, 9 June 1941, Treasury meeting pp.157-165 and memo. for President pp.166-171.
31. Memo. 9 June 1941, Hopkins Papers, box 307, folder: Period Between Trips to London. For comparison of drafts see memo. to President, 9 June 1941, at same location, and Treasury draft at H.M. Diary 406, pp.166-171.
32. See memo. by Redvers Opie, 12 Aug. 1941, T160/1105/F17660/02/1.
33. Halifax to Wood and Churchill, 10 June 1941, ibid.
34. Wood to Eden, 10 June 1941, ibid.
35. Churchill and Wood to Halifax, 15 June 1941, and Wood to Churchill 14 June 1941, ibid. For Wood's reservations about the commission see Wood to Eden, 23 June 1941, W7782/426/49, F0371/28901.
36. Memo. 20 June 1941, Roosevelt PSF, box 156, folder: Lend-Lease.
37. Wood to Churchill, 28 June 1941, T160/1105/F17660/02/1.
38. Chancellor of the Exchequer to Washington, 8 July 1941, W8340/39/49, F0371/28802.
39. Washington to F0 (dispatched 3.20 p.m.), 8 July 1941, W8340/39/49, F0371/28802.
40. Washington to F0 (dispatched 2.58 p.m.), 8 July 1941, ibid.
41. Memo. of conversation Keynes and Acheson, 7 July 1941, 841.24/635½. There is disagreement between British and American records about the date Halifax and Keynes met Roosevelt. Acheson's memo. of 7 July refers to Keynes informing him of the substance of the talks he had had with the President, whereas British records indicate the meeting did not occur until the following day. In Washington to F0 (3.20 p.m.), 8 July 1941, W8340/39/49, F0371/28802, it is stated 'J.M.K. [Keynes] and Halifax saw President today', also the 8 July was a Tuesday and in Chancellor of Exchequer to Washington, 29 June 1941, W7905/37/49,

F0371/28801, it is mentioned that Halifax and Keynes 'are to meet with F.D.R. [Roosevelt] on the following Tuesday'. On this evidence it looks as if 8 July is the correct date.

42. Washington to F0 (3.20 p.m.), 8 July 1941, W8340/39/49, F0371/28802, and Keynes to Wood, 8 July 1941, T160/1105/F17660/02/1.

43. Waley to Hopkins, 9 July 1941, T160/1105/F17660/02/1.

44. Churchill and Wood to Washington, 14 July 1941, W8377/37/49, F0371/28802.

45. Wood to Keynes, 14 July 1941, ibid.

46. Stirling to Board of Trade, (received) 4 July 1941, W8681/426/49, F0371/28901.

47. Washington to F0, 4 July 1941, W9465/426/49, F0371/28901.

48. F0 to Washington, 16 July 1941, W8738/426/49, F0371/28901. An interesting line taken in this telegram was that while there was a provision in the 1938 agreement which allowed economic controls to be imposed in wartime, there was no mention as to when they should be removed. Eden, Duncan and Wood thought this might provide Britain with legitimate grounds for continuing controls after the war. This was a rather cavalier interpretation of the treaty and did not provide a solution to the trade talks.

49. Ibid.

50. See Acheson, **Present at the Creation**, p.29, and Keynes to Wood, 15 July 1941, W9078/37/49, F0371/28803. Keynes in a rather I-told-you-so fashion explained to Wood that he did not think they could get excused from repayments without being more forthcoming about the economic policy declaration, however as we shall see Keynes was not prepared to go as far as the State Department wanted.

51. Opie memo. 12 Aug. 1941, T160/1105/F17660/02/1.

52. Berle Diary, 17 and 23 July, Berle Papers, box 213.

53. Acheson to Welles, 15 July 1941, Roosevelt PSF, box 96, folder: Welles Correspondence June to Dec. 1941.

54. Roosevelt to Acheson, 18 July 1941, ibid.

55. Ibid.

56. Welles memo. 27 July 1941, 841.24/646½. The author owes this point to D. Reynolds, **The Creation of the Anglo-American Alliance 1937-41** (Europa, London, 1981), p.275.

57. Hull to Roosevelt, 19 Nov. 1941, Roosevelt PSF, box 16, folder: Lend-Lease III.

Trade Talks and Lend-Lease Consideration

58. Hawkins memo. to Hull, Welles and Acheson, 4 Aug. 1941, Roosevelt PSF, box 90, folder: State Department.
59. See Wood to Eden with draft attached, 8 Aug. 1941, W9748/37/49, F0371/28804.
60. Acheson, *Present at the Creation*, p.30.
61. Keynes to Acheson, 29 July 1941, 841.24/648½.
62. Keynes memo. 28 July 1941, T160/1105/F7660/02/1.
63. Acheson memo. 28 July 1941, 841.24/820.
64. Hawkins to Acheson, 1 Aug. 1941, 841.24/643 , and Halifax to London, 3 Aug. 1941, W9552/37/49, F0371/28803.
65. Reynolds in *Anglo-American Alliance.*
66. Wood to Eden with draft attached, 8 Aug. 1941, W9748/37/49, F0371/28804.

Chapter Three

THE ATLANTIC CHARTER AND LEND-LEASE

A declaration of intent by Britain about postwar economic policy had become of the utmost concern for the State Department in the context of Anglo-American economic relations by August 1941. After some uncertainty about the procedure by which Britain was to be brought to a commitment to postwar liberal economic policies, Acheson, Welles, Berle and Hawkins decided by mid-summer 1941 that such a statement should be included in the Consideration Agreement (i.e. article seven of the Mutual Aid Agreement). Their decision, however, did not preclude the possibility of seeking a similar commitment in a different context as well, and in fact this is exactly what Undersecretary of State Welles did at the meeting between Roosevelt and Churchill at the Atlantic Conference.

Roosevelt first began to think of a meeting with Churchill after receiving the latter's message of 7 December 1940, in which Britain's imminent bankruptcy was declared and in which a series of political and strategic issues were raised. The President believed that a meeting would enable them to sort out those issues quickly and he hoped that a personal rapport between him and Churchill might develop which would facilitate future decision-making[1]. In the months that followed the night-time blitz on Britain's cities, and German victories in North Africa and the Mediterranean prevented Churchill from leaving the UK and Roosevelt's hopes for a meeting between them from being quickly realised. Harry Hopkins partly compensated for the President's disappointment with his trip to London as a special envoy in February 1941. Hopkins was a great success; the account of one meeting between him and Churchill, which has perhaps been embellished for dramatic effect,

The Atlantic Charter and Lend-Lease

illustrates the informal, no-nonsense friendship they established in early 1941 upon which Churchill was to rely often in the coming years in order to sound out Roosevelt on delicate matters. The scene was after dinner and Churchill had launched into one of his famous perorations. He sought to persuade Hopkins that England was fighting the war for the same goals that had been pursued in the New Deal.

> He wound up after about half an hour. Nobody spoke for a moment after he had finished; everyone else was waiting uneasily for the reaction of President Roosevelt's representative, who had slumped farther and farther down on his spine. "Well, Mr. Prime Minister", Hopkins finally said, "neither the President nor myself gives a damn about what you've been saying. All we're interested in in Washington is how we can beat that son of a bitch in Berlin". Churchill smiled...and pulled out a fresh cigar.[2]

Hopkins did much to pave the way for the friendship which later developed between Roosevelt and the Prime Minister.

On the 22 June 1941, the anniversary of Napoleon's march on Moscow, Hitler invaded the Soviet Union. With Germany's attention now focused mainly to the East, Hopkins, in July during his second trip to London, found the time was ripe to conclude arrangements for a meeting between Roosevelt and Churchill. The date set was early August and the place eventually decided upon was Placentia Bay, Newfoundland.

The Atlantic Conference was an organisational shambles and this had important consequences for Anglo-American economic relations. The Americans were not prepared for substantive talks and a British memorandum shows that there was no formal agenda. The meetings were haphazardly arranged and the participants were often unsure about what they were supposed to be discussing[3]. Neither Churchill nor Roosevelt had specified what the purpose of the meeting was to be, though they were both keen to establish a closer relationship, and a number of issues begged attention such as the battle for the Atlantic, the German invasion of the Soviet Union, the Japanese threat in the Far East and the problem of secret wartime agreements which might

The Atlantic Charter and Lend-Lease

adversely affect the peace settlement after the war. This latter point combined with propaganda considerations to produce the Atlantic Charter which was one of the main achievements of the meeting.

Roosevelt suggested to Churchill on the first evening of the conference that they should issue a joint statement which would identify common goals for the two liberal democracies and which would offer the world an alternative vision to that presented by the Axis Powers. Churchill agreed, and the result was the Atlantic Charter which was the first Anglo-American declaration of war aims. References to the future and to the ideals which the two leaders hoped to see fulfilled were necessarily involved but point four of the declaration, which dealt with economic policies, developed during the course of negotiations along more specific lines than either Roosevelt or Churchill had anticipated. The man responsible for giving the declaration its unexpected twist was Sumner Welles who saw the joint statement as a chance for getting Britain to make that elusive commitment to postwar policies of freer trade and non-discrimination which the State Department so keenly wanted. How Welles fared in this attempt was determined mainly by the attitudes of Roosevelt and Churchill, and before looking at the conference a few words need to be devoted to the two leaders and their views on postwar policy.

There were a number of occasions in the months preceding the Atlantic Conference when Roosevelt had cause to think about the problem of postwar policy, and as we have seen there was more than a hint of a difference about this between him and members of the State Department. Just how different their views were becomes apparent in their respective attitudes towards a major speech by Eden on British war aims at the Mansion House in London on 30 May. The address echoed the sentiments expressed by Hull earlier in the month at the inauguration of the National Foreign Trade Week but it was much less specific. Eden spoke of Britain's commitment to social security at home and abroad, and concerning economic policy he went on to say, 'When peace comes we shall make such relaxation of our war-time financial arrangements as will permit the revival of international trade on the widest possible basis'[4]. A week later Leo Pasvolsky, a senior economic adviser in the State Department, wrote a lengthy memorandum to Hull pointing out the shortcomings of Eden's speech. Pasvolsky was particularly worried by the absence of any mention of specific means of attaining the rather vague objectives mentioned by Eden. He noted that the speech was far less acceptable to the State Department than the one made by the Prime Minister, Chamberlain, on 31 January 1940, when a clear statement of intent was made to return to the Most Favoured Nation Principle and multilateral channels of trade after the war. In the light of Eden's less satisfactory statement Pasvolsky suggested that there should be a joint Anglo-American exploration, 'to work out a more or less precise post-war program'[5]. In correspondence which took place a few days later between Berle and Roosevelt a rather amusing irony is evident concerning Pasvolsky's views.

Berle like other members of the State Department, feared that secret wartime diplomacy might cause a repeat of the kind of catastrophe which had occurred at the Paris Peace conference in 1919. He did not want the State Department to have its hands tied and its principles compromised by commitments made by Britain, or any other power, on the basis of short-term expediency. At the end of June 1941 Berle's worst suspicions were aroused by rumours reaching Washington of secret British agreements concerning postwar Yugoslavia. He promptly asked Roosevelt for permission to sketch out American policy for the future which would indicate among other things opposition to secret arrangements for the postwar world. The President granted Berle his request though he insisted that any plans should be kept confidential. He then most significantly went on to say,

> When I saw Keynes three weeks ago, I told him I did not like the proposed speech of Eden's [i.e. the Mansion House Speech] because while we could all agree on objectives, we could all fight about the machinery to attain them. He got Eden to eliminate the methods...and we should follow that idea over here[6].

Thus Keynes and Halifax were quite right in July when they reported to London that Roosevelt did not wish for details and definitions regarding postwar policy. The President was only prepared to state US goals in general terms. There was therefore a substantial difference between his position and the State Department line as advocated by Pasvolsky on 7 June.

The Atlantic Charter and Lend-Lease

During early July Berle continued to caution his colleagues about British secret commitments and in addition he expressed his fear that Britain intended to develop a controlled trading system on the lines developed in Germany by the economist Schacht[7]. Sumner Welles, Hopkins and Roosevelt were all concerned and the result was a letter to Churchill on 14 July in which Roosevelt asked the Prime Minister to release a statement, which he would publicly support, indicating that, 'no post-war peace commitments as to territories, populations or economics have been given'[8]. The tone of the letter was quite insistent but Roosevelt received no response. This lack of forthcomingness which was also evident to Acheson in the 15 July meeting with Keynes that we considered in the previous chapter prompted Roosevelt, with some nudging from the State Department, to lend more support to the idea of extracting a declaration of postwar intent from Britain. In July the President had instructed Hopkins that during his trip to London he should tell Churchill not to expect any talk of American entry into the war or of territorial and economic matters at the Atlantic Conference; but by the time Roosevelt got to Placentia Bay he had changed his mind[9]. The propaganda value of a joint declaration and his desire to prevent secret agreements which might compromise postwar settlements overcame his wariness about speaking on postwar policy. He did not confer with Churchill or prepare a draft prior to the conference, but in informal talks with Welles he made it clear that a declaration of principles, which would prevent Britain entering secret agreements of the kind she had made in World War I, was uppermost in his mind[10]. He also talked casually about the future of Britain's restrictive trade policies with his son Elliott shortly before the British arrived at Placentia Bay[11], but there was little, if any, specific preparation for the joint statement though Welles, no doubt with it in mind, took to the conference a copy of the draft Mutual Aid Agreement which Acheson had given to Keynes on 28 July. The draft contained the kind of declaration the State Department sought from Britain but, as we noted in the previous chapter, although Roosevelt had formally approved the draft for negotiation it is unlikely that he realised it contained the kind of detail about methods which he had told Berle to steer clear of on 26 June. Events at the conference show that Roosevelt had not

The Atlantic Charter and Lend-Lease

significantly changed his opinions; he wanted a general declaration of intent but he would not support Welles when he attempted to plagiarise article seven of the draft Mutual Aid Agreement in the joint declaration. In Roosevelt's opinion mention of such detailed means and formulations would have had a divisive effect on Anglo-American relations at a time when it was crucial to maintain harmony and accord.

Churchill was even more cautious than Roosevelt about public statements concerning postwar policies. A few months prior to the Atlantic Conference he had 'blown up' over matters of this kind, which had been leaked to the press by Harold Nicolson who was, ironically, in Duff Cooper's Ministry of Information[12]. Concerning the State Department's ideas Churchill had strong grounds for reticence. His government was virtually unanimous in its opposition to the way in which the State Department wanted Britain to abandon her economic controls. Even those well disposed to State Department objectives, such as members of the Board of Trade, the Economic Section of the Cabinet Secretariat and the North American Department of the Foreign Office, were worried about how Britain was to move towards them. Churchill himself was well known as a liberal imperialist who had originally opposed Imperial Preference but it was a mistake, which Ambassador Winant and other Americans made, to think that under the circumstances Britain faced during the war that Churchill would be prepared to give up economic controls. He was far from being ignorant of economic matters; he had been Chancellor of the Exchequer from 1924 to 1929 and so he was well aware of the difficulties confronting Britain. Furthermore, as Colonial Secretary in 1922 he had proved to be a willing compromiser of liberal economic principles when major imperial economic interests were at stake. In that year he supported and implemented the Stevenson Plan to restrict the out-put of rubber in Malaya and Ceylon in order to raise prices[13]. Faced with the grim facts of Britain's wartime economic situation and in the knowledge of widespread opposition in his government to the demands made by members of the State Department Churchill was unwilling to take a doctrinal stance on free trade.

Although Churchill had made no arrangements for a joint declaration before his arrival at Placentia Bay he was delighted to seize the opportunity offered by Roosevelt for identifying common

The Atlantic Charter and Lend-Lease

Anglo-American aspirations in a statement of general principles because this would help to bring the two countries closer together and because it would provide beneficial propaganda. He knew as well as Roosevelt, however, that any resort to details might raise divisive issues which would damage the prospects for wartime collaboration and destroy the propaganda value of the conference.

Churchill and Roosevelt travelled to Placentia Bay respectively on *HMS Prince of Wales* and the *USS Augusta*. Churchill was accompanied by his personal friend and adviser Lord Cherwell, by the Permanent Undersecretary at the Foreign Office Sir Alexander Cadogan, by the Chiefs of Staff and by Harry Hopkins who had just returned from Moscow. Hopkins suffered one of his frequent bouts of ill-health on the voyage but he was sufficiently recovered to advise Roosevelt at the Conference. Churchill's entourage was enlarged on the last day of the conference, 12 August, by the belated arrival of Max Beaverbrook the Minister of Supply, who was too late to influence the course of events. Roosevelt took with him Undersecretary of State Welles, Averell Harriman, who had been given the job of expediting Lend-Lease in London, and his Chiefs of Staff.

Churchill arrived at the rendezvous a few hours after Roosevelt on 9 August. Cadogan and Welles got straight down to business that afternoon. Ambassador Halifax had primed Cadogan for the discussions by advising him to be accommodating as Welles had recently been friendly and helpful[14]. This might explain why Cadogan's response was not completely candid when Welles raised the question of Britain's intentions concerning postwar economic policy. Welles produced a copy of the extant American draft of the Mutual Aid Agreement and there was some discussion of article seven, which was the consideration part, and of economic discrimination. Cadogan was diplomatic; he said he had always disliked the Ottawa Agreements but then added that decisions on such matters would have to be taken by Churchill of whose views he professed ignorance. Cadogan may sincerely have disliked Imperial Preference, however, he disliked American proposals for its removal even more. A few months later he described the American version of article seven as, 'impertinent blackmail', but he gave Welles no inkling of such views on 9 August. Indeed, Welles commented later that there was complete accord on the new American draft between him and Cadogan.

The Atlantic Charter and Lend-Lease

This seems to have led Welles to the mistaken belief that proposals like those in article seven would not be uncogenial to the British[15].

A few hours after the exchange of views between Cadogan and Welles, Churchill and Roosevelt dined aboard the USS Augusta. During the course of the evening the President suggested that they should issue a joint statement of principles and intent. Churchill eagerly responded and took the initiative by offering to draw up the first draft. Early on Sunday morning he sketched the overall format for Cadogan who swiftly knocked it into shape. Churchill made some minor amendments and then it was handed to Welles after the Sunday service on the deck of the Prince of Wales in which they had all appropriately sung 'Onward Christian Soldiers'. Churchill and Cadogan had produced a broad, general statement which tried to identify common ground between the British and the Americans. Divisive issues were deliberately avoided and as the paragraph on economic policy shows there was thus an inevitable element of blandness.

> Fourth they will strive to bring about a fair and equitable distribution of essential produce, not only within their territorial boundaries, but between the nations of the world.[16]

Within twenty four hours Welles had re-cast point four in a radically different vein, which was strikingly similar to that embodied in article seven of the Mutual Aid Agreement.

> Fourth they will strive to promote mutually advantageous relations between them through the elimination of any discrimination in either the United States of America or in the United Kingdom against the importation of any product originating in the other country; and they will endeavour to further the enjoyment by all peoples of access on equal terms to the markets and to the raw materials which are needed for their economic prosperity.[17]

When Roosevelt saw this he revised it in accordance with views he had previously expressed. It is possible that an irritable exchange between Roosevelt and Churchill the previous evening over free trade and Britain's imperial arrangements reinforced the President's belief that they should avoid discussing means and stick to stating ends, but the President had been convinced of the desirability of this for some time[18]. He changed the phrase concerning the elimination of discrimination in Welles' draft from being a description of a means so that it specified an end.

> Fourth they will endeavour to further the enjoyment by all peoples of access without discrimination and on equal terms, to the markets and to the raw materials of the world which are needed for their economic prosperity.[19]

On Monday morning 11 August Roosevelt, accompanied by Harry Hopkins and Welles, gave the re-draft of the joint declaration to Churchill. The Prime Minister read through the first three points quite happily but then of point four he said he was in no position to accept it because it might be taken to call into question the contractual obligations of the Ottawa Agreements. He went on, in reply to a protest from Welles, to point out that in the past British free trade had been met by successive doses of American protectionism. While the Undersecretary was digesting this, the Prime Minister proposed that, 'with due respect for their existing obligations' should be inserted into point four, that 'trade' should be substituted for 'markets' and that 'without discrimination' should be deleted. Welles refused to capitulate; he tenaciously pressed for a commitment from Britain to abandon discrimination. He pointed out that Britain was only required to commit herself to moving towards freer non-discriminatory trade; he did not of course mention that his original draft had been more demanding. Churchill replied by reminding Welles that he had opposed the Ottawa Agreements for a long time but he went on to reiterate his legal difficulties and to explain that if Welles wanted to retain his version then the Dominions would have to be consulted, which would take no less than a week, and that even then their verdict would probably be unfavourable[20]. This was a game of foxes and hounds. The views Churchill expressed for American consumption were slightly different from those he relayed to the Cabinet later in the day.

The Atlantic Charter and Lend-Lease

> The fourth condition would evidently have to be amended to safeguard our obligations contracted in Ottawa and not prejudice the future of imperial preference. This might fall into its place after the war in a general economic settlement with decisive lowering of tariffs and trade barriers throughout the world. But we cannot settle it now.[21]

In an effort to de-fuse the situation Hopkins suggested that Cadogan and Welles should re-draft point four. He commented that, 'it was inconceivable that the issuance of the joint declaration should be held up by a matter of this kind'[22]. Poor Welles was not as perceptive as Hopkins, and instead of graciously accepting defeat he expostulated that it was not a question of words but principles and that this paragraph embodied the ideal for which the administration had striven for the past nine years. The end nevertheless came quickly as Roosevelt sided with Hopkins. It was decided that Churchill and Cadogan should re-draft point four and then consult with Welles later in the day.

After the meeting Welles made one last attempt to change the President's mind. He suggested to him that Churchill should be persuaded to expedite communications with the Dominions so that the commitment to non-discrimination could be included in point four. He specifically argued that if Churchill's phrase 'with due respect for their existing obligations' was adopted then, 'the article would have no application to the Ottawa Agreements, and its force would be gravely weakened'[23]. Welles' idea that the problem could be resolved by expediting communications with the Dominions evinces a lack of diplomatic finesse if not downright naivety. Roosevelt did not take Welles' advice. It might have been, as Welles speculated later, that Hopkins brought pressure to bear to give way to Churchill on point four, but it is unlikely he did anything more than reinforce Roosevelt's already existing disposition[24]. Roosevelt knew the issue of discrimination was too controversial and potentially divisive to be resolved in the context of the joint declaration. Why Welles ever thought the British would renounce discriminatory controls is difficult to imagine; he may have been encouraged by the false impression he acquired from talks with Cadogan on 9 August but he certainly had no other grounds apart from a rather inflated opinion of his own abilities.

A few minutes before Welles went to see Cadogan about point four he received the President's response to his arguments.

> Dear Sumner,
> Time being of the essence I think I can stand on my own former formulas - to wit: access to raw materials. This omits entirely the other subject which is the only one in conflict: discrimination in trade.
> The fourth would then read "of access to the raw materials of the world" etc.
> Yours,
> F.D.R. [25]

When Welles met Cadogan he was a little surprised and rather pleased to find that the declaration still had some teeth in it - teeth which Roosevelt would have been content for the British to extract. Churchill had retained the phrase 'access on equal terms to trade' which could be construed as a general commitment to non-discriminatory policies. As this was more acceptable to Welles than the minimum which Roosevelt had instructed him to accept, he agreed to the British re-draft and it became the final version of point four[26]. Thus the economic part of the declaration was equivocal; for the British its main value was the American acknowledgement that existing controls were not to be unconditionally abandoned, while for Welles the salient point was the commitment to move towards equal access to trade.

> Fourth, they will endeavour, with due respect for their existing obligations, to further the enjoyment of all States, great or small, victor or vanquished, of access, on equal terms, to the trade and to the raw materials of the world which are needed for their economic prosperity.[27]

When Welles took this to Roosevelt the latter remarked that even this version was 'better than he had thought Mr. Churchill would be willing to concede'[28]. If further proof were needed to establish Roosevelt's belief that it would be difficult and therefore at this stage of the war unwise to try to extract detailed commitments from Britain then this comment provides it.

Welles made a grave tactical error in raising the question of economic discrimination at the Atlantic Conference. He failed to coordinate fully with the President concerning his intentions and the result was a declaration which compromised the State Department's principles. There is no doubt that the wording of point four was closer to the position the British were defending in the Supplementary Trade Talks and in the Consideration Talks than to the one espoused by the State Department. Welles had suffered a diplomatic defeat which weakened his department's negotiating position for the future.

The text of point four agreed upon by Cadogan and Welles was not finally authorised by Roosevelt and Churchill until the early afternoon of the following day. In the meantime the Deputy Prime Minister Attlee, unaware of the outcome of Cadogan's discussion with Welles, called an emergency meeting of the Cabinet which took place in the early hours of Tuesday morning (London was five hours ahead of local Newfoundland time). Members of the Cabinet discussed the Welles/Roosevelt text of the declaration and Churchill's counter-proposals. Churchill put them under considerable pressure to accept his amendments without further ado; he suspected that the phrase 'equal access to trade' would arouse opposition in the Cabinet but he did not want to antagonise the Americans by making further demands. He was of course ignorant of the fact that Roosevelt had told Welles that he was prepared to leave the whole question of discrimination in trade entirely to one side. Churchill, like Roosevelt, was willing to compromise for the value to be gained from stating common Anglo-American aims and by projecting an image of cooperation.

The Cabinet sent Churchill a revision of point four and added a new paragraph-point five.

> Fourth, they will endeavour to further enjoyment by all peoples of access, without discrimination and on equal terms, to raw materials of the world which are needed for their economic prosperity, and to promote greatest possible expansion of markets for the interchange of goods and services throughout the world.
> Fifth, they desire to bring about the fullest collaboration between all nations

in the economic field, with the object of securing for all improved labour standards, economic advancement and social security.[29]

Attlee informed Churchill that these were only the preliminary views of the Cabinet; he explained that Kingsley Wood and Duncan, the two men concerned most with economic policy, had been absent from the meeting and that a more considered view would be sent later in the morning[30]. The Cabinet had already adopted a more defensive position than Churchill; the prohibition against discrimination was left in point four but it was now only to apply to raw materials, and point five could be used to argue against dismantling economic controls if such action was seen as likely to endanger either the domestic economy or social security. Churchill's response to this was simply to increase the pressure on the Cabinet to agree to the Welles/Roosevelt version plus his amendments, and in fact in the early afternoon of 12 August Churchill went ahead and agreed with Roosevelt on that version without waiting for the 'considered proposals' of his Cabinet to arrive (at least that is what he later reported to Attlee, though there is circumstantial evidence to suggest that he did receive the Cabinet's considered opinions before concluding the Atlantic Charter but chose to ignore them)[31]. He put the preliminary views of the Cabinet to Roosevelt who accepted point five but rejected the re-formulation of point four. Thus the social security clause which helped to stengthen Britain's economic defences was included in the Atlantic Charter but the phrase about equal access, contrary to what became the considered opinion of the Cabinet, stayed in [32].

When the Cabinet re-convened at ten o'clock it had no less than three drafts of article four before it; the Welles/Roosevelt draft as amended by Churchill, the Cabinet's draft of earlier that morning, and a draft put forward by Kingsley Wood which was actually Keynes' new draft of the Consideration Agreement which we discussed at the end of the previous chapter. In the meeting Wood drew the attention of his colleagues to the fact that the problems connected with point four had also arisen in relation to article seven of the Mutual Aid Agreement. He read an extract from a letter by Amery, 'which stressed the importance of not permitting any doubt as to our right and

The Atlantic Charter and Lend-Lease

determination to pursue a policy of inter-Imperial Preference'[33]. Eden also favoured a defensive strategy; he said that there would be grave economic dangers for Britain after the war if America insisted on the abandonment of exchange controls[34]. After considerable discussion the Cabinet wrote to Churchill that they 'greatly preferred' their version of point four, which they had sent him earlier, subject to the additional amendment that the promotion of the greatest possible expansion of markets should be done with due respect for existing obligations. They wanted a clear distinction to be drawn between trade and raw materials: in the latter case, and this might have been partly a consequence of the Wheat Talks we shall be looking at shortly, the Cabinet favoured equal terms of access and saw no reason to qualify this by reference to existing obligations. 'We are, however, bound to make this reservation in dealing with trade in order to safeguard Imperial preference and, e.g. to prevent our markets from being undercut by countries with a low standard of living like Japan'. The Cabinet also feared that 'access on equal terms to trade' might be interpreted in terms of 'extreme laissez-faire' which was unacceptable as indeed was anything which might prevent Britain from using exchange controls after the war. Even with Churchill's amendments the Cabinet was still unhappy but at the end of the telegram they conceded that if the Prime Minister had 'great difficulty' in getting their proposals accepted then they would accept the American draft subject to his amendments[35].

As we have observed the Cabinet's arguments were to no avail, but they need to be borne in mind in the context of developments in Anglo-American economic policies after the Atlantic Conference. Point four thus committed America and Britain, with due respect for their existing obligations, to the goal of equal access for trade and raw materials. This was not a total victory for the British over the State Department but it was good enough for Amery to congratulate Wood on, 'the comparatively innocuous character of Points Four and Five in the Joint Declaration'[36]. Duncan, Wood and the Minister Without Portfolio Arthur Greenwood were also pleased because they believed point four provided a defence of Imperial Preference which could be incorporated into the Consideration Agreement[37].

Once Hull received the text it did not take him long to see the threat posed by the economic provisions of the Atlantic Charter, and as international economic policy was one of Hull's main concerns and one of the few areas of foreign affairs over which Roosevelt did not take direct command during the war, Hull was understandably sensitive about the charter's fourth and fifth points. The anger he came to feel over their content was fortified by the context in which the charter had been born, for while Hull was politically important because of his influence in Congress and because the right wing of the Democratic Party thought he was a sound moderating influence upon New Deal radicalism, his relationship with the President was cool and formal and he was often excluded from important decision-making. Roosevelt much preferred to work with his old school friend Sumner Welles and this caused friction both within the State Department and between Hull and the President. With regard to the Atlantic Conference Hull had been denied any knowledge of it and more pointedly he had discovered that there had been a directive so denying him[38]. The final straw was that his immediate junior, Welles, who Hull personally and professionally disliked, had been privy to the preparations, had attended the conference and had botched up the economic part of the declaration.

Rumours at a press conference on 14 August tended to confirm Hull's fear that London meant to use point four to defend Imperial Preference. Hull was determined that this should not be done. On 18 August he began to work on the President; he sent him the paper by Hawkins of 4 August in which the latter had painted a vivid picture of the dangers posed by Britain's economic controls. Whether Roosevelt read it or not is unclear but a few days later when Hull pressed upon the President the need to clarify point four he agreed that Hull could send the following to Churchill.

> The fourth point in the statement by the President and Mr. Churchill is a forthright declaration of intention by the British and American Governments to do everything in their power, now and in the post-war period by means of the reduction of trade barriers and the reduction or elimination of preferences and discriminations, 'to further the enjoyment...etc.'[39]

The Atlantic Charter and Lend-Lease

This attempt to cut through the equivocation of point four was passed on to Eden and Churchill by US Ambassador Winant. The reaction of the British leaders was not helpful to Hull. There was certainly no inclination in Churchill's Cabinet to give away what safeguards had been won at the Atlantic Conference and while the Prime Minister believed that there could be, 'no great future for the world without a vast breaking down of tariffs and other barriers', he was not prepared to take decisive action at that time, nor was he prepared to countenance British action in the future without reciprocal moves from the US and other countries. He suggested, 'vexatious discriminations as part, of a general scheme to further the enjoyment...etc.' to Kingsley Wood as an alternative which might placate Hull. Wood, cautious as usual, thought the less sensitive term restrictions would be better than discriminations. The Prime Minister agreed and with the further substitution of 'harmful' for 'vexatious' Churchill's re-wording of point four was sent to the State Department via the US Embassy in London[40].

Winant proved to be sympathetic towards Churchill's defensive reply. He told Hull that he thought Churchill favoured Hull's re-phrasing but had been prevented from adopting it because of fears about splits within the Conservative Party if the future of Imperial Preference was placed in question. This assessment was not entirely accurate. Churchill was worried about splitting his party but he was also concerned that the methods adopted for implementing a liberal world economy should not damage British interests. Winant also told Hull that he had been warned that if the Americans insisted on their clarification then it would have to be referred to the Dominions, which would delay things, and that in any case the Dominions would probably reject it in the end. The threat of complicating talks by involving the Dominions or the claim that the Dominions would not agree was frequently and ingenuously used by the British. On this occasion Winant was convinced of Churchill's difficulties and he urged Hull not to press matters[41]. Churchill's re-wording was of no use to Hull but he took Winant's advice and dropped the matter even though he and his deputies were apprehensive about the effect point four might have on the Consideration Agreement.

There were two factors in addition to point four of the Atlantic Charter which each had an

The Atlantic Charter and Lend-Lease

impact upon the re-drafting of the draft Consideration Agreement in London. The first factor was the role played by Arthur Greenwood, Minister Without Portfolio and a leading light in the Labour Party. In February 1941 he had been placed in charge of a new committee, which was often referred to as the Greenwood Committee, to deal with postwar reconstruction policy. In August 1941, he set up a non-ministerial counterpart 'The Committee on Postwar External Economic Policy and Anglo-American Cooperation'[42]. These committees met infrequently and Greenwood has been described as a weak chairman, but until his exit from the government in February 1941 he was an influential figure in Anglo-American economic policy-making. This was largely because of the coordinating role he performed by virtue of his suzerainty over the economic policy committees. In particular, he had a vantage point from which he could see that the position the Americans adopted in the Wheat Talks during the summer of 1941 was directly at odds with the economic principles the State Department had advocated for inclusion in point four of the Atlantic Charter and which were embodied in the American draft of article seven. The second factor was the Wheat Talks themselves which require some detailed explanation.

The abolition of the Corn Laws in 1846 had made Britain an open market for foreign grains and an obvious destination for American wheat. The export of New World cereals burgeoned at the end of the Nineteenth Century and a steady pattern of trade was established with Britain. Doubts about massive reliance on overseas food supplies emerged in Britain with the U-boat blockade during the Great War, but it was not until the Depression that Britain moved drastically away from agricultural free trade with the Agricultural Marketing Acts of 1931 and 1933, and the Wheat Act of 1932. The Second World War accelerated this trend and sparked off consideration of long term measures to foster and expand British agricultural production. The farm lobby, rural interests and an influential section of the Conservative Party led by the Minister of Agriculture, R. S. Hudson, began to think in terms of more protection and of subsidies for farmers to lessen the strategic vulnerability of Britain's reliance on imported foods. Given the Conservative Party's dependence on the electoral support of rural Britain such views were politically powerful. In addition to this the Treasury began to look with favour on any policy which would reduce

The Atlantic Charter and Lend-Lease

Britain's postwar import bill - grain had been Britain's largest single pre-war import item.

The problem with wheat on the American side of the Atlantic was over-production. The depression in the 1930s hit the farming community cruelly. While the industrial unemployed starved and ranks of farmers left the land, as so vividly portrayed in Steinbeck's 'The Grapes of Wrath', the corn of Oklahoma stood as high as an elephant's eye: the problem was that not enough people had the wherewithal to buy it[43]. European and British moves towards economic nationalism exacerbated the problem of American agricultural surpluses and presented the New Deal with one of its most intractable and politically explosive problems.

Henry A. Wallace, born into a farming community in Iowa in 1888, the 'one world idealist' who carried the radical, some claimed left-wing, conscience of the New Deal through to the end of the 1940s, was given the job of sorting out America's agricultural problems by Roosevelt. Wallace's solution was two-fold; he 'retired' thousands of acres of marginal farmland by paying farmers not to produce, and secondly he supported Hull's trade programme in the hope of recovering overseas markets[44]. The British wartime controls which reduced her purchases of American agricultural products was thus a considerable blow to the hopes of the US Department of Agriculture and as we have seen, Hull was quick to complain on its behalf to the British Government. One result of these complaints was the Supplementary Trade Talks; however, wheat was so important that it merited negotiations on its own. Before leaving the Department of Agriculture to become Roosevelt's running mate in the 1940 election, Wallace began to address the problem of the world production of and international trade in wheat. He decided that free trade alone was not the solution; both domestic production and market supply of wheat were too important strategically, economically, philanthropically and politically to be left to the vagaries of weather, man and the free market. He devised a plan, despite his professed hatred of parochial self-interest, which envisaged a controlled market in the interests of the US. As Vice President he continued to busy himself with economic matters and the emergence of the American Wheat Proposals in August 1941 had his strong backing. Some time later, Ronald Campbell, British Minister in Washington, explained that Wallace's

The Atlantic Charter and Lend-Lease

commitment to American agriculture combined with his arrogance had led him to formulate the Wheat Proposals in a manner which embodied the kind of economic nationalism he deplored in others, but that unfortunately he could not be made to see this[45].

Claude Wickard, 'Roosevelt's farmer from Indiana', and Wallace's successor at the Department of Agriculture, shared Wallace's commitment to promoting American agriculture. One of the pitfalls he and the Vice President wished to avoid was a postwar slump in agricultural prices after American farmers had been encouraged to produce more for the war effort[46]. Thus it was with the objective of establishing prosperous and stable wheat farming in the US that the Americans entered into talks in Washington with the other main producers, Argentina, Canada and Australia, and with Britain who was the main buyer of wheat, between 10 July and 3 August, 1941.

On the same day that Churchill began his journey to Placentia Bay the first round of the Wheat Talks was concluded. The British were shocked by the draft proposals which the US had pushed through the preliminary talks. They knew that they had been drawn up in the US Department of Agriculture but they were surprised that the State Department, whose responsibility it was to negotiate with foreign countries, evinced neither embarrassment about the proposals, which were to control the wheat trade in America's interests, nor any reluctance about pressing them on the British when in all previous talks they had preached the merits of free trade.

The draft which emerged on 3 August had some similarities to proposals for the stabilisation of the wheat trade which had been made in 1939 but there were three unpalatable novelties. Firstly, a minimum price was to be applied to all wheat production, not to seventy five per cent as had previously been the case. Secondly, the minimum price was to be raised from 35/6d. to 38/6d. per quarter; this caused apocalyptic visions in London about Britain's international balance of payments. Thirdly, the Americans were suggesting that the onus of enforcing the agreement should lie with the importing countries. Not only was Britain to accept a vendor's charter and reduce her own cereal production, she was also to be obliged to embargo wheat imports from those who did not join the agreement. London feared that acts of embargo would provoke retaliatory action against British exports

The Atlantic Charter and Lend-Lease

and that the big producers and Britain might appear to be foisting an agreement upon the Soviet Union and the major western European importers and producers when they were in no position to contribute to the discussions[47].

The aspect of the agreement which worried and angered British ministers and officials most was the blatant way it contradicted the much vaunted economic principles of the State Department. The suspicion harboured by some ministers and officials, including Wood and Greenwood, that Hull's pursuit of free trade was simply a guise for pursuing American national interests rather than an altruistic commitment to free trade seemed to be confirmed. The State Department appeared self-righteous and hypocritical because as soon as something arose over which it was in America's interests to have economic controls it immediately stopped talking about laissez-faire and equal access. This had been borne in mind on the 12 August when the Cabinet cabled Churchill that they favoured equal access to raw materials, which of course included wheat. On 15 August in a note expressing his views on the Consideration Agreement, Keynes commented,

> The draft Wheat Agreement is a good illustration of the extreme difficulty of strictly interpreting "discrimination" in the post-war world. On the one hand we are here asked by the United States Government to abjure "discrimination". Yet, in the draft Wheat Agreement, which they press on us in the same week, we are asked to commit ourselves to "discrimination" in the most extreme form against any country which does not accept the wheat plans of the big four.[48]

R. S. Hudson, the Minister of Agriculture, wanted to know where the quid pro quo lay in the wheat proposals; he was so incensed he thought they warranted the removal of restrictions on Britain's cereal acreage and as Leith-Ross of the Ministry of Economic Warfare explained to Winant, 'Hudson even speaks privately of new post-war policy to maintain fertility as[a]long range measure of national defense'[49].

In the latter part of August informal Anglo-American talks on wheat were begun in London between Leith-Ross, Lloyd Steere the Agricultural Attache at the US Embassy, Appleby the US

The Atlantic Charter and Lend-Lease

Undersecretary of Agriculture and R.M. Evans the Director of the US Agricultural Adjustment Agency. It fell to Leith-Ross, who was pro-American and one of the few in the British Administration who favoured the American proposals for long-term price fixing, to explain to Steere that the British Government would not accept the American price formula and that it disliked the idea of reducing the British wheat acreage[50]. This news was ill received in Washington where matters were placed in the unsympathetic hands of Assistant Secretary of State Breckinridge Long who was certainly not an Anglophile. On 4 September in a letter on Hull's behalf Long explained the basis of the American position to Winant. It was a painfully crude exposition of American self-interest, which reflected the thinking of some members both of the Agriculture Department and of the State Department, and it was hardly likely to afford much assistance to the US negotiators in London in their attempts to present an acceptable case to Britain. Long argued that it was America's intention to recover the European wheat market it had lost in the 1920s and to charge the European countries fair prices. He went on,

> It is of course in the interest of wheat-exporting countries that European wheat-importing countries should learn as soon as possible of the new policy which they will at the appropriate time be pressed to adopt. It is before, and not after, their urgent postwar needs have been relieved, that they should appreciate the necessity of international collaboration in working out an effective solution of the world wheat problem.[51]

As these views filtered into the Foreign Office they fuelled the indignation that was already smouldering. Nigel Ronald the department's adviser on postwar economic reconstruction and its representative on Greenwood's committee on external economic policy and Anglo-American cooperation, vitriolically commented on Long's reasoning,

> This is too much like selling one's birthright for a mess of pottage. Do not let us allow ourselves to be manoevred into the position of selling our birthright for a mess of pottage and give

The Atlantic Charter and Lend-Lease

> way too far to meet the Americans on Article VII of the Draft Consideration Agreement.[52]

On 17 September Winant reported to Hull that the British thought that the format of the Wheat Proposals might appear as an objectionable diktat to other countries, and that they disliked the provisions concerning importing nations. The Americans had dropped their proposals for policing prices, but the British were still supposed to police quotas. Winant went on to say that the British were frightened that exchange difficulties would arise, that they objected to the price formula and the proposed reduction of wheat acreage in importing countries and that they regarded the absence of the Soviet Union from the talks as a major problem[53]. On the same day Winant, still surprisingly optimistic that a settlement could be reached, sent a letter to Eden urging the necessity of reaching an accord, but rather imprudently he also passed on verbatim some of Breckinridge Long's arguments[54]. These had already caused violent reactions in London and when they were formally communicated to Eden they provided the pretext for taking the wheat issue to the highest level.

In a telegram on 8 October Churchill wrote to Roosevelt that,

> The draft seems to give the impression that it is contemplated to force on the wheat importing countries of Europe, as a condition of immediate post-war relief, a series of obligations including a drastic restriction of their wheat production, which would vitally affect their agricultural systems.[55]

Churchill said that he thought the propaganda effect of the proposals would be harmful and that the Soviet Union should be a party to any agreement that was to be made but that, given her delicate strategic situation, he thought it would be unwise to distract her with the Wheat Proposals. The Prime Minister wanted to emasculate the American proposals, allowing only anodyne provisions for 'an ever normal granary', a relief pool and export quota arrangements among the big four producers to go forward. Even after this Winant continued to place the most favourable construction possible on the British position. Just before the beginning of the second round of the Wheat Talks in Washington, Winant wrote to Hull on 12 October that,

> In a very frank talk with the Prime Minister he told me that the wheat problem as it affected Great Britain was not a matter of concern to him and I believe he is in agreement with us on our general proposals.[56]

This was somewhat at odds with the tone and substance of Churchill's letter to Roosevelt. Perhaps Winant had misunderstood Churchill or maybe the Prime Minister had not been entirely candid with him; whatever the case may have been Winant misread the situation. He knew that the original reaction of the British to the Wheat Proposals had been caustic but he believed that the talks in London between Leith-Ross and Appleby had done much to dilute the corrosive effect on Anglo-American relations. There was some truth in this but much ill feeling and substantial differences remained. Winant, however, continued, almost to the point of perversity, to construe the atmosphere in London in the Consideration as well as the Wheat Talks as more favourable to American demands than was actually the case. In so doing, he communicated a very misleading impression to Washington.

The Wheat Talks jaundiced British views of American economic plans at the very time that the review of the American July draft of article seven got under way in London. A number of British ministers and officials perceived the inconsistency in American economic demands as a symptom both of bad faith and entrepreneurial avarice. There was widespread determination, bolstered by what was seen as a victory at the Atlantic Conference, not to exchange Britain's economic future for a 'mess of pottage'. Contrary to the reports that Winant later gave Washington that article seven was being reviewed at lowly bureaucratic levels by anti-American officials, it was dealt with by senior ministers including Wood and Greenwood, who were members of the War Cabinet, as well as by Amery, Duncan, Cranborne, Moyne and Dalton the Minister of Economic Warfare[57]. In addition Churchill, Attlee and Eden were all involved directly at various times and also tangentially during Cabinet discussions and in correspondence about identical matters raised by point four of the Atlantic Charter. Winant contributed further to the State Department's misperceptions by suggesting that it was only the arch-Tories - virtually imperialists as he once indignantly referred to them - who were opposing American demands. On a number of occasions he reported favourably about Churchill's attitudes on the Consideration and Wheat Talks and he advised Washington that the Labour Party would unanimously support article seven whereas in fact many in the party were opposed to it, particularly Arthur Greenwood being one of the focal points of ministerial opposition[58].

We may recall that on his return to London Keynes had proposed an alternative to the American July draft of article seven.

> They shall provide for joint and agreed action by the U.S. and the U.K., each working within the limits of their governing economic conditions, directed to the progressive attainment of a balanced international economy which would render unnecessary policies of discrimination and other impediments to the freedom of trade.

This was the starting point for Britain's response to the State Department. It was followed by a constellation of factors, to wit: point four of the Atlantic Charter, Churchill's refusal to be moved by Hull's plea for a more forthright statement on economic policy, and American proposals for a wheat agreement, all of which conspired to stengthen the defensive stance the British Government was already inclined to take on article seven.

During the latter part of August Greenwood, who had taken charge of and coordinated work on the re-draft of article seven, accepted a number of safeguards for Britain's economic interests. By 8 September Amery had got the caveat concerning respect for existing obligations, culled from point four of the Atlantic Charter, added to the new draft. A query from Cranborne about the phrase 'avoidance of special discriminations' which was already a more anodyne re-phrasing of Keynes' version, resulted in the word discrimination being deleted altogether[59]. The substance of article seven now read as follows,

> they shall provide for joint and agreed action by the Government of the United States and the Government of the United Kingdom, (each working within the limits

of their governing economic conditions and
existing obligations/established policies)
directed to the progressive attainment of
a balanced international economy and the
enjoyment by all States,...etc.[60]

It went on to repeat the text of points four and five of the Atlantic Charter and ended with the commitment that the two countries should begin talks as soon as convenient to implement the aims of article seven.

This version was considered by the Foreign Office and its legal advisers in early September and Nigel Ronald explained the conclusions in a lengthy memorandum which he sent to Mr. Daish of the War Cabinet Offices, with copies to the Treasury, the Board of Trade and the Dominion and Colonial offices. The main problem that the Foreign Office identified in article seven arose from the attempt to safeguard three things for Britain: the right to use exchange controls and other measures of trade regulation, the right to take protective measures against cheap goods from countries with lower standards of living, and Imperial Preference. The Foreign Office believed that points four and five of the Atlantic Charter, so long as discrimination was not involved, achieved the first two objectives and therefore there was no point in reproducing their text in article seven. On the third objective, the department thought that the phrases in parentheses were too broad and as their main purpose was to protect Imperial Preference Ronald suggested it would be better either to include an explicit phrase to that effect in article seven or else, and here he put forward a proposal which was eagerly taken up later, the British and Americans could informally minute or agree that article seven was not intended to exclude the use of Imperial Preference[61]. This sparked off a further round of amendments centring on the discrimination issue, the upshot of which was a new draft which in some ways returned to Keynes' version of early August. Keynes was against the line argued by Amery in particular that Britain should just repeat points four and five of the Atlantic Charter in article seven. He correctly pointed out that as the commitments in points four and five had already been given they could not provide a quid pro quo for Lend-Lease. Keynes wanted Britain to be more forthcoming; he noted in a letter to Richard Hopkins, Second Secretary in the Treasury, and Lord Catto, financial adviser to Wood,

The Atlantic Charter and Lend-Lease

that the Americans had many other ways of pressurising the British on economic policies and it was best not to antagonise them in the Consideration Agreement[62]. Keynes' hopes were partly fulfilled; the new draft, in accordance with Foreign Office arguments, dropped Amery's amendment concerning 'existing obligations' and now simply referred to the Atlantic Charter rather than repeating its text. The draft also went some way towards accommodating the American desire for talks on postwar economic policy by stipulating that the date for talks should not just be 'as soon as convenient', which was the phrase used in the Greenwood draft of early September, but that they should be held at an early convenient date. Finally, the term discrimination was re-incorporated into the draft and after considerable debate over how it should be used Churchill himself settled the matter by adopting the same wording he had offered Hull in clarification of point four of the Atlantic Charter; 'harmful' was now to prefix discrimination[63]. By late September the following draft had been approved by Churchill.

> The terms and conditions upon which the Government of the United Kingdom receives defence aid from the Government of the United States of America and the benefits to be received by the United States of America in return therefor, as finally determined, shall be such as not to burden commerce between the two countries, but to promote mutually advantageous economic relations between them; they shall provide for joint and agreed action by the United States and the United Kingdom, each working within the limits of their governing economic conditions, directed to securing as part of a general plan the progressive attainment of balanced international economics, the avoidance of harmful discriminations and generally the economic objectives set forth in the joint Declaration made by the President of the United States of America and the Prime Minister of the United Kingdom on August 12, 1941.
>   And furthermore it is agreed that at an early convenient date conversations should be begun between the two Governments with a view to discussing the best means of attaining the above objects

and generally the better ordering of economic intercourse between nations in future conditions of settled peace.[64]

It had taken the British over two months to produce what they considered to be satisfactory counter-proposals on article seven for the Americans. The Consideration Talks were now renewed in Washington and they coincided and interacted with the second round of the Wheat Talks. The atmosphere in Anglo-American economic relations soon began to deteriorate as it became clear that the State Department would not accept the safeguards the British had woven into article seven, and that the British would not accept the American proposals on wheat. A double impasse loomed large upon the horizon.

NOTES

1. For background and accounts of the Atlantic Conference see, T. A. Wilson, The First Summit: Roosevelt and Churchill at Placentia Bay 1941 (Houghton Mifflin, Boston, 1969), H. V. Morton, Atlantic Meeting (Methuen, London, 1943), and A. P. Dobson, 'Economic Diplomacy at the Atlantic Conference', Review of International Studies, 10, 2 (April 1984), pp. 143-163.
2. Quoted from an article on Hopkins by G. T. Hellman in Hopkins Papers, box 338.
3. Wilson, First Summit, p.151, Bridges memo. to Churchill, 31 July 1941, A6942/18/45, F0371/26151; F. J. Merli and T. A. Wilson (Ed.), The Makers of American Diplomacy (Scribners, New York, 1974), T. A. Wilson and R. D. McKinzie, 'Franklin D. Roosevelt and the Conduct of American Foreign Policy', p.483.
4. For extracts from the text of Eden's Mansion House Speech see, L. Broad, Eden: The Chronicles of a Career (Hutchinson, London, 1955), pp.154-155.
5. Pasvolsky memo. to Hull, 7 June 1941, 840.50/232½.
6. Berle to Roosevelt and his reply 21 and 26 June 1941, Roosevelt PSF, box 90.
7. Berle to Hopkins, 7 July 1941, Berle to Welles 7 and 8 July 1941, Berle to Roosevelt 8 and 9 July, 1941, Berle Papers, box 54, folder: Allied Commitments for Postwar Settlements June to November 1941.

8. W. F. Kimball, *Churchill and Roosevelt: The Complete Correspondence*, 3 Vols. (Princeton University Press, New Jersey, 1984), Vol.I, p.221 Roosevelt to Churchill, 14 July 1941.
9. Editorial comment, ibid, p.227.
10. S. Welles, *Where Are We Heading?* (Harper Bros. New York, 1946), p.6.
11. E. Roosevelt, *As He Saw It* (Duell, Sloan and Pearce, New York, 1946), p.24.
12. H. Nicolson *Diaries and Letters 1939-45* (Collins, London, 1968), pp.143-144.
13. J. Brandes, *Herbert Hoover and Economic Diplomacy* (University of Pittsburg Press, New York, 1962), pp.84-87.
14. D. Dilks (Ed.) *The Diaries of Sir Alexander Cadogan 1938-45* (Putnams, New York, 1972), editorial note, p.397.
15. Ibid pp.430-31, and memo. of conversation between Welles and Cadogan, 9 Aug. 1941, 740.0011 European War 1939/14007.2. Some authors have mistakenly claimed that Welles took a prepared draft of a joint declaration to the Atlantic Conference which suggests that more thought and preparation went into the draft than is suggested in this narrative, see, Roosevelt *As He Saw It*, p.39, Wilson, *First Summit*, and W. L. Langer and S. E. Gleason, *The Undeclared War* (Harper Row, New York, 1968). Nothing apart from article seven of the draft Mutual Aid Agreement is mentioned in the documents and W. M. Franklin who has had access to Welles' papers wrote to the author, 'In response to your letter of June 7, I can say that I did not find in the papers of Sumner Welles any draft of joint principles which he might have prepared and taken to the Atlantic Conference of 1941' Franklin to Dobson, 16 June 1982 with permission to cite.
16. W. S. Churchill *History of the Second World War: The Grand Alliance* (Cassell, London, 1948), p.386.
17. Welles, *Where Are We Heading?* p.9.
18. Roosevelt, *As He Saw It*, pp.35-37.
19. Welles, *Where Are We Heading?* pp.10-11.
20. Churchill memo. to War Cabinet, 20 Aug. 1941, WP(41)202, CAB 66, Churchill, *Grand Alliance*, pp.387-388, Welles, *Where Are We Heading*, p.13.
21. Churchill to Attlee, Tudor 15, 11 Aug. 1941, WP(41)203, CAB 66. Telegrams during the Atlantic Conference were code-named Tudor and Abbey respectively from Churchill to the Cabinet and from the Cabinet to Churchill.

22. Memo. of conversation between Roosevelt, Churchill, Welles, Cadogan and Hopkins, 11 Aug. 1941, 740.0011 European War 1939/14007.6.
23. Welles, *Where Are We Heading*? p.15.
24. Ibid, p.15.
25. Ibid, p.16.
26. Memo. of conversation between Welles and Cadogan, 11 Aug. 1941, 740.0011 European War 1939/14007.8.
27. Churchill, *Grand Alliance*, pp.443-444.
28. Memo. of conversation between Welles and Cadogan, 11 Aug. 1941, 740.0011 European War 1939/14007.8.
29. Attlee to Churchill, Abbey 31, 11 Aug. 1941, WP(41)203 CAB 66.202.
30. Ibid.
31. Churchill to Attlee, Tudor 20, 12 Aug. 1941, ibid. For details of the circumstantial evidence see Dobson, *Economic Diplomacy*, pp.158-161.
32. Churchill to Attlee, Tudor 23, 12 Aug. 1941, WP(41)203, CAB 66.
33. War Cabinet, 12 Aug. 1941, WM81/41, CAB 65.
34. Ibid.
35. Attlee to Churchill, Abbey 35, 12 Aug. 1941, WP(41)203 CAB 66.
36. Amery to Wood, 18 Aug. 1941, T160/1105/F17660/02/1.
37. Duncan to Wood, 19 Aug. 1941 and Greenwood to Wood, 22 Aug. 1941, ibid.
38. Breckinridge Long Desk Diary, 31 Aug. 1941, Library of Congress, Long Papers, box 5.
39. Hull to Roosevelt, 23 Aug. 1941, Roosevelt PSF, box 2, folder: Atlantic Charter. Hull to Roosevelt 18 August 1941, Roosevelt PSF, box 90, folder: State Department 1941. Hull to Winant, 25 Aug. 1941, 740.0011 European War 1939/14454.
40. Churchill to Wood and his reply, 28 and 29 August 1941, W10659/426/49, FO371/28805.
41. Winant to Hull, 1 Sept. 1941, 740.0011 European War 1939/14570.
42. Minutes, 24 Feb. 1941, RP(41) CAB 87, and notes, 8 Aug. 1941, W9915/426/49, F0371/28903.
43. The author is indebted to Professor David Adams for the contrasting images of American agriculture painted by 'Oklahoma' and Steinbeck.
44. For Wallace's views on foreign policy see, J. S. Walker, *Henry A. Wallace and American Foreign Policy* (Greenwood Press, Connecticut, 1976).

45. Campbell to Sargent, 1 April 1942, W5914/19/49, FO371/32413.
46. Wickard's statement 23 Sept. 1941, Hearings before House Sub-committee of Appropriations Committee, Lend-Lease: quoted in D. Albertson, *Roosevelt's Farmer: Claude R. Wickard in the New Deal* (Columbia University Press, New York, 1961), p.235.
47. R. J. Hammond, *History of the Second World War, U.K. Civil Series, Food I* (HMSO and Longmans Green, London, 1951), p.351.
48. Keynes to Sir H. Wilson, 15 Aug. 1941, T160/1105/F17660/02/1.
49. Winant to Hull, 23 Aug. 1941, 102.78/2959.
50. F. Leith-Ross, *Money Talks: Fifty Years of International Finance. The Autobiography of Sir Frederick Leith-Ross* (Hutchinson, London, 1968), pp.290-292. Winant to Hull, 23 Aug. 1941, 102.78/2959.
51. Breckinridge Long (for Secretary of State) to Winant, 4 Sept. 1941, 561.311 F1 advisory committee/1033b. For Long's views on Britain see, Long Desk Diary, 4 March and 29 Jan. 1942, Long Papers, box 5.
52. Minutes by N. B. Ronald, 29 Sept. 1941, W10969/37/49, FO371/28806. The contradiction in the State Department position did not go unnoticed in the Board of Trade: see Willis to Holland, 6 Sept. 1941, where it is noted that the proposal that Britain police the Wheat Agreement could conflict with the idea of free access to primary products. Public Record Office, Board of Trade records, BT11/1733/CRT10071/41.
53. Winant to Hull, 17 Sept. 1941, 561.311 F1 advisory committee/1935. On 15 Sept. Leith-Ross indicated his willingness to accept British policing of export quotas but others higher in the government i.e. Wood and Greenwood, disagreed, Leith Ross to Willis, 15 Sept. 1941, BT11/1733/CRT10071/41.
54. See Winant to Hull, 12 Oct. 1941, 561.311 F1 advisory committee/1049.
55. Churchill to Roosevelt, 8 Oct. 1941, 561.311 F1 advisory committee/1055.
56. Winant to Hull, 12 Oct. 1941, 561.311 F1 advisory committee/1049.
57. Winant to Hull and Acheson, 16 Nov. 1941, 841.24/1002.
58. Winant to Hull, 29 Sept. 1941, 841.24/814.
59. Amery to Greenwood, 27 Aug. 1941 and Cranborne to Greenwood, 7 Sept. 1941, both at W10480/37/49, FO371/28805.

60. Attached to, Ronald to Daish, 8 Sept. 1941, ibid.
61. Ibid.
62. Keynes to Hopkins and Catto, 27 Aug. 1941, T160/1105/F17660/02/1.
63. See margin note in Smith to Butler, 26 Sept. 1941, W11797/37/49, F0371/28808.
64. Ibid.

Chapter Four

THE WHEAT TALKS AND THE MUTUAL AID AGREEMENT

In late September Winant was finally able to tell an impatient State Department that details of a new British draft of article seven had been sent to Halifax for informal discussion and that Redvers Opie, who was a member of Halifax's staff and who was in London at that time, was shortly to take the full text to Washington. Winant was now less sympathetic towards British prevarication than he had been when Hull had sought clarification of point four of the Atlantic Charter and he reported to Hull that, 'contrary to the advice of September 1, ...I believe we should insist on articles [of the Mutual Aid Agreement] including the provision against discrimination'[1]. He thought that the political climate was now more conducive to the success of article seven and wrote that if the matter came up in Parliament the majority of the Conservatives, the Liberals and the entire Labour bloc would vote for it. Winant conveyed the misleading impression that only the Tory imperialists were opposed to article seven; his failure to discern any opposition to it from the Labour Party is probably attributable to a doctrinal reluctance to do so. He had been posted to London with the possibility in mind that the Labour Party might succeed to power, and Breckinridge Long described him as,'an intense, melodramatic theorist with a philosophy embedded in humanitarianism and directed by sympathy for labor' (epithets used by Cadogan were less charitable: 'inaudible', 'spineless', 'ass')[2]. In addition to the rose-tinted view he had of the Labour Party Winant also failed to discern how the Wheat Talks had soured the attitudes of men like Greenwood, Ronald and Wood who were key decision-makers in the Consideration Talks. In the light of all this and the British success at the Atlantic Conference

The Wheat Talks and the Mutual Aid Agreement

Winant's assessment of the situation in London seems singularly unapt.

The growing misperceptions in Washington were strengthened by Halifax who told Acheson after a brief trip to London that Churchill had said that an economic accord with the US was second only in importance to winning the war[3]. The mistake Halifax and Winant made was to infer that such statements meant Churchill was prepared to capitulate to American economic demands.

On 3 October Halifax outlined the British re-draft of article seven to Acheson. He pointed out that the British were now prepared to enter talks as soon as possible to implement its aims, and he mentioned Keynes among others as a possible negotiator; also, he explained that Keynes and Wood thought that 'harmful' should qualify 'discrimination'. Acheson did not object to early talks (he had suggested this himself in July with the idea of a joint Anglo-American commission), but he dryly commented that a harmful restriction was, 'usually a restriction which somebody else proposed'[4].

Disappointment with the British proposals was mitigated by Halifax who encouraged members of the State Department to believe that they could still achieve an agreement which would be satisfactory to them. On 9 October he told Welles that while there was a split in the British Cabinet over the current draft of article seven strong opposition was restricted to extreme Tory elements, i.e.imperialists. This misleading information was added to when Halifax claimed that, 'Mr. Churchill strongly supported the position taken by this [i.e. the US] Government'[5].

Even before Opie arrived from London with the full text of the British proposals Acheson's drafting committee, which consisted of Hawkins, Feis and John Hickerson of the department's European Division, was set to work to strengthen the State Department's case. Hawkins was quick off the mark but he misconstrued Halifax's comment that Keynes might negotiate the impelementation of article seven to mean that he might participate in the current discussions over its content. He wrote to Acheson that, 'if Mr. Keynes himself comes, I think it highly unlikely that we will ever be able to reach an agreement on a draft...'[6]. The misunderstanding is trivial but it throws light on a cast of mind existing in the State Department that viewed opposition to American proposals as coming mainly from imperialists and oddballs such as Keynes. Hawkins thought that if article seven was submitted to the highest government circle in London that it would by-pass its opposition and provide a rallying point for high ranking British liberals. Hawkins had got it almost entirely wrong. Sympathy towards the aims of article seven was to be found most at the lower bureaucratic and political levels, i.e. Halifax and his staff, Richard Law the Parliamentary Undersecretary for Foreign Affairs, the North American Department of the Foreign Office, and officials of the Economic Section of the War Cabinet Secretariat, of the Board of Trade, and of 'S Branch' which Cherwell had helped to set up to advise Churchill on scientific and economic matters. Furthermore, it was not just Imperial Preference that occasioned opposition to American policy; the majority of ministers in London were also concerned that the prohibition of discrimination would prevent Britain from using exchange controls to help salvage her economic fortunes after the war.

Hawkins produced a new version of article seven on 10 October which was intended to strengthen the American bargaining position in the Supplementary Trade Talks which were still teetering along and to get Britain committed to the abandonment of bilateralist economic policies. He wanted Britain to eliminate Imperial Preference and join the US in reducing tariffs. The two countries, he suggested, should commit themselves to early talks to achieve these objectives[7]. Thus by the time Opie arrived in Washington with the new British draft the Americans were already revising it.

Halifax and Opie handed the draft to Acheson on 17 October; they explained that the Prime Minister wanted an agreement but that he was worried about domestic political problems if Imperial Preference was discarded without a viable alternative economic strategy on the table to help Britain. According to the official record Acheson and Hawkins simply took the proposals saying that they would have to take the matter up both with Hull and possibly with the President. Halifax reported to London that Acheson's initial reaction seemed 'OK' though he wanted to reserve his position on the word 'harmful'. In Acheson's memoirs more colourful reactions are recorded, though the account is also slightly confused as the author has conflated the two meetings with Halifax of 3 and 17 October into one event.

The Wheat Talks and the Mutual Aid Agreement

A glance was enough to show that the insertion of some slippery words and phrases had robbed of all meaning our prohibition of discrimination...Instead, their proposed settlement would commit the two countries "each working within the limits of their governing economic conditions [an escape clause large enough for a Sherman tank]...to securing as part of a general plan [that is, British obligations in return for lend-lease to be conditioned upon, say, Latin America's accepting the same] the progressive attainment of a balanced international economy, [here were two Humpty Dumpty words which could mean whatever one wished them to mean] the avoidance of harmful discriminations, [harmful discriminations I said to Halifax, are always the other fellow's discriminations never one's own]..."[8]

Acheson's drafting committee renewed their efforts and again Hawkins proved industrious. He tried his hand at a formula which would extract from Britain a commitment to the abandonment of discriminatory policies without causing her political embarrassment by mentioning Imperial Preference. He proposed the following alterations to the British draft: delete 'joint and agreed' because there might be agreed action which was not joint; omit 'each working within the limits of their governing economic conditions' because it was too similar to point four of the Atlantic Charter; omit 'as part of a general plan' because it could provide a let-out clause if no general plan emerged; and delete 'harmful'. He suggested that embarrassment in London could be avoided by omitting references to Imperial Preference, but the British should be told plainly that its abolition was intended by article seven and in order to avoid any subsequent misunderstanding the two countries could exchange confidential notes of interpretation[9]. We may recall that an identical procedure had been proposed by Ronald though his intention was to exclude Imperial Preference from article seven altogether.

Adolf Berle declared Hawkins' re-draft to be 'the best yet' and only added that 'like minded governments' should be invited to participate in the talks to implement its objectives. Herbert Feis

The Wheat Talks and the Mutual Aid Agreement

raised the solitary voice of dissent in the department, but he was not influential. He was Jewish and had mixed in radical circles while at the London School of Economics in 1919; thus he was unhappy about Hull's pro-Vichy policy, the lack of concern among his colleagues for the plight of European Jewry and about his department's attempts to force the British Empire into economic policies it was clearly reluctant to adopt. Acheson, when Feis put the last point to him, brushed it aside remarking that the Dominions would fall in line with American policy because of their growing dependence on the US for defence[10].

On 16 November Winant again advised the State Department to persist with their economic objectives and he reinforced the impression that opposition to American demands in London was located in small pockets and generally at junior levels. 'The Secretary of State should know' he wrote, 'that future US-UK economic relations are being left to ranking civil servants and government economic advisers...excepting for intermittent references in the Cabinet to the wheat agreement'[11]. He added that it was a good time to press the British because of their favourable reaction to the recent repeal of the remnants of the US Neutrality Law.

Acheson and his drafting committee were now coming to the end of their work despite many time-consuming distractions caused by the growing crisis with Japan. After the re-draft had been approved by the various interested parties in Washington, including the Lend-Lease Administration, Hull sent it to Roosevelt with the comments that it simply put into effect instructions the President had given Acheson in July, though as we have seen the State Department had construed them rather liberally. The President nevertheless approved the new draft, and thus ensured that a critical phase in the negotiations with the British was about to be embarked upon[12].

On 2 December Acheson and Feis gave their new draft of article seven to Halifax. It read as follows,

> In the final determination of the benefits to be provided to the United States of America by the Government of the United Kingdom in return for aid furnished under the Act of Congress of March 11, 1941, the terms and conditions thereof shall be such as not to burden commerce between the two

countries, but to promote mutually advantageous economic relations between them and the betterment of world-wide economic relations. To that end, they shall include provision for agreed action by the United States of America and the United Kingdom, open to participation by all other countries of like mind, directed to the expansion, by appropriate international and domestic measures of production, employment, and the exchange and consumption of goods, which are the material foundations of the liberty and the welfare of all peoples; to the elimination of all forms of discriminatory treatment in international commerce, and to the reduction of tariffs and other trade barriers; and, in objectives set forth in the Joint Declaration made on August 14, 1941, by the President of the United States of America and the Prime Minister of the United Kingdom.

At an early convenient date, conversations shall be begun between the two Governments with a view to determining in the light of governing economic conditions, the best means of attaining the above stated objectives by their own agreed action and of seeking the agreed action of other like minded Governments.[13]

The Americans had made some cosmetic alterations to their July draft. They now mentioned tariff reductions as well as the abolition of discrimination, and Acheson pointed out that their new draft of article seven emphasised that the specified aims were to be achieved by concerted international action in the context of an expanding world economy. The most important cosmetic change, however, was the omission of a specific reference to Imperial Preference. Acheson and Hawkins had come to believe that there were two causes of the opposition in London to the State Department version: one was the Tory imperialists' commitment to the Ottawa trade arrangements; the other was the fear of the political embarrassment that would arise if Britain were seen to abandon Imperial Preference at the behest of the State Department. They calculated that if this embarrassment could be avoided then a majority of British officials and members of the government would accept the American version of article seven and swamp the opposition to it from the imperialists. Acheson explained to Halifax that they had taken pains to avoid upsetting British sensitivities over Imperial Preference, but that the intention of article seven was nevertheless to abolish it; however, if the Americans were asked about this in public they would evade a direct reply by simply stating that nothing was excluded from its scope.

Halifax pointed out that the commitment to abolish discrimination might not be seen in London as commensurate with the undertaking to reduce tariffs. Acheson was unmoved; he made it clear that an unequivocal commitment to abolish Imperial Preference was crucial for him and his colleagues. He had explained earlier in the meeting that they had put 'in the light of governing economic conditions' in the second paragraph of the article so that it qualified the means of implementation and not the aims of the article; he now warned Halifax that if agreement was not reached soon or if a loop-hole for Imperial Preference was again suggested, the suspicions and impatience this would arouse in the US could prove disastrous. He cautioned that further delay might result in the US service departments becoming involved which would not be helpful to Britain; there was also the problem of congressional appropriations for Lend-Lease in January to think about, and furthermore if Britain's exasperating behaviour continued even those well disposed towards her might feel like throwing in the towel. Halifax in his report to London, whilst acknowledging that some risks were involved, favoured acceptance of the American position. He emphasised how much he agreed with the sentiments Acheson had expressed and he declared his faith in American goodwill[14]. Halifax had been won over: perhaps he should have paid more attention to Lord Chesterfield's anecdote that politicians are moved by interest, not by sentiment.

The view championed by the British Treasury, which prevailed in London, was that the unqualified commitment to abolish discrimination was imprudent, especially when article seven did not specify what a commensurate tariff reduction would be. On the face of it this draft of article seven seemed more favourable to British interests than did the American July draft, but as Acheson had made clear much of it was political window-dressing. Its

The Wheat Talks and the Mutual Aid Agreement

purpose remained the same; the difference was that it now depended upon an understanding extraneous to the text. Halifax, frightened by the prospect of a breakdown in the talks, was prepared to put his faith in American goodwill and accept their interpretation of the article, and he urged London to do likewise; London, however, was not prepared to do so. Kingsley Wood and others were unhappy with the text and with Acheson's interpretation. An equally worrying factor was that the draft could be interpreted in various ways and the British Government was not prepared to trust to American goodwill in interpreting it in the future. In the light of the substantial difficulties the British saw with the American version it is doubtful whether the consideration issue could have been resolved in December 1941 even if an abundance of faith in American economic goodwill had existed in London. In fact, by early December, there was a distinct absence of such faith and this was largely because of the second round of the Wheat Talks to which we must now turn.

On 14 October, the British, led by the head of the Merchant Marine Commission in Washington Sir Arthur Salter, and the Americans, led by Paul Appleby, began the second round of the Wheat Talks. At the same time L. A. Wheeler of the US Department of Agriculture was preparing a reply to Churchill's letter of 8 October to the President which we considered in the previous chapter. Roosevelt's reply was rather bland which is not surprising considering its origins. The President acknowledged the difficulty of imposing an agreement on countries which were not participating in the talks, but he said that an agreement should still be sought and that it should be possible to include a formula which would enable the Soviet Union to enter into the agreement at a later date. He mentioned an equitable sharing of the export market, an 'ever normal granary' and the cooperation of Britain as the main importer as crucial goals which should be pursued in the talks. Some British officials saw this as a move towards accepting the position Churchill had outlined on 8 October but, in fact, it left matters wide open[15].

In five meetings from 20 to 27 October Salter explained British reservations about the Wheat Proposals. In reply the Americans persisted with immoderate demands: for example, on the question of levels of production they would not compromise and insisted that Britain should reduce her acreage even

The Wheat Talks and the Mutual Aid Agreement

though this would damage her agricultural system and adversely affect the quality of rural life by forcing farmers off the land. 'They even went so far as to argue that these [importing] countries would be directly benefited and that in any case they would share in the direct advantages arising from a prosperous overseas farming population.' T.N. Whitehead of the Foreign Office North American Department minuted the view that, 'This failure to take effective notice of the British representative's criticisms' strongly suggested that the arguments the Americans adduced to defend their position, 'were not the real reasons which were prompting them. This was in fact obviously the case'[16].

On 31 October Hull entered the fray once again. He called for British acceptance of the Wheat Proposals and commented that, 'it should...be made clear that the ultimate objectives of the agreement are in accordance with the liberal trade principles of Anglo-American collaboration as expressed in the Atlantic Charter'[17]. Just how Hull could perform this somersault in economic logic is difficult to see, but he was not alone in his intellectual gymnastics. On 10 November the Australian Minister in Washington passed on to the British details of a conversation with Acheson in which he had used the terms 'broad-minded' and 'liberal' in referring to the Wheat Agreement. However, two days later when Salter suggested to Acheson and Hawkins that there was an apparent conflict between 'American proposals in the wheat agreement and their proposals in Article 7...regarding the post-war international trade system', the two State Department officials looked distinctly 'uneasy'[18]. Nevertheless, in the weeks that followed both Hull and Acheson continued to bring pressure to bear on the British. The need to appease Congress and the faction in the Department of Agriculture which favoured restrictive commodity agreements, the adverse affect non-agreement might have on Lend-Lease and the damage to Anglo-American economic cooperation in general were all used to try to get Britain to agree to the Wheat Proposals, but by late November there was little chance of that happening[19].

On 26 November Hull wrote to Winant that except for wheat prices the US had met all the British objections, but this was not entirely accurate[20]. The Americans still wanted Britain to police quotas which were to be allocated to non-members of the agreement and a Board of Trade paper pointed out in

The Wheat Talks and the Mutual Aid Agreement

early December the dangerous consequences that such an agreement would have: it would offend the Soviet Union because she had not participated in drawing up an agreement which would greatly affect her; the policing arrangements would have repercussions on Britain's trade relations; Britain might be the only importing country to accept the agreement if the high prices suggested by the US were accepted; it might also set a precedent for high prices in other commodity agreements which would further damage Britain's balance of payments[21]. In addition to these factors Hull had overlooked an important aspect of the Wheat Talks which was caused by the blatant contradiction between the Wheat Proposals and the principles which the State Department constantly enunciated. This angered the British, made them suspicious of American intentions in economic policy and thus contributed to their resolve not to give in to American economic demands. In the light of developments in the Wheat Talks it is little wonder that Halifax's plea for faith in American goodwill in relation to article seven went largely unheeded in London.

On 7 December the Japanese attacked Pearl Harbor and the following day the US formally entered the war becoming Britain's co-belligerent. The determination in London to resist American economic demands was immediately strengthened and a more robust attitude towards dealings in general with the US was soon evident, for example, when Churchill was asked whether the military ought to continue cautiously to make representations to the US he replied, 'Oh! that is the way we talked to her while we were wooing her; now that she is in the harem, we talk to her quite differently'[22]. Those who had resisted American demands before her entry into the war saw even less reason to make what one Treasury adviser described as a 'unilateral sacrifice of our policy to theirs'[23]. They thought that consideration for what was now being used in a common war effort was inappropriate. Amery advised great caution concerning Halifax's recommendations about the American 2 December draft of article seven and it was soon clear that the ambassador's pleas were going to fail[24].

On 9 December Hull and Winant repeated the arguments for British acceptance of article seven as it stood yet again; Hull told the ambassador he should let the British know, 'With respect to the provision concerning discrimination, all that we ask is that the British sit down with us to work out the

The Wheat Talks and the Mutual Aid Agreement

problems which lie ahead'[25]. But this was clearly a misleading gloss on the text as far as the British were concerned; Acheson had made it clear that they would sit down at the negotiating table with the future of a major bargaining counter already decided: Imperial Preference was to be abolished. Winant tried to take up the matter of article seven at the highest political level without success. On 14 December he reported on his failure but advised Acheson and Hull that they should continue to argue their views on article seven which he believed would win through in the end, though he was now less sanguine about the Wheat Talks, which he thought the British would try to postpone until they could become part of a wider economic settlement[26]. In fact, decisions had been taken in London which were more drastic than Winant realised.

On 13 December a telegram which reflected the views of Wood and Greenwood more than those of the Foreign Office was sent to Washington. It informed Halifax that it was preferable, in the changed circumstances i.e. American entry into the war, not to make a hurried decision concerning article seven, and that more general talks with the Dominions and the US were under consideration, 'requiring no final decision on Imperial Preference or any other large issue'. In the light of the idea of pooling US and UK resources for the war effort Wood and others hoped that article seven might become redundant, but, so far as the new draft was concerned, Halifax was told that

> Apart from Imperial Preference, the...introduction of the word "discrimination" without any qualifying adjective shows the importance the Administration attach to it. Our comment, for your information, is that the word "discrimination" admits of varied interpretations, and it becomes essential that we should review very carefully to what extent we can at this stage wholeheartedly subscribe to it...We need to review carefully how far we can afford to divest ourselves of this power to use protective measures unless and until better arrangements can be found.[27]

Halifax did not agree and in the following weeks he and his staff encouraged the Americans to sustain their pressure for agreement on consideration.

The Wheat Talks and the Mutual Aid Agreement

On 12 December Churchill journeyed to Washington for a council of war with Roosevelt. The State Department now had an opportunity to argue their case at the highest level and on their own ground. Winant informed Hull that to the best of his knowledge Churchill had neither read nor seriously considered the American arguments about article seven; this was corroborated from a 'reliable source' in the British Embassy in Washington who also told Acheson that if article seven were raised with the Prime Minister in Washington there would be unanimous advice from the embassy to accept it. Acheson was also cautioned that if the matter were not resolved in Washington it would probably get bogged down in bureaucracy in London, which was a diplomatic way of telling the Americans that they should try to circumvent the Prime Minister's advisers there[28]. For some days the issue of consideration was to hang fire in Washington as the British Embassy and the State Department tried to arrange things so that Churchill would make a final decision about this matter. While those manoeuvres were going on dramatic developments in the Wheat Talks broke the brooding impasse that had been apparent there for some time.

On 12 December the Treasury and the Foreign Office agreed that Churchill should be given briefs both on the Wheat Talks and on article seven for his discussions in the US. Instead, apparently by mistake though possibly with the collusion of Greenwood and Wood, the briefs were sent as instructions to Washington. Ronald and Richard Law thought that the 'briefs' would unintentionally and unnecessarily give a harsh picture of the British position if they were conveyed to the Americans. Ronald's fears were not so much for 'the corpse of the Wheat Agreement' as for future economic talks and he and Law wanted a note of clarification to be sent to Washington. Kingsley Wood would have none of this; Ronald recorded that,

> The Chancellor...was inclined to take up the wholly indefensible line that it was not for the Foreign Office to interfere in these matters. Both he and Mr. Greenwood, he said, had agreed with the Prime Minister that we could never accept what the Americans were asking us to do in connexion with the Wheat Agreement: we could neither accept the price formula or

The Wheat Talks and the Mutual Aid Agreement

> [sic] the suggestion we should undertake to police non-signatories.[29]

Just before Christmas other voices joined the debate on the Wheat Proposals, urging accommodation; Leith-Ross favoured the draft agreement and Salter thought that it might be necessary to accept it for otherwise anti-British sentiment might be strengthened and there might be adverse effects in the State Department with regard to Lend-Lease[30]. It was at this point, when serious differences of opinion were emerging in the British camp, that the impasse in the Wheat Talks was broken. It began around the 11 December with exchanges of information between Eden and Winant. Eventually Winant's economic adviser, Professor E. F. Penrose was given the minutes of the October talks.

> He was at once struck by the fact that Sir A. Salter had put the U.K. case with great cogency and lucidity, but that no one had even bothered to try to answer him. The first consequence of Prof. Penrose's researches was that U.S. Ambassador withdrew...charges...and actually asked our [i.e. British] help in rebutting the charges which the State Department levelled against us.[31]

Penrose told Winant that the Consideration Talks were being jeopardised because of doubts about American sincerity when they advocated free trade in one breath and in the next demanded that Britain, instead of seeking the cheapest source for her most vital import, should buy at fixed prices from four designated markets[32]. On 28 December Winant reported on the unease in London and he specifically mentioned the difficulties that the British saw with non-signatories and the fact that moderates were being forced to side with the hard-liners led by Hudson because of American policy[33]. The American Wheat proposals were already under pressure because of the tepid support from the other big producers and because of British criticisms, and the intervention of Penrose and Winant tipped the scales decisively. On 19 January Salter reported that the State Department now believed that it was injudicious to conclude an agreement of the kind it had argued for up to now without the participation of the Soviet Union[34]. This was not the whole story but it was a convenient way of saving face and

The Wheat Talks and the Mutual Aid Agreement

falling back on an anodyne provisional agreement along the lines Churchill had suggested on 8 October. As Ronald wryly put it, it was 'vaguely disquieting' that the US Embassy in London was able to put across the British case better than 'our own Embassy' in Washington[35]. The talks dragged on in a desultory fashion for some months but the British had won a postponement of all the sensitive issues.

Thus after much controversy the Wheat Talks fizzled out. Their most important effect was on the development of attitudes in London towards economic cooperation with the US. Lord Chesterfield was only partly right when he said that politicians are motivated by interest and not by sentiment, because the identification of interest is often determined by the sentiments that men hold. Both during and after the Wheat Talks British policy-makers became more inclined to formulate policies in a manner which assumed an absence of good faith and an adversary spirit in their American opposite numbers.

With the American withdrawal of proposals in the Wheat Talks that contradicted the economic principles of the State Department it was now possible for Hull and his acolytes to argue more cogently for laissez-faire. On 16 December a new initiative was taken to try to show Britain the error of her economic ways. The 'Pasvolsky Memorandum' was deliberately leaked to the British Government via their embassy in Washington; this was a confidential State Department paper by Pasvolsky which attacked Britain for her lack of cooperation on economic policy[36]. Pasvolsky was the leading economist in the department but while his analysis of the opposition in London to American economic policy was more perceptive than Winant's he still attributed it largely to doctrinal disaffection with free trade whereas, although that existed, the bulk of the opposition was more concerned with ensuring that the means of moving towards freer trade would not damage Britain. Failing to grasp this, Pasvolsky thought Britain should accept article seven as currently drafted at once, and then detailed economic talks which would cater for Britain's economic difficulties could get underway. The British, of course, were unsure that such talks could solve their problems if certain policies were excluded by article seven in the first place.

Four days after sending the 'Pasvolsky Memorandum' to London Halifax entered his own impassioned plea for British acceptance of article seven. He wrote that the substance of London's telegram of 13 December would have a 'deplorable effect' if he communicated it to the Americans. He went on,

> Above all we simply cannot afford to allow suspicion to arise in the mind of the President or his advisers that we are organising entry of the United States into the war as a pretext for evading the commitments which we might otherwise have been not unwilling to undertake...'[37]

In a second letter Halifax reported that the Americans did not envisage the abolition of discrimination in isolation from other developments. The talks which would issue from the Mutual Aid Agreement would provide for, 'a very substantial reduction of United States tariffs', and so, fully convinced of the need for Britain to accept article seven, Halifax re-kindled the idea of exchanging notes of interpretation as a tactic that might produce agreement[38].

London dismissed Halifax's arguments with the duplitious claim that the Dominions were unhappy with article seven as it stood and with the observation that neither government could risk publishing an ambiguous agreement that might prejudice future cooperation. On the suggestion that notes of interpretation should be exchanged the reaction was more favourable and Halifax was told to bring Churchill up to date on the arguments for and against acceptance of article seven which had been made since his departure from London and to seek his opinion about an exchange of notes[39].

Kingsley Wood asked Winant on 27 December what he thought about exchanging notes which would link the abolition of discrimination to postwar reductions in American tariffs; he also mentioned Britain's 'problems' with the Dominions. Winant evaded a reply telling Wood he had received no directives on this from Washington. Winant was angered by Wood using the Dominions as an excuse for not accepting article seven because Bruce, the Australian High Commissioner in London, had told him that the Dominions favoured acceptance. Winant expressed the hope to Hull that talks with Churchill in Washington would make the proposed exchange of notes unnecessary[40].

For two weeks the hopes of those who wanted progress on article seven hinged on direct appeals to Churchill. All the signals from the British Embassy indicated that agreement was possible. Hickerson reported to Hull that Noel Hall, the British Minister in Washington, thought that if Hull or the President expressed an interest in the Consideration Agreement then it would be signed at once. A similar message came from Opie who added that Halifax now regarded agreement as a matter involving his own personal prestige; even the dour and wily Phillips favoured acceptance, though with an exchange of notes of interpretation. However, worrying signs began to emerge when Halifax's first approach to Churchill about article seven was rebuffed by him with the curt comment that he was too busy to take up the matter[41].

On 29 December Halifax talked with Hull and they decided that Acheson should approach Roosevelt and that Halifax should speak again with Churchill, after the Prime Minister returned from his excursion to Toronto, to see if the two leaders could be persuaded to take decisive action on article seven[42]. Halifax told the Foreign Office he was determined not to leave the matter in cold storage and he reported that he and all his senior advisers saw not the slightest chance of the US altering its position. He strongly recommended acceptance of the current draft of article seven and he sent to London his own draft of a bland statement of interpretation which made no attempt to protect Imperial Preference or to construe the term 'discrimination' in such a way as to protect British economic interests[43].

While Halifax fulminated in Washington, Greenwood spelt out the difficulties over article seven for the War Cabinet. He reported that the Prime Minister was unable to take up the matter in Washington and that progress would have to await his return to London[44]. The Foreign Office was not entirely happy about this and while it had more reservations about article seven than Halifax had it was beginning to doubt the wisdom of further delays and equivocation. At the end of December Richard Law summed up the situation as follows,

> One difficulty about Consideration is that while we [i.e. the Foreign Office] regard it, in the main as a political problem affecting, possibly, our whole future relations with the U.S.A., the Chancellor regards it as a financial problem. The Prime Minister seems to support the Chancellor...[who] aided and abetted by

The Wheat Talks and the Mutual Aid Agreement

> the Greenwood Committee, acts in these matters as his own Foreign Secretary. ...Another difficulty is this. It is the view of the Greenwood Committee that on Consideration as well as on Wheat that the Americans are determined at all costs to get the better of us.[45]

In general the Foreign Office agreed with Halifax on the desirability of signing the Mutual Aid Agreement, but they thought that a better note of interpretation than the one which he had sent on 29 December was required. Law drew up a new note which emphasised joint action in the context of an expanding world economy. It concluded with, 'It is against this background and in conjunction with it that there are added the objectives of eliminating, by agreed and if necessary by gradual stages, discriminatory treatment, reducing tariffs and achieving the other objectives of the Atlantic Charter'[46]. Eden's position on all this is rather difficult to decipher. On 5 January, reacting to the 'Pasvolsky Memorandum' and to the analysis of it which was then emerging in London, he wrote that, 'My own point of view is that from a political point of view Imperial Preference is an Imperial domestic matter and as such should not be lightly described as discriminatory, though from the economic view it is undoubtedly discriminatory in effect'[47]. This line of thinking was soon to become important but then Eden began to have similar doubts to those that Law had expressed and he eventually argued for giving way to the Americans. Of more immediate concern is Keynes' evaluation of the 'Pasvolsky Memorandum'.

Keynes first damned it with faint praise and then ridiculed Pasvolsky himself.

> The bulk of this paper, which is a very able one, within its limitations, is a dogmatic statement of the virtues of laissez-faire in international trade on the lines familiar forty years ago,...Mr. Pasvolsky looks like Rip Van Winkle and evidently is, in fact, he![48]

The 'Pasvolsky Memorandum' was subjected to intellectual destruction by Keynes who along with other British officials believed with characteristic arrogance that much of the problem in Anglo-American

The Wheat Talks and the Mutual Aid Agreement

economic relations lay in American lack of understanding. There was some truth to this but one feels that Keynes had missed the point here: the 'Pasvolsky Memorandum' was not a university paper embodying the latest ideas of economic theory; it was primarily a political document which was intended to indicate both American dislike of British policies and American determination to get article seven accepted. In fact Keynes now wanted Britain to accept article seven because he thought it would necessarily remain vague without detailed talks and because further delays would only antagonise the Americans. He was otpimistic about the outcome of detailed talks because he had a plan for an International Clearing Union which he hoped the Americans would accept (at least in a modified form), making it unncessary for Britain to continue discriminatory monetary exchange policies after the war. Their perceived need to engage in such policies was of course one of the main reasons for the British Cabinet to be opposed to article seven, with its prohibition of discrimination. Ironically, Keynes' analysis of the 'Pasvolsky Memorandum' gave more ammunition to those who were resisting American demands. Towards the end of his analysis Keynes commented that,

> The chief moral I draw from this paper is the inadvisability (which I wish Lord Halifax could be made to appreciate) of our being asked to sign up ambiguous undertakings on the dotted line <u>in advance</u> of face to face discussion about the principles of future policy.[49]

This view was taken by the majority of the British Government as grounds for continuing to seek a more satisfactory note of interpretation of article seven.

On 5 January the Cabinet asked Greenwood to draw up arguments for and against acceptance of the current draft of article seven. Within a few days Greenwood produced a lengthy document; the arguments for acceptance were: i) that it would keep American goodwill, ii) that Lend-Lease appropriations were imminent, iii) that a new postwar economy needed to be planned, iv) that article seven provided some quid pro quo for the abandonment of Imperial Preference, v) that acceptance would prevent a return to protectionism, vi) that the Dominions favoured agreement providing

The Wheat Talks and the Mutual Aid Agreement

a quid pro quo was received. The catalogue of arguments against agreement was notably longer: i) that as the US was now a co-belligerent article seven was inappropriate, ii) that America would not damage the war effort because of non-agreement i.e. Lend-Lease would continue as before despite hints to the contrary from the State Department, iii) that Britain needed to know specifically what her quid pro quo would be (the British reasoned that with America in the war payment for Lend-Lease was inappropriate and thus the Americans needed to give something to the British in exchange for her abandoning Imperial Preference), iv) that Imperial Preference was more important politically than economically, v) that agreement would weaken imperial ties at a sensitive time, vi) that there was no strong feeling in the US about Imperial Preference, vii) that it would be acceptable if there was an interpretation safeguarding Imperial Preference, viii) that it might allow cheap exports into British markets, ix) that there was a disparity between the abolition of preferences and the reduction of tariffs[50].

Amery predictably opposed acceptance, Cranborne thought that a note of interpretation was essential and Kingsley Wood believed that the idea of pooling US and UK resources for the war effort made article seven redundant, but that if the Americans insisted on it then he thought that Imperial Preference should be removed entirely from its scope[51]. The views of key ministers in London were consolidating into a stongly anti-American position, contrary to those expectations widely held in the State Department which had been propagated by Winant and the British Embassy in Washington. American hopes that they would be able to break the deadlock on article seven by approaching Churchill directly also proved to be fruitless.

On 17 January Churchill reported to the Cabinet that while he was in the US he had taken the line that article seven, 'need not be settled as a matter of urgency, and that he had not been pressed on the point'[52]. When Halifax first raised the matter Churchill had brushed it aside and when he raised it a second time after talking with Hull Churchill told him in no uncertain terms that the matter should be postponed on the grounds which had been repeatedly argued from London by Wood and Greenwood[53]. Roosevelt also tried his hand with Churchill on a number of occasions, only to be told that article seven was not in the Prime Minister's brief[54].

The Wheat Talks and the Mutual Aid Agreement

The one dramatic confrontation came between Churchill and Hull on the eve of the former's return to London. Breckinridge Long recorded that,

> Churchill has refused to include in the contract for our compensation for Lend-Lease the agreement to discard the Empire tariff and trade program. Hull secured the President's acceptance. Churchill has got it eliminated. They dined side by side last night and Hull approached the subject only to have Churchill say he definitely refused to agree to it and would not accept it.[55]

Halifax and his embassy staff had miscalculated badly: instead of Churchill acceding to a request from a high ranking member of the US Administration he had strongly rejected it.

On 22 January Acheson, anxious to reach agreement on article seven, wrote to Hull saying that he was unaware of what had transpired between Roosevelt and Churchill but that he wanted a clear indication as to whether the President was prepared to put pressure on the British to agree[56]. Roosevelt's comments at the Cabinet meeting the following day would undoubtedly have heartened Acheson: he 'spoke of the British being hard to work with. He said they were high hat and selfish'[57]. As it was Acheson did not have long to wait; he got an audience with the President on 29 December and Roosevelt said that he wanted an agreement. Acheson explained that as Churchill was worried about domestic political problems they had drawn up a memorandum which gave the British two options: they could either accept article seven as it stood, or the entire issue of repayment and Anglo-American economic cooperation could be deferred. Roosevelt realised the threat to the British implicit in the second option but to ensure that they did not fail to get the message he wrote in long-hand that 'I strongly hope the British will accept the first course because the second leaves them in a much more difficult future economic position' and he told Acheson that some way should be found to unofficially disclose this to them[58].

That evening Acheson and Feis showed the President's comment to Halifax and told him that if the matter was postponed the British might discover Congress to be more demanding when discussions were renewed. Halifax, following instructions from

The Wheat Talks and the Mutual Aid Agreement

London, suggested that the concept of pooling resources had rendered article seven redundant, but Acheson replied that Lend-Lease was the only legal mechanism by which such pooling arrangements could go forward. In his report to London Halifax said that it would now be a profound mistake not to sign the agreement[59].

London was used to hearing such arguments from Halifax but a number of other developments were proving to be more persuasive and they began to reduce the government's ability to resist American pressures. There were serious military reverses in North Africa and in the Far East which undermined the prestige of Churchill's government, and there was also the fact that the Dominions, partly because of their need for American defence assistance, were 'actually resentful' that Britain had not signed the Consideration Agreement[60]. Britain was facing crises on several fronts, but the government still refused to succumb to American pressure although it was now split in its opinions.

In the Cabinet on 2 February Eden, amidst a long wrangle, 'put up a fight to meet the State Department'. He acknowledged that the Americans had considerable scope for interpreting the agreement as it stood in ways damaging to Britain, but he thought that if it was not signed now worse conditions might be set in the future and that in the meantime relations with the State Department would deteriorate. The Secretary of State for Air, Sinclair, true to his liberal colours sided with Eden, and so did Lord Cranborne, largely because of representations made by the Dominions. The unholy alliance of Churchill, the old Chamberlainite Kingsley Wood, the imperialist Amery and the leading Labourite Arthur Greenwood opposed signing on the grounds marshalled for the Cabinet by Greenwood in early January though now with emphasis on the need for a specific quid pro quo for the elimination of Imperial Preference and on the unacceptability of article seven's infringing upon Britain's sovereign relations with the Empire. As Cadogan put it in his diary, 'P.M. carried the day against A. [Anthony Eden]' and it was decided that Eden and Wood should draw up a note, interpreting article seven, which would safeguard Imperial Preference[61].

A few hours after the Cabinet meeting Winant sent details about it to Acheson. The source of his information is unclear though it was presumably the Foreign Office. Winant mentioned in particular that

The Wheat Talks and the Mutual Aid Agreement

members of the Cabinet thought that the US Administration would not have political difficulties if amendments were made to the wording of article seven, which they believed lacked strong support in its present form outside the State Department. Winant suggested that Roosevelt and Morgenthau should disabuse them of this belief; he thought that the latter would be especially influential with Wood because he still felt a debt of gratitude to Morgenthau for helping with Britain's supply problem[62]. Acheson acted quickly. He brought the letter to the attention of Roosevelt, Hull, Morgenthau, Welles, Wallace and Hawkins. Hawkins was livid. He said the British were attempting to repudiate the Atlantic Charter (which was rather ironical as they thought they were consolidating the position achieved therein) and that before the British Cabinet reneged on it, it should consider that there might be, 'repercussions of the gravest character on the unity of the war effort'[63]. On 4 February Roosevelt and Acheson, who was acting on Morgenthau's behalf, took a strong line. Acheson, using Morgenthau's name with his permission, wrote to Wood expressing the opinion that the Mutual Aid Agreement was fair and that it should be accepted to avoid both impediment to the war effort and the danger of adverse effects on more long-range matters[64]. Roosevelt's letter to Churchill was a similar mixture of personal appeals and veiled threats.

> I am convinced that further delay in concluding this agreement will be harmful to your interests and ours. I am likewise convinced that the present draft is not only fair and equitable but it meets the apprehension, which some of your colleagues have felt and which Halifax has brought to our attention...failure to sign this agreement would do much mischief.[65]

While this was going on Eden and Wood had come up with an interpretation which excluded Imperial Preference from the scope of article seven. Eden, however, soon began to have doubts because of a letter from Winant which disclosed the President's view that it would probably be worse for Britain if she did not agree to settle matters now. The letter also contained the blunt statement that, 'The United States Government believes that further attempts to refine the language of article seven would be time consuming and wholly unprofitable'. This and the arrival of the letters from Morgenthau and Roosevelt requesting agreement persuaded Eden that the note interpreting article seven drawn up with Wood would not be acceptable to Washington. He therefore drafted a second version which did not require the exclusion of Imperial Preference; instead it called for gradual stages of joint and agreed action with no imposition of unilateral obligations[66].

The Cabinet on 6 February would not accept Eden's second draft; ministers strongly favoured the first, which they decided should be sent to Halifax. They advised Churchill that in his response to Roosevelt's letter of 4 February he should explain this decision[67]. Churchill duly wrote to the President that the Cabinet was more resolved than ever not to trade Imperial Preference for Lend-Lease and that they felt that if article seven was accepted as it stood it would entail interference in the domestic affairs of the British Empire, which would occasion difficult debates in Parliament. It would also provide material for German propaganda and might provoke suggestions that Britain was becoming a dependent territory of the US. The Prime Minister said he had always been 'opposed' or 'lukewarm' to Imperial Preference and he rather ingenuously claimed that, 'we are all for sweeping away trade barriers'. Britain, he went on, wanted to work with the US in, 'constructing a free, fertile economic policy for the postwar world' but that he hoped that Roosevelt would make allowances for British difficulties. He asked for the President's help in getting the British note of interpretation accepted; the crucial part of which stated that,

> The representatives of the United Kingdom Government have stated that they do not understand the word 'discrimination' as applying to special arrangements between members of the same Commonwealth or Federation, such as the British Commonwealth or the United States of America and its Possessions, and that before accepting any definite commitments involving modification of the existing system of Imperial Preference, the Government of the United Kingdom would naturally require to consult with the Governments of the Dominions.[68]

The Wheat Talks and the Mutual Aid Agreement

Winant sent a rather garbled account of the Cabinet meeting to Washington, but there was no misunderstanding of its outcome; he commented in the note that it, 'is a negation of most we have asked for'[69].

In Washington Halifax did as he was bid and argued, albeit half-heartedly according to Welles, that the note of interpretation was all right. He said that Churchill did not want to upset the Conservative Party and as everyone would favour liberal trade policies after the war there was no harm in asking the Dominions to acquiesce before starting talks on Imperial Preference. Welles, knowing full well the position of the Dominions, said that if they were so acquiescent why had they not been asked already, to which Halifax candidly replied that they had and that they favoured the position of the US. Welles commented later, 'I would say no more beyond emphasising the fact this issue was fast becoming a very serious issue and that I feared the British did not realise how serious an issue it really was'[70]. Further meetings the following day made it clear that the State Department still wanted a commitment from Britain which would eventually result in the abolition of Imperial Preference. Welles described the situation as 'grave' and Acheson said the US could not accept that talks on Imperial Preference were to be conditional upon Dominion agreement. When Halifax suggested that Imperial Preference was purely a domestic matter Feis and Acheson 'turned it down flat' and, 'Halifax did not dissent'[71].

After spending the weekend with Churchill at Chequers, Winant reported to Hull that seventy-five per cent of the Cabinet opposed article seven in its present form. The Prime Minister had told him, however, that he and some of his colleagues had little faith in preferences and discrimination and that they would be happy to begin separate talks on those issues[72]. This was nothing new, as apart from the imperialists most members of the government wanted economic cooperation with the US, but they did not want to give away the bargaining chips before specific talks got underway.

On 10 February Acheson produced the first draft of a reply to Churchill's letter and the proposed note of interpretation. Acheson specifically rejected the idea of excluding Imperial Preference from the scope of article seven but he went on that, 'There is no suggestion...of bartering Empire sovereignty to meet a debt', and that, 'The Article

The Wheat Talks and the Mutual Aid Agreement

makes it plain that all conclusions must be reached by agreement after discussions of all the objectives mentioned'. Acheson's draft made no attempt to qualify the aim of eliminating discrimination, of which Imperial Preference was regarded as an instance, indeed the draft contained the statement, 'I still believe that a simple acceptance of the draft would be far the best method of achieivng the purposes of both our countries'[73]. When Acheson had finished his draft Welles informed Roosevelt that a reply for Churchill had been prepared as requested[74]. The following day Welles sent another note to Roosevelt saying that Acheson and Harry Hopkins had re-worked the draft letter for the Prime Minister and Welles said he thought it was an improvement[75]. It is this draft which is generally held to have been sent to Churchill; however, in the light of the role which Welles had played in Anglo-American economic diplomacy since 1940 it is inconceivable that he could have described the letter Roosevelt actually sent to Churchill on 11 February as an improvement on Acheson's 10 February draft. If the second re-draft, which Acheson had helped with, was the letter Roosevelt sent to Churchill then it is odd that Acheson should later comment rather disparagingly that, 'If this did not illumine the subject, as Professor Whitehead said of a lecture by Lord Russell on higher mathematics, it did not deepen the surrounding darkness'. Hull also peremptorily dismisses Roosevelt's letter with the simple comment that it led to a final agreement[76]. One suspects that both Acheson and Hull handle this matter rather gingerly because the letter queered the State Department's pitch just as Roosevelt himself had done at the Atlantic Conference. The answer to the question of authorship of the final draft of Roosevelt's letter to Churchill is to be found in R. E. Sherwood's account of the relationship between Hopkins and the President.

> A reply to the Prime Minister, drafted by the State Department, was couched in the usual formal terms, but Roosevelt rejected this and wrote a cable in his own intensely personal and considerate manner.[77]

The State Department must surely have thought that Roosevelt's letter was too considerate. He wrote that,

The Wheat Talks and the Mutual Aid Agreement

> I want to make it clear to you, that it is the furthest thing from my mind that we are attempting in any way to ask you to trade the principle of imperial preference as a consideration for lend-lease...
> What seems to be bothering the Cabinet is the thought that we want a commitment in advance that empire preference will be abolished. We are asking for no such commitment, and I can say that Article 7 does not contain any such commitment. I realize that that would be a commitment which your government could not give now if it wanted to; and I am very sure that I could not, on my part, make any commitment relative to a vital revision of our tariff policy.[78]

Churchill and his Cabinet immediately seized the life-line. The Prime Minister wrote that 'I am deeply grateful to you for all you say, which entirely meets my difficulties'. He continued, 'Of course when I am asked I shall state my view of the public document from my own standpoint in terms which lie within your assurances'[79].

It has been suggested on the basis of Cabinet minutes that Churchill accepted article seven because he thought that Roosevelt had agreed to exclude Imperial Preference from its scope. This seems an unlikely mistake and one that would have been corrected by Wood. A possible explanation of the error contained in the minutes is that it was made by the secretary who took them rather than by Churchill. Whatever the case might be a draft letter to the Dominions of the following day clearly shows the government understood that Imperial Preference fell within the scope of article seven. Another reason which has been suggested for Churchill's acceptance is that the British did not want to antagonise Roosevelt when he was about to consider whether or not to relieve Britain of $800 million worth of pre-Lend-Lease contracts, but the evidence to support this hypothesis is weak. Both these attempts to explain Churchill's behaviour assume that he and his Cabinet were still very reluctant to accept the agreement whereas this was no longer the case[80].

The British negotiating position had been weakened since the entry of Japan into the war. On 26 February Ronald commented that after the losses of crucial components of the Sterling Area such as Malaya, 'The Americans could hardly be expected to treat seriously any suggestion by us that, unless they fell in with our ideas for the co-ordination of post-war policy, we should be forced back on a closed Empire trading system. Such a trading system henceforward is probably an illusion'[81]. Thus economic cooperation with the Americans was more necessary than ever and probably unavoidable: the question was on what terms it should be undertaken. Article seven as it stood was unacceptable but the interpretation of it by Roosevelt was not.

Members of the State Department had consistently striven for an unequivocal commitment from Britain to eliminate discriminatory economic practices, including Imperial Preference, and this was to be part of the consideration for Lend-Lease. They envisaged cooperative talks between Britain and the US which would determine the means by which those aims, along with other liberal economic policies, were to be implemented. Roosevelt now repudiated much of that and contrived to throw discriminatory policies and Imperial Preference back into the bargaining arena in such a way that Britain would be able to use them as bargaining chips. Furthermore, the President postponed their elimination into an indeterminate future that effectively qualified the stated aims of article seven. Two years later in the House of Commons Churchill, to some people's surprise though why is difficult to see as he was only paraphrasing the President's message of 11 February 1942, said that,

> I did not agree to Article 7...without having previously obtained from the President a definite assurance that we were no more committed to the abolition of Imperial Preference, than the American Government were committed to the abolition of their high protective tariffs.[82]

Churchill had rather conveniently overlooked much of the ambiguity which arose from article seven when it was interpreted in the light of Roosevelt's letter, but the Mutual Aid Agreement was a successful rearguard action by the British. The State Department attempt to eliminate the equivocation embodied in the Atlantic Charter had failed and Roosevelt had proved once again to be less sanguine about free trade and less keen to get detailed commitments on economic policy than Hull and his acolytes. It is true that the British were now committed to early economic talks with the Americans, and as Lionel Robbins, the head of the Economic Section of the War Cabinet Secretariat, correctly states in his memoirs the British would have been foolish to go completely against the economic spirit which had motivated the State Department in the Lend-Lease Consideration Talks; nevertheless they had more room to manoeuvre than the State Department had intended that they should have[83].

Towards the end of this book we shall have occasion to look briefly at the talks which issued from article seven and at the way 'discrimination' and Imperial Preference raised their heads again at the end of the war, but now we must turn to the political and economic consequences of Lend-Lease in operation.

NOTES

1. See: Hull to Winant and his reply, 27 and 29 Sept. 1941, 841.24/811; and Winant to Hull, 30 Sept. 1941, 841.24/814.
2. Breckinridge Long Desk Diary, 15 Feb. 1945, Long Papers, box 5; and D. Dilks (Ed.), The Diaries of Sir Alexander Cadogan 1938-45 (Putnams, New York, 1972), pp.364, 642 and 699.
3. Memo. of conversation between Halifax and Acheson, 3 Oct. 1941, 841.24/1059.
4. Ibid, and Acheson memo. for Hull and Welles, 22 Oct. 1941, 841.24/1059.
5. Memo. of conversation between Halifax and Welles, 9 Oct. 1941, 841.24/1074.
6. Hawkins to Acheson, 10 Oct. 1941, 841.24/902½.
7. Ibid.
8. D. Acheson, Present at the Creation (W. W. Norton Company, New York, 1969), p.31. The statement in the last parentheses was made on 3 Oct., see memo. of conversation between Halifax and Acheson, 841.24/898. For official record see memo. of conversation between Acheson, Hawkins, Halifax and Opie, 17 Oct. 1941, 841.24/1019; and Halifax to FO, 17 Oct. 1941, T160/1105/F17660/02/2.
9. Hawkins to Acheson, 24 Oct. 1941, 841.24/921½.
10. See: Berle to Acheson, 24 Oct. 1941, 841.24/921½; Feis to Acheson, 841.24/922½; M. F. Healey, 'Witness Participant and Chronicler: The Role of Herbert Feis As Economic Adviser To The

The Wheat Talks and the Mutual Aid Agreement

State Department 1931-43', Ph.D. Thesis, Georgetown University, Washington, 1973; and Acheson, *Present at the Creation*, p.31.

11. Winant to Hull, 16 Nov. 1941, 841.24/1002.

12. Hull to Roosevelt and his reply, 19 Nov. 1941, Roosevelt PSF, box 16, folder: lend-lease 1941(3).

13. The final text may be found in, *A Decade of American Foreign Policy, Basic Documents* (US Government Printing Office, Washington 1950). December text is at Halifax to FO, 4 Dec. 1941, W14596/37/49, FO371/28812.

14. See: Halifax to FO, 4 Dec. 1941, W14596/37/49, FO371/28812; and minutes by N. Butler and P. Dean of the FO North American Department, 7 and 11 Dec. 1941, W14652/37/49, FO371/28812.

15. Roosevelt to Churchill, 17 Oct. 1941, 561.311 F1 advisory committee/1053. For British reactions see 'The Wheat Conference Situation' a draft document for ministers circulated by T. Padmore, 5 Dec. 1941, BT11/1734/CRT10072/41.

16. Minutes by T. N. Whitehead of the FO North American Department on records of five meetings 20 to 27 Oct. 1941, 10 Feb. 1942, W19/19/49, FO371/32410.

17. Hull to Winant, 31 Oct. 1941, 561.311F1 advisory committee/1049.

18. Washington to FO, 10 Nov. 1941, T160/1105/F17660/02/2; and Halifax to FO, 27 Nov.1941, concerning informal talks between Salter, Acheson and Hawkins on 12 Nov., BT11/1734/CRT 10072/41. Acheson repeated his view that a satisfactory conclusion of the Wheat Talks was important for future Anglo-American economic talks at a Board of Economic Operations meeting on 17 Nov. minutes of BEO meeting 17 Nov. 1941, Berle Papers, box 56, folder: BEO Oct. to Dec. 1941.

19. Needless to say Halifax was a willing agent for passing these warnings on to London, see Halifax to FO, 27 Nov. and 1 Dec.1941, BT11/1734/CRT10072/41

20. Hull to Winant, 26 Nov. 1941, 561.311 F1/advisory committee/1060.

21. 'The Wheat Conference Situatuion', a draft document for ministers circulated by T. Padmore, 5 Dec. 1941, BT11/1734/CRT10072/41.

22. A. Bryant, *The Turn of the Tide: Based on the War Diaries of Field Marshall Viscount* Alanbrooke (Collins, London, 1957), p.282.

23. Memo. by Hubert Henderson, 8 Dec. 1941, T160/1105/F17660/02/2.

24. Memo. by Amery, 10 Dec. 1941 ibid.

The Wheat Talks and the Mutual Aid Agreement

25. Hull to Winant (dispatched 8.00 p.m.), 841.24/1039b.
26. Winant to Hull, 14 Dec. 1941, 841.24/1095.
27. FO to Washington, 13 Dec. 1941, W14652/37/49, F0371/28812.
28. Winant to Hull, and memo. by Acheson, both dated 26 Dec. 1941 and at 841.24/1107.
29. Minutes by Ronald, 18 Dec. 1941, W193/19/49, F0371/32410.
30. Leith-Ross memo. on wheat policy, 24 Dec. 1941, and notes by Salter on the Wheat Conference, both at W302/19/49, F0371/32410.
31. See: Winant to Eden, 11 Dec. 1941, T160/1105/F17660/02/2; and minutes by Ronald, 20 April 1942, W5914/19/49, F0371/32413.
32. E. F. Penrose, Economic Planning for the Peace (Princeton University Press, New Jersey, 1953), p.66.
33. Winant to Hull, 28 Dec. 1941, 561.311F1 advisory committee/1066.
34. Salter to FO, 19 Jan. 1942, W1004/19/49, F0371/32410.
35. Minutes by Ronald, 20 April 1942, W5914/19/49, F0371/32413.
36. Halifax to Eden with the 'Pasvolsky Memorandum' enclosed, 16 Dec. 1941, W367/81/49, F0371/28856.
37. Halifax to FO, 20 Dec. 1941, W15249/37/49, F0371/28813.
38. Halifax to FO (telegram 5954), 20 Dec. 1941, ibid.
39. FO to Washington, 24 Dec. 1941, W15273/37/49, F0371/28813.
40. See: Winant to Hull, 29 Dec. 1941, 841.24/III; and Penrose, Economic Planning, p.31.
41. See: Hickerson to Hull, 29 Dec. 1941, 841.24/1135; memo. of conversation between Opie, Pasvolsky and Achilles, 30 Dec. 1941, 841.24/1156; and Phillips to FO, 31 Dec. 1941,T160/1105/F17660/02/2.
42. Memo. of conversation between Halifax and Hull, 29 Dec. 1941, 841.24/1129; and Hull to Roosevelt, 30 Dec. 1941, 841.24/1154A.
43. Halifax to FO, 29 Dec. 1941, W15637/37/49, F0371/28813.
44. Greenwood, WM(1)42, 1 Jan. 1942, CAB 65.
45. Minutes by Law, 30 Dec. 1941, W193/19/42, F0371/32410.
46. See: Law to Cranborne, 7 Jan. 1942, W15677/37/49, F0371/28813; and Law's draft proposals for a note of interpretation, 7 Jan. 1942, ibid.

The Wheat Talks and the Mutual Aid Agreement

47. Eden to Halifax, 6 Jan. 1942, W367/81/49, FO371/32481.
48. 'Notes on the Pasvolsky Memorandum' by Keynes, 5 Jan. 1942, W789/81/49, FO371/32481.
49. Ibid.
50. Memo. by Greenwood in response to a request by the Cabinet on 5 Jan. 1942, WP(42)21, CAB 66.
51. Memo. by Amery, WP(42)23, 12 Jan. 1942, CAB66; Cranborne to Greenwood 13 Jan. 1942, W585/122/49, FO371/32491; WP(42)25, 17 Jan. 1942, CAB 66.
52. WM(8)42, 17 Jan. 1942, CAB65.
53. Halifax to FO, 30 Jan. 1942, W1508/122/49, FO371/32491.
54. Acheson to Hull, concerning his conversation with the President, 29 Jan. 1942, 841.24/1224.
55. Breckinridge Long Desk Diary, 13 Jan. 1942, Long Papers, box 5; C. Hull, The Memoirs of Cordell Hull, 2 Vols. (Hodder and Stoughton, London, 1948), Vol.II, p.1153.
56. Acheson to Hull, 22 Jan. 1942, 841.24/11256/12.
57. Wickard Diary, 23 Jan. 1942 (entered 25 January 1942), F. D. Roosevelt Library, Wickard Papers.
58. Acheson to Hull, 29 Jan. 1942, 841.24/1224.
59. Halifax to FO (for War Cabinet circulation), 30 Jan.1942, W1508/122/49, FO371/32491.
60. Bruce to Dominions Office, 31 Jan. 1942, W1508/122/49, FO371/32491.
61. Dilks, Cadogan, 2 Feb.1942, pp.430-431; and WM(14)42, 2 Feb. 1942, CAB 65.
62. Winant to Acheson, 3 Feb. 1942, 841.24/1183.
63. See: Hull to Winant, 4 Feb. 1942, 841.24/1183; and Hawkins to Acheson, 4 Feb. 1942, 841.24/1125.
64. Morgenthau to Wood, 4 Feb. 1942, but, as Acheson to Morgenthau, 4 Feb. 1942 shows, Acheson drafted and signed the letter on Morgenthau's behalf. Both letters are at 841.24/1184C.
65. W. F. Kimball, Churchill and Roosevelt: The Complete Correspondence, 3 Vols. (Princeton University Press, New York, 1984), Vol.I, pp.344-345, Roosevelt to Churchill, 4 Feb. 1942.
66. Winant to Eden, 4 Feb. 1942, W1725/122/49, FO371/32491, and Eden's second draft of a note of interpretation WP(42)66, 5 Feb. 1942, CAB 66.
67. WM(17)42, 6 Feb. 1942, CAB 65.

The Wheat Talks and the Mutual Aid Agreement

68. Kimball, *Correspondence*, Vol.I, pp.349-351, Churchill to Roosevelt, 7 Feb. 1942: text of note can be found at FO to Halifax, 6 Feb. 1942, W1508/122/49, FO371/32491, or at 841.24/1186.
69. Winant to Acheson, 6 Feb. 1942, 841.24/1186.
70. Memo. of conversation between Halifax and Welles, 6 Feb. 1942, 841.24/1186.
71. See: Halifax to FO, 8 Feb. 1942, W1979/122/49, FO371/32491; and memo. of conversation between Halifax, Opie, Acheson and Feis, 7 Feb. 1942, 841.24/1225; and Acheson, *Present at the Creation*, p.33.
72. Winant to Hull, 841.24/1192; and Penrose, *Economic Planning*, p.24.
73. Kimball, *Correspondence*, Vol.I, pp.356-357, draft letter by Acheson (not sent), 10 Feb. 1942.
74. Welles to Roosevelt, 10 Feb. 1942, 841.24/1125.
75. Welles to Roosevelt, 11 Feb. 1942, 841.24/1243A. Acheson in his memoirs corroborates this but he then goes on to say that it was this draft which was 'fired off', Acheson, *Present at the Creation*, p.33.
76. See Acheson, *Present at the Creation*, p.33, and Hull, *Memoirs*, Vol.II, p.1153.
77. R. E. Sherwood, *The White House Papers of Harry L. Hopkins*, 2 Vols. (Eyre and Spottiswoode, London, 1948), Vol.II, p.512.
78. Kimball, *Correspondence*, Vol.I, pp.357-358, Roosevelt to Churchill, 11 Feb. 1942.
79. Ibid, pp.360-361, Churchill to Roosevelt, 12 Feb. 1942.
80. See D. Reynolds, *The Creation of the Anglo-American Alliance 1937-41* (Europa, London, 1981), pp.278-279. The Cabinet minutes upon which Reynolds bases his claim that Churchill misunderstood the President's letter of 11 February are at WM(42)20, 12 Feb. 1942, CAB 65, however, the minutes first state that the Prime Minister read Roosevelt's letter to the Cabinet and then they go on to summarise some of it. It is possible that the summary, in which the mistake is contained, was made by the secretary taking the minutes rather than by Churchill (why should he first read the letter and then summarise it?). In any case this would only be an important issue if the Cabinet would have refused to agree to article seven on the basis of what Roosevelt actually said in his letter; evidence of later reactions, when the matter was definitely clear, indicates this would not have happened.

The Wheat Talks and the Mutual Aid Agreement

81. Memo. of conversation between Ronald and Sir Hubert Henderson, 26 Feb. 1942, W2458/27/49, F0371/32423.
82. Churchill, House of Commons Debates, April 1944, 399:579-580.
83. Lord Robbins, *Autobiography of an Economist* (Macmillan, London, 1971), p.195.

Chapter Five

RESERVES, EXPORTS, AND RECIPROCAL AID

Lend-Lease was not an economic panacea. The British Government continued to worry about the low level of her monetary reserves and about the prospective difficulties of reconverting from wartime to peactime production. By June 1944 American aid had made it possible for Britain to have 33 per cent of its labour force engaged in war duties and 22 per cent in the armed forces. In 1943 Britain's exports were 25 per cent of what they had been in 1937, once munitions were taken out of the account, and the situation changed little until the end of the war. The government estimated that exports would have to expand to 150 per cent of what they had been in 1938 in order to get the postwar economy on an even keel: thus exports and the intimately allied issue of gold and dollar reserves were crucially important[1].

In February 1942 at a US Treasury meeting Jacob Viner, seemingly with flawless economic logic, stated that if Britain received all her US requirements on Lend-Lease there would be no need for her to replenish her dollar reserves[2]. It would, however, have been insufferable for the world's greatest trading nation to have accepted such humiliating economic circumstances. After Lend-Lease came into being Britain continued to export in order to obtain supplies unavailable in the US, and to sustain foreign economies which provided materials essential for the war effort. Some of these exports had the potential for arousing criticisms in the US because they were similar to or identical to Lend-Lease supplies. The British therefore argued for an increase in their dollar reserves so that they could pay for items which were vulnerable to criticism instead of receiving them on Lend-Lease. There was also the matter of international confidence in sterling; the British claimed that they needed gold and dollar reserves to hold against sterling liabilities rapidly accumulating in India, Egypt and elsewhere because of war expenditure. Underlying the arguments put to the Americans were British convictions that they should try to protect their economic independence and sustain a sterling-based economic system which, if it could not provide an alternative to close cooperation with the US, might at least provide a viable position from which to bargain.

A highly complex and troublesome network of relationships soon developed between the US and the UK involving Lend-Lease, its British equivalent - Reciprocal Aid, and Britain's dollar reserves and exports. The tension which was often apparent on the surface of these relationships was reinforced by a long-standing commercial rivalry between the two countries. Britain was determined to recapture export markets, abandoned because of the war, and to accumulate sufficient reserves to facilitate postwar trade and to provide herself with a degree of economic independence: America was equally determined to expand her presence in the international economy and to ensure that Britain was not in a position which could hamper that growth. American production quadrupled during the war and as this was before the great consumer society had come into being there were widespread fears in the US business community and government that a depression would ensue if foreign markets were not found for this excess production. American policies which developed largely as a consequence of these convictions were also partly influenced by domestic political considerations and by different views within the Roosevelt Administration as to how America's economic interests could best be realised: the detailed effects of these factors will become evident as the story unfolds.

The sale of assets and South African gold and a timely loan from the Belgian Government failed to plug the gap between Britain's dollar holdings and her expenditures in the weeks before Lend-Lease became law. Morgenthau did much to help: he set a plan in motion for the head of the government's Reconstruction Finance Corporation (RFC), Jesse Jones, to extend a loan to Britain, and he used his good offices to keep the American supply line open even when it was unclear how Britain would requite new dollar commitments[3]. The British Government hoped that Lend-Lease funds might be used retrospectively but a few days after the Lend-Lease

Reserves, Exports and Reciprocal Aid

Bill became law the Director of the Budget, Harold Smith, testifying before Congress, declared that Britain had enough dollars to meet her existing obligations and that appropriations under the act would only be used for British orders placed after 11 March 1941[4]. It now looked as if Britain's interim finance crisis would become permanent.

Churchill and Kinglsey Wood were worried and they wrote to the President that they did not think that Britain's reserves should sink below $150 million. Since Phillips' journey to Washington to seek financial help in the autumn of 1940 the British had regarded $600 million as a viable working balance and this was frequently mentioned to the US Treasury. On 18 March Morgenthau told Arthur Purvis, a Canadian businessman in charge of the British Purchasing Commission in Washington, that Lend-Lease was now in the hands of Hopkins but that he would give 'help without responsibility', and the following day true to his word he informed Phillips that he had got Hopkins and the President to agree that Britain should be relieved of between $300 million and $400 million of pre-Lend-Lease contracts[5]. The British, hoping to take advantage of this, sent Keynes to Washington in May to try to sort out Britain's financial position.

On 13 May at a meeting with Morgenthau and one of his assistants, Merle Cochran, Keynes thanked the Secretary for his past help and then rather gingerly broached the subject of Britain's reserves. A few days earlier Hopkins had refused Lend-Lease items for India, and Keynes said that he agreed with this because it was preferable for Britain to pay for sensitive items and have a working dollar balance which would enable her to do this. Morgenthau asked whether a dollar reserve was necessary for the war or for financial reasons: Keynes was evasive but admitted it was necessary on both counts. After the meeting, as Keynes was collecting his hat from Cochran's office, the latter urged him to be more direct with Morgenthau. He said that neither of them fully understood what Keynes was getting at when he had referred to making Britain's financial position more secure. Keynes explained that he hoped that there would be additional Lend-Lease appropriations in July and clearly implied that they might be used so that Britain's dollar position could be strengthened. Cochran cautioned him that there would be 'some objections to the British building up too important cash balances while the Lend-Lease program was in operation'[6]. That caution was to echo in British ears for the next four years.

In the following weeks Keynes persisted in trying to get American assistance so that Britain could accumulate $600 million of reserves and, despite antagonising American officials including Morgenthau, by July he was able to report some success. The Americans would not agree to take over all the dollar liabilities that the British wanted them to but a package deal was put together which would at least cover Britain's immediate dollar debts. In June the Neutrality Law had been amended to enable the RFC to extend a loan of $425 million to Britain against $700 million of collateral in the form of British investments in the US, and an agreement was concluded in July. In addition to this Morgenthau promised that the administration would try to relieve Britain of between $400 million and $600 million worth of pre-Lend-Lease contracts. Britain would then be left with about $300 million of debts to be covered by current dollar income from sales of gold and assets, and from trade receipts[7].

These arrangements prevented Britain from becoming dollarless, but they did not provide a sufficient working reserve. Furthermore, the pre-Lend-Lease take-outs did not materialise to the extent hoped for. The State Department, perhaps a little surprisingly given the friction between it and the British over economic questions, consistently favoured a handsome amount of dollar relief for Britain, however, the US Treasury had a change of heart and became less sanguine about this. Morgenthau was offended by Keynes' attitude during the summer, and he complained bitterly about his canvassing for support in Washington for a rise in Britain's dollar balances. Morgenthau was sensitive about the Treasury's jurisdictional authority and was of the opinion that the clever Keynes was going behind his back and trying to make a sucker out of him. There was also a backcloth of growing acrimony over economic relations between Britain and the US which included a spate of complaints about Britain's misuse of Lend-Lease. In February the President decreed that the time was not appropriate for relieving Britain of pre-Lend-Lease contracts, mainly for aircraft, worth $800 million, and although this was not the end of the matter - among other things US service departments took over $290 million of British contracts in May - Britain's finances were once again critically strained[8].

Reserves, Exports and Reciprocal Aid

The entry of the US into the war did not help matters here as a growing flow of British supplies began to go to the US via Reciprocal Aid thus losing more dollar income for Britain.

It was in the light of these developments that Harry White, who was becoming the key figure in the US Treasury concerned with Anglo-American economic relations, began a line of thinking which was to be of great consequence. In an inter-departmental meeting on 6 February, which unanimously agreed that the US should accept Reciprocal Aid, White with typical arrogance and perception said this decision would have a bearing upon Britain's reserve position and he suggested that the US really needed to decide the amount of dollars that Britain should be allowed to accumulate[9]. The idea, and later the practice, of America controlling Britain's economic fortunes in this way became a subject of major political controversy, but before we take the story of Britain's reserves any further we must pause to see what happened with regard to Britain's export policy in the autumn of 1941 because exports, reserves, Lend-Lease and Reciprocal Aid all became inextricably entwined in the following months.

In late June and early July 1941 the uneasy state of Anglo-American trade relations was aggravated by American businessmen who alleged that Britain was misusing Lend-Lease. This resulted in the tabling of a resolution in Congress which called for an investigation into the continuation of Britain's trade with Latin America. After discussing these embarrassing accusations Keynes, Oscar Cox, and later the President himself, defended the British handling of Lend-Lease. Nevertheless, even though many of the allegations were unfounded and had arisen because of the competitive rivalry between American and British exporters, the Americans came to the conclusion that it was politically necessary for the British to publicly commit themselves to a standard of good behaviour with regard to their exports and Lend-Lease. On 9 July Hopkins asked Winant to take up the issues of profiteering in the distribution of civilian Lend-Lease, and of Lend-Lease items entering Britain's export trade, with ministers in London[10].

Over the following weeks two parallel sets of talks took place: one was in Washington between Arthur Purvis and officials from the US Treasury and the Lend-Lease Agency (OLLA), and the other was in London between Winant and Wood. Lend-Lease profiteering did not become a major issue, but the decisions about British exports had important consequences. In Washington they developed a criterion to prevent competition between British and American exports, and this was embodied in the 'Burns Letters' so-called after the nominal head of the OLLA. In London they developed a criterion of control based on goods being in scarce supply in the US. Hopkins, who visited London in July, instructed Winant to present this criterion to Wood and to urge him to accept it. Back in Washington his deputy Cox and the US Treasury were unaware of this; they came to think that scarce supply had been suggested by Wood as an alternative to the 'Burns Letters'. When Cox realised his mistake he then suggested that both criteria should be applied and after some pressure on the British, and with some amendments to the original American wording, Kingsley Wood and Duncan, the President of the Board of Trade, accepted that both criteria should be incorporated into the statement of policy, which emerged on 10 September as the Export White Paper. It was a unilateral declaration in form but in practice it was a binding Anglo-American accord[11].

The export restrictions appear Draconian: Britain was not to use Lend-Lease articles in her export trade except where it was impossible to segregate them from other sources of supply, in which cases the British domestic consumption of the material in question had to be at least equal to the amount supplied under Lend-Lease (this was known as the substitution principle); articles similar to those supplied under Lend-Lease were not to be used by Britain to expand her export markets at America's expense and she committed herself to reduce exports to the 'irreducible minimum necessary to supply or, obtain materials essential to the war effort'; articles similar to Lend-Lease supplies but not in short supply in the US were not to be exported in excess of what Britain produced or bought from any source; and finally under 4(i)a of the White Paper, which eventually caused the most problems, no materials in short supply in the US, whether supplied for cash or under Lend-Lease, were to be used for export except where they were needed overseas in connection with war supplies which were essential to the war effort and which could not be obtained from the US, or where small quantities were needed for components of exports which were otherwise made of non-scarce materials, or where repair parts for British machinery were needed, or where plant was required for contracts already undertaken[12].

The British did not accept these terms with relish but unlike the proposals that the State Department espoused for article seven during 1941 they could see some justice in them, and in any case Britain's exports had already shrunk to an irreducible minimum. Furthermore, Purvis had begun to nudge the Americans towards an Anglo-American war supply programme which involved the US reducing civilian production[13]; these proposals would have had little appeal if there was even the slightest hint of Britain abusing American generosity. By September 1941 the British also calculated that their future freedom to export would not be unduly hampered because they expected that America would soon enter the war and that then unilateral restrictions on British exports could be abandoned. The Americans were motivated by equity and self-interest in the Export White Paper Talks; firstly they observed that in law Lend-Lease was justified in terms of defending the US not on the basis of maintaining or recovering Britain's commercial standing; secondly that it would have been politically unacceptable for the US to subsidise British exports at the expense of its own; and thirdly, there was an element of commercial opportunism involved, particularly with regard to American wishes to break Britain's hold on Latin American markets. Until December 1941 Britain's export policy was restrained and American criticisms of it were largely unjustified, however, with America's entry into the war and the continuation of the White Paper things began to change.

When Churchill was discussing war strategy with Roosevelt at the Arcadia Conference in the US during December 1941 and January 1942 there was much talk of pooling resources and the British hoped that this signalled the end of the Export White Paper. At the end of December Edward Stettinius, who had become the Lend-Lease Administrator on 28 October, agreed that Britain could export items for the war effort to the Empire and allied countries in the Eastern Hemisphere, which were vulnerable under 4(i)a of the White Paper, by assuming their unobtainability in the US. In return the British were to keep the Americans informed about their exports and begin plans for joint programming [14]. Unfortunately for the British their hopes for the complete abandonment of the White Paper remained unfulfilled. The US Administration still saw a forceful sense of justice

Reserves, Exports and Reciprocal Aid

in restricting Britain's use of Lend-Lease and this was reinforced by desires both to appease Congress and to pursue commercial interests. At the end of January Breckinridge Long noted bitterly that Lend-Lease oil pipes which the British had installed in Iran were for their own exclusive use; he said Britain's policy was to 'suck the United States dry', and then ally with the Soviet Union! In the US Cabinet on 13 February, 'The President spoke about the British being "caught" using precious shipping to maintain their commercial trade rather than the war effort. He indicated we ought to have someone studying the situation apparently because we can't trust the British'[15]. Thus the Americans rejected the idea of truly pooling resources in the discussions about export policy in much the same way as they rejected it when the British suggested that pooling made the idea of Lend-Lease Consideration redundant.

Apart from the Eastern Hemisphere waiver and the supersession of the White Paper provisions in the cases of a few materials where the Combined Production and Resources Board and the Combined Raw Materials Board (CPRB and CRMB, both set up in early 1942) agreed on joint programmes, there was no further formal, effective relaxation of the export restrictions until VE-day. On 20 April 1942 Chalkley, the commercial counsellor at the British Embassy in Washington, was informed by the OLLA that, 'We are of the opinion... - in case there should be any question as to this - that the White Paper, as such, should remain in effect'[16]. The only legitimate way available to Britain to gain further relief from export controls was to develop joint programmes with the US and in July 1942 with a view to doing this the CRMB set up the Combined Export and Marketing Committee (CEMC), and we shall shortly consider how this fared.

By mid-February 1942 it was apparent to the British Government that America's entry into the war was not going to alleviate Britain's economic problems substantially. The final Consideration Agreement was a partial victory for the British and the worst elements of the American Wheat Proposals had been side-stepped, but the prospects for her exports whilst Lend-Lease continued were not auspicious, and her reserve position was unhealthy and as the Treasury informed Phillips in early 1942, both were about to become more complicated because of Reciprocal Aid which could deplete Britain's dollar reserves even further[17]. This possibility had been noted by Harry White and Acheson, though the former from the point of view of how it might limit the growth of Britain's reserves whereas the latter was more concerned that they should be adequate both to meet Britain's world-wide economic obligations and State Department demands that she adopt liberal trading policies. The State Department was in charge of the Reciprocal Aid Discussions, but Acheson had to work closely with the US Treasury because of the monetary and financial questions which were involved and he and his department were far from being in a position to decide policy unilaterally on the American side.

On 23 February 1942 Reciprocal Aid was officially authorised though there had been an unofficial trickle of supplies and valuable information since the beginning of Lend-Lease[18]. Talks, instigated by Acheson, soon began in Washington about the expected increase in Reciprocal Aid and the effect this would have on Britain's reserve position. On 28 February Acheson told US Treasury officials that he thought certain issues should be considered before advancing with Reciprocal Aid; firstly what level of reserves would give Britain a working balance - he noted in this respect that Keynes had mentioned $600 million; secondly the drain on British dollar reserves needed to be assessed - for example - her liabilities under pre-Lend-Lease contracts; thirdly some estimate of the likely income to the Sterling Area dollar pool should be made; and fourthly they should consider guaranteeing Britain an adequate dollar reserve. If the US did this, Acheson said it would be necessary to reach an understanding about British and Dominion policy in maintaining the gold and dollar position of the Sterling Area and in spending dollars provided by the US, and to establish a small standing committee to monitor things. Within this framework the US could fulfill its guarantee to Britain by adopting one or more of the following tactics: buying sterling for dollars, taking over British dollar contracts, enlarging the scope of Lend-Lease, reducing the scope of Reciprocal Aid, and extending a dollar loan to Britain. Acheson's intention was to be generous and helpful to Britain but the list of tactics available to the US also indicated how vulnerable the British were to possible American manipulation[19].

On 17 March Acheson's views were discussed with Treasury and other interested officials. It soon became clear that Harry White's attitude, which was representative of his department, was less generous and forthcoming than Acheson's. When asked by the latter if he had told the British that some way would be found to provide them with a working balance of $600 million or some other figure White replied, 'we have never told them definitely and I think there is possibly some reason to avoid telling them specifically the amount'[20]. White wanted to retain manoeuvrability so that he could react to changing circumstances and, as we shall see shortly, to influence unilaterally the amount of reserves Britain could accumulate. He told Acheson that he wanted to fulfill Morgenthau's promise to the British to provide them with enough dollars for the prosecution of the war but he would not commit the Treasury any further than this. In fact White and leading members of the Treasury did not want to take Britain's wider monetary and commercial circumstances into account. This became increasingly clear during April and May when they and State Department officials discussed a memorandum from London on Britain's financial position which argued for measures that would strengthen Britain's overall economic position.

The British Teasury was profoundly worried by Britain's economic weakness; it suspected American motives and wanted to recover some kind of economic independence. In a memorandum of 18 April it made a bold attempt to achieve some level of economic security. It brought to the attention of the Americans that sterling liabilities, particularly in India and the Middle East, were growing rapidly, and to off-set this and to strengthen Britain's position it suggested that newly mined gold in the Sterling Area should be set aside and held against sterling debts, that in addition to the relief from pre-Lend-Lease contracts - which had been more or less agreed - the US should also take over a further $450 million of aircraft contracts, that there should be no more capital transfers from Britain to the US, and that Britain's lone stand from 1940 to December 1941 and the projected increase in Reciprocal Aid should be taken into account. In return Britain would not attempt to build up anything more than a working dollar balance, would extend Reciprocal Aid to the amount desired by the US and would remove sensitive items from Lend-Lease[21].

Acheson found himself in a minority of one when discussing these proposals in Washington. He sympathised with the British arguments and wanted to give further relief on pre-Lend-Lease contracts, though the figure used in the American discussions was $235 million not $450 million. White claimed that Britain's case was only persuasive if her gold holdings were taken out of her reserve account, which he was opposed to doing. He indicated that Britain could liquidate her pre-Lend-Lease contracts and still have $700 million of gold and dollar reserves. Morgenthau and Cox thought further dollar relief for Britain would be difficult to justify politically and all the representatives, excepting Acheson, from the departments and agencies involved in the discussions agreed. They thus decided not to take over further dollar commitments from the British and Acheson, while commenting that this was a mistake, agreed to inform the British of the decision. On 29 May Morgenthau also told Phillips that the US would not accept the suggestion that Britain should hold gold separately from her reserves to offset sterling liabilities[22].

The attempt in the April memorandum if not exactly to feather-bed Britain's reserve and export position at least to give it some measure of strength failed. Nevertheless, there were still grounds for some optimism in London. On 31 May, Roosevelt in his 'Fifth Report to Congress on the Lend-Lease Operations' continued to speak of pooling resources. He noted that rich countries would give more in absolute terms than poorer countries but providing that sacrifices were made equally in proportion to resources then this was fair. This notion of equity was reflected in the agreement the British and Americans reached on Reciprocal Aid in September: the Americans made two major allowances for Britain's reserve position which meant that Reciprocal Aid was not truly reciprocal. Britain was to supply US forces and undertake military construction work for America when she could do so more effectively than the US, but both raw materials and GI pay in the Sterling Area were excluded from the agreement[23].

By the autumn of 1942 the only question remaining in relation to Reciprocal Aid was whether a financial record of operations should be kept. The British argued that they did not have the man-power to cost Reciprocal Aid and that too much emphasis on sterling and dollar signs would create the impression of debts and credits and undermine the idea of pooling resources. There was also the fact that the amount of Reciprocal Aid, partly because of the allowances for Britain's reserve position, was not very impressive when compared with that of Lend-Lease. Stettinius and Averell Harriman, who had been appointed in September 1941 to head a US mission in London to expedite Lend-Lease supplies, both supported the British in their desire not to cost Reciprocal Aid, and for the time being a compromise was struck whereby the Americans simply kept a rough quantitative record of the supplies they received[24].

It is noteworthy that there were differences between Reciprocal Aid and Lend-Lease. We have already mentioned some but there were also differences in procurement practices which require consideration. Lend-Lease operated within a legalistic framework, procurement was centralised and easily monitored by the service departments and OLLA. The framework within which Reciprocal Aid operated was more flexible than that for Lend-Lease; it had developed largely through practice and under the general authority of the government rather than from specific legislation. Procurement was de-centralised because it mainly occurred at the various places of use throughout the UK, North Africa, the Middle East etc. Consequently, monitoring under these circumstances would have been difficult and extravagant with man-power. These differences were eventually to cause difficulties for Britain and the US but for the time being both sides were satisfied. However, the failure of the British to achieve what they wanted as expressed in their April memorandum meant that their reserve position was still vulnerable and uncertain, and that Britain's international commercial standing was precarious. The dangers of this weakness were exacerbated by the low level of British exports and as 1942 progressed officials from the Treasury and the Board of Trade began to chafe under the Export White Paper restrictions.

The British had hoped that the CEMC would develop joint Anglo-American export programmes thus superseding the White Paper provisions but progress was only made with a small number of materials. Partly because of this, and partly because they thought that after America's entry into the war that the export restrictions were unjustifiably one-sided the British began to interpret broadly both the Export White Paper and Stettinius' concession regarding Eastern Hemisphere exports. Complaints about British misuse of Lend-Lease supplies were contained in a report by OLLA officials who had travelled abroad during 1942 to investigate

Reserves, Exports and Reciprocal Aid

Lend-Lease operations; it was known as the 'Shirer-Hyde Report', and while noting that there had been numerous irregularities they were not deemed serious though more careful monitoring was recommended particularly as the Harriman Mission seemed to have become 'an advocate for the British rather than an outpost to watch our interests'[25]. Criticisms of the way Britain handled Lend-Lease supplies had a cumulative effect in Washington where there was now an official focal point which catalogued and broadcasted them within the US Administration. OLLA, as part of its monitoring duties established a White Paper Committee to ensure that the export restrictions were observed by Britain, and in August 1942 Harry L. Whitney was appointed as its chairman. Whitney was angered by breaches of the regulations governing the operation of Lend-Lease and he became a constant source of pressure both for tightening controls and for reducing Lend-Lease aid to Britain.

In July Sir Samuel Beale, who worked closely with the Board of Trade, tried to persuade Stettinius to extend the Eastern Hemisphere export concession to the Western Hemisphere and to accept an interpretation of the White Paper phrase 'unobtainable in the US' which would give Britain more export freedom. Whitney, who was already complaining about British abuses of the Eastern Hemisphere concession, adamantly opposed Beale's suggestions and drafted a reply for Stettinius which was sent to Beale on 14 November. Stettinius refused to extend the Eastern Hemisphere concession, 'nor could he accept interpretation of unobtainability to mean on terms satisfactory as regards delivery and price'. He reminded Beale that the concession had been given as a temporary relaxation of the White Paper controls on the understanding that joint export programming would develop. As this had not materialised, 'it was time to reconsider the problem and to establish some effective means of consultation and agreement in advance of proposed exports as the principles of the White Paper must be maintained effectively'[26].

Beale did not reply to Stettinius' letter. Over the next few months criticisms of Britain's export policy increased in Washington, and in London resentment grew larger over export controls; however attention in Washington was soon focused on Britain's dollar reserves and no major developments occurred on the export front for some months. Despite the low level of Britain's exports, her provision of Reciprocal Aid, and the refusal by the

Reserves, Exports and Reciprocal Aid

the US to take over pre-Lend-Lease contracts to the extent desired by the British, her reserves grew during 1942 mainly because of the receipt of dollars from American servicemen's pay in the Sterling Area.

On 23 November Cox sent Stettinius a memorandum indicating that Britain's gold and dollar reserves were approaching $1 billion. Stettinius took up the matter with Morgenthau suggesting that they should discuss how Britain's reserves could be prevented from rising above what he described as a relatively high figure[27]. It is doubtful if he realised the implications of this suggestion: Stettinius was an able and amiable administrator - he had a penchant for brass bands and was known in Latin America with some affection as *Los Dientes* - but he lacked political skills and was easily swayed by whatever pressure was most immediate. In this instance Cox's memorandum worried him because he thought that there might be difficulties with the forthcoming Lend-Lease appropriations in Congress on 11 January if the rise in British dollar balances became public knowledge. Stettinius was an Anglophile, but on this occasion he set events in motion which led to the most serious challenge to Britiain's economic sovereignty during the war.

The issue of Britain's dollar reserves was seized on by Vice Pesident Wallace, who was one of the most radical New Dealers; he had little love for the British Empire or its economic policies. Wallance was in charge of the Board of Economic Warfare (BEW) and was an ubiquitous figure on the domestic economic front. The BEW was also involved in acquiring materials from abroad and this opening into foreign economic affairs provided Wallace with the pretext for setting up a committee on 17 December to look into Britain's dollar reserves. Some days later, because of parallel developments in the US Treasury, a meeting between Hull, Morgenthau, Stettinius, Wallace and Acheson decided to reconstitute that committee with White as its chairman. At the end of the month it recommended that Britain's gold and dollar reserves should be limited to between $600 million and $1 billion. Acheson objected to this but the recommendation was approved by the Cabinet Dollar Committee consisting of Hull, Stimson, Stettinius, Wallace and on this occasion Daniel Bell acting on behalf of Morgenthau[28]. Hull's concurrence was somewhat out of line with his department's policy and with his subsequent actions. It can perhaps be explained by the pique he felt over the bitter Anglo-American dispute about who should lead the Free French. As Nigel Ronald quipped, 'the unhappy tale of events in North Africa has cast a black and murphy cloud over relations between the State Department and the Foreign Office'[29]. Robert Murphy was the leading American diplomat involved in the affair. On New Year's Day the Cabinet Committee sent their recommendation to Roosevelt who approved it on 11 January.

Two days later White's Dollar Committee decided that, 'the Treasury should inform Sir Frederick of the situation in broad outline'[30]. Subsequently there was considerable controversy among American officials because within days Phillips knew the precise parameters which had been set for Britain's dollar reserves. Phillips said he was given the information by US Treasury officials but White denied this and it is clear he certainly wanted to keep a low profile on the US decision to limit Britain's reserves. In early February he told Morgenthau that, 'Our position so far has been that it involves no new policy, that the range is merely a guidepost for the implementation of our present policy'[31]. The British were not so easily deceived.

Confronted with a unilateral decision to restrict their reserves and simultaneous suggestions that civilian tobacco and Icelandic fish should be removed from Lend-Lease supplies, which would entail more dollar expenditure by the UK, the British mounted a defence of their economic interests. On 19 January Kingsley Wood wrote to Morgenthau saying that Phillips had informed him that their dollar balances might not be allowed to rise any further. He pointed out that Britain's net financial position was still deteriorating because of the growth of sterling liabilities and he suggested that Britain's dollar reserves should not be subjected to unilateral actions by the US but that the matter should be a subject for joint discussions. In talks and in memoranda during the next two months the British continued to argue their case but at first it seemed with little success[32].

In March civilian tobacco was taken off Lend-Lease and at the end of the month White submitted a Treasury memorandum to his Dollar Committee which suggested four ways of reducing Britain's dollar reserves: Britain could re-pay short-term dollar liabilities, Reciprocal Aid could be extended, Lend-Lease could be reduced, and Britain could transfer stock-piles and interests in

Reserves, Exports and Reciprocal Aid

the US to the American Government. On 1 April it was decided that extending Reciprocal Aid was the best option, but within days of this decision being made Stettinius and his assistants, partly swayed by Phillips' arguments about Britain's sterling liabilities and partly because Congressional appropriations for Lend-Lease were now out of the way, began to have second thoughts about unilaterally imposing an arbitrary limit of $1 billion on Britain's reserves. When Morgenthau got wind of this he was displeased with Stettinius for changing his mind and with Phillips for persuading him to do so[33].

In a letter of information for Harry Hopkins, drawn up by Cox and Stettinius, the new position of the OLLA was made clear. Stettinius wanted Reciprocal Aid to be extended to raw materials and GI pay in the Sterling Area. He thought that the level of Britain's reserves made such extensions politically necessary and he asked for support from Hopkins and from the President in case Churchill opposed these proposals[34]. In fact the British were never asked to pay GIs (there was concern in Washington about the possibility of American soldiers being described as mercenaries), but up to this point it appears as if Stettinius was taking a hard line; however he made a distinction between the political desirability of expanding Reciprocal Aid, which would reduce Britain's dollar income to some extent, and the imposition of an arbitrary limit on Britain's reserves. At the end of the letter Stettinius said that while he was not prepared at this stage to accept the British arguments about their dollar reserves that,

> the international ramifications such as the effect on the British financial structure, on Anglo-American relations, and the economic stability of the post-war world indicate that more than only domestic issues should be considered in the settlement of the problem.

On 20 April Charles Denby, probably the most pro-British official in the OLLA, told Stettinius' senior assistant Bernhard Knollenberg that a number of their colleagues were unhappy with the situation and he urged that the decision to limit Britain's reserves should be reconsidered and that they should come clean with the British about what they were doing[35]. At the end of April Stettinius decided

Reserves, Exports and Reciprocal Aid

to follow Denby's advice, and in a formal letter to Morgenthau, who was so annoyed with the OLLA that he had insisted that Stettinius should put this in writing, he suggested that the decision about limiting Britain's balances should be reviewed in the light of her international financial position and that, 'We should reconsider whether or not it may not be advisable to canvas the whole problem frankly and openly with representatives of the British Treasury before arriving at any final decision with respect to her reserves'[36].

An identical view was taken in the State Department but there was strong opposition from White and Morgenthau because they wanted to keep within the letter of the Lend-Lease Law and because they did not want Britain to have the monetary wherewithal to pursue independent policies. As Morgenthau put it in a letter to Truman after the war, it had been his policy as Secretary of the Treasury to shift the financial centre of the world from Wall Street and the 'City' in London to the US Treasury[37]. Part of that plan was running into difficulties in early 1943 in the talks with Keynes which eventually led to the International Monetary Fund (IMF), and the more financial strength the British had the more difficult it would be to bend them to the wishes of the US Treasury. Thus Morgenthau did not engage the British in frank discussions about the reserves question, but OLLA and the State Department did force their own government to make an internal review of its policy on the British dollar balances.

Stettinius and Acheson managed to put the brake on things for a time, for example an attempt by White to centralise the discussions about Reciprocal Aid and the dollar balances in his hands - a proposal Denby described as preposterous - was foiled[38]. Nevertheless, the review did not substantially alter American policy; it was agreed that America should not use anything other than Reciprocal Aid for reducing Britain's balances for the time being but that a request to Britain for an expansion of Reciprocal Aid to cover $200 million to $300 million worth of raw materials ought to go forward. On 27 May White formally made this request of Phillips, at the same time he rather ominously asked him to summarise, 'your views on the appropriate reserve of gold and dollars which this Government should assist the British Government to maintain'[39].

Reserves, Exports and Reciprocal Aid

When White's letter reached London it set off two chains of thought: one of which was directly concerned with the extension of reciprocal Aid and its implications for Britain's dollar balances; the other was to do with Britain's exports.

The British thought that if they extended Reciprocal Aid it would begin to be a real reciprocation of Lend-Lease, in which case there would be even less justification for the one-sided restrictions of the Export White Paper. Hugh Dalton, President of the Board of Trade, pointed out to his colleagues in May that industrialists were unhappy with the Export White Paper and that they were growing suspicious that it was being used by the Americans for their own commercial advantage. The Board of Trade now began to think about replacing the White Paper with a joint Anglo-American declaration on exports, but in the meantime less orthodox methods were used to redress the situation, to wit: a liberal interpretation of the White Paper restrictions and particularly of Stettinius' concession on exports to the Eastern Hemisphere. These developments, which in fact had begun well before May 1943, did not go unnoticed in Whitney's White Paper Committee. Complaints from there became so strident that the OLLA set up another committee under Robert Stevens, which included some representatives from the State Department, to investigate the extent of British non-compliance with the White Paper and to recommend future action.

So at the same time as the British were about to seek release from the Export White Paper, Whitney, the Steven's Committee and later the US Treasury began to press for its tighter enforcement. The dominant groups, however, within both the OLLA and the State Department, were sympathetic towards Britain, and reports to Stettinius from the Harriman Mission in London and State Department memoranda at this time disclose a growing awareness of the complexity and the seriousness of Britain's economic difficulties. One State Department official, noting the disappearance of Britain's international trade during the war, commented that, 'not all the King's (and the President's) dollars and men can put it together again'. Yet despite this decline the State Department knew that Britain could still foil its hopes for a liberal postwar international economy, and it wanted to avoid adopting policies which would push Britain into a defensive policy of economic protectionism; 'Herein lies the particular interest of the United States' commented another State Department memorandum, 'in a satisfactory solution of Britain's postwar international problems'. Thus on Britain's export policy, just as in the case of her dollar balances, there were two clearly different views in Washington, and both issues were now on the verge of becoming embroiled in very complex negotiations[40].

The more direct implications of White's request for an expansion of Reciprocal Aid were considered in the light of two important factors by the British. Firstly, because of pressures from the US War Department, it was now obvious from comments that Stettinius made in June that Reciprocal Aid would have to be costed because if the British did not do it then the Americans would[41]. The British realised that this would facilitate direct comparisons between Lend-Lease and Reciprocal Aid and that if the latter was not expanded these comparisons would not be favourable for Britain. The second factor was the extent of the drain on Britain's dollar balances which would result from the expansion of Reciprocal Aid; this had to be weighed in the balance against the favourable impression the increase in British supplies to the US was expected to create in Washington, hopes that it would help them in their arguments for being relieved of the Export White Paper restrictions, and the enhancement of the idea of pooling resources.

On the 25 June important and heated discussions took place, about extending Reciprocal Aid, between Stettinius, Acheson, Feis, Opie and Phillips. Phillips was described as being 'very tough' by the Americans and he seemed to them to, 'regard the difficulties presented by the propsal as not limited to those arising from the proposal itself, but also from the point of view of the propsal as a first step in a continued policy of restricting the growth of British balances'. Phillips was sceptical about the existence of American domestic pressure for extending Reciprocal Aid and he wanted some assurance that Britain would be allowed an adequate dollar reserve. The American response, apart from firmly asserting that there were already domestic pressures for extending Reciprocal Aid, was equivocal. Stettinius said that no guarantees about future policy could be given but that if Reciprocal Aid were not extended and Britain's dollar balances continued to rise then pressures for the reduction of Lend-Lease would be irresistible. If, on the other hand, raw materials were provided by Britain,

Reserves, Exports and Reciprocal Aid

Stettinius said that this might enable them to be more generous with Lend-Lease and to defend a level of $1.5 billion for Britain's reserves, 'if it could be shown that the British were pooling their resources with ours'. The following day Stettinius consolidated the American position in a letter to Phillips in which he stated that the present list of raw materials the US wanted under Reciprocal Aid would have no further significant additions. This reassured the British that the OLLA was not trying to reduce her reserves incrementally, and it was with this understanding combined with Stettinius' statements of the previous day that Phillips discussed matters when he went to London[42].

The British Government now decided to proceed with the extension of Reciprocal Aid though before doing so they prepared the ground for a simultaneous advance on export policy. This may have been prompted by knowledge of the highly critical report being compiled by the Stevens Committee (Whitney certainly thought it was) and the need for a pre-emptive strike. On 10 July Halifax and Llewellin, the British Resident Minister for Supply in Washington, sent copies of a memorandum to Hull and Stettinius stating that as the US was a co-belligerent, as combined organisations had been set up, and as US and UK competition for markets was no longer a factor (sic) the Export White Paper was inappropriate and should be superseded by a joint declaration along the following lines:

> His Majesty's Government attach importance to the principle that no advantage in world markets shall accrue to either country at the expense of the other by reason of sacrifices made in the interests of the effective prosecution of the war.[43]

The prevailing opinion within the State Department and OLLA favoured an Anglo-American declaration on export policy. As one official observed if the British extended Reciprocal Aid, 'they might need a White Paper from us'[44]. The State Department took its cue from this logic and began to consider a joint export declaration. Consequently when the Steven's Committee reported towards the end of July that Britain was ignoring the White Paper completely with regard to Eastern Hemisphere exports, and recommended that tighter controls should be instituted its advice was shunted to one side in favour of developing plans for the supersession of the White Paper[45]. This frustrated and angered Whitney and his like-minded colleagues and while they were unable to do much then, a reorganisation of the bureaucracy in charge of American foreign economic policy which began in July was soon to give them more power. However, as far as the British were concerned the immediate prospects looked good for the changes they wanted in economic policy.

In a memorandum for the Cabinet on 22 July, Eden, Wood and Dalton expressed their hopes for settling a number of issues concerning Lend-Lease and Reciprocal Aid, 'in the course of which we expect to obtain substantial relief from the limitations at present imposed on our export trade', and they added, with what proved to be ill-founded optimism, that, 'It is desirable to take advantage of the favourable atmosphere which these arrangements are likely to produce'[46]. There were hopes for approaching the Americans informally in order to reach an understanding that no limit should be placed on Britain's level of dollar reserves because of her sterling liabilities, and the British also made sure that the Americans saw a link between the extension of Reciprocal Aid and relief from the Export White Paper restrictions, though there was no suggestion at this time that the former was conditional upon the latter. Progress on Reciprocal Aid with OLLA and the State Department was proceeding satisfactorily to a conclusion when literally hours before a scheduled announcement about it in the Commons by Kingsley Wood a 'bombshell' arrived from Washington - Morgenthau had effectively vetoed acceptance of the agreement.

On the 3 and 4 of August the US Treasury, which had been kept largely in the dark about the Reciprocal Aid Negotiations, was suddenly confronted with proposals which Stettinius had more or less agreed to: Morgenthau decided that he could not publicly state that they were acceptable. In the light of information from one of his advisers, Bernstein, that Britain's reserves would be $1.6 billion by the end of the year Morgenthau thought that Stettinius' list of raw materials was too limited and in any case Britain had only committed herself to supplying $70 million worth; the rest from the Sterling Area would have to be negotiated for with India and the Dominions. He also objected to 1 October as the starting date for the new arrangements and to the proposal that the supply of Reciprocal Aid should be centralised in the same way as Lend-Lease. This would be highly complicated because of the decentralised points of supply and it would allow the British to control the flow of Reciprocal Aid administratively[47].

Charles Denby rather indiscreetly explained to Opie the background to Morgenthau's veto and the motive for it. From what Denby said it was clear that while Stettinius and Acheson wanted to nurture the idea of pooling resources and to present Britain's efforts in a favourable light to make a rise in her dollar reserves defensible, Morgenthau viewed Reciprocal Aid simply as a means of reducing them to a satisfactory level and all his objections were levelled at those features of the proposals which he believed would prevent Reciprocal Aid from being such a means of reducing Britain's reserves. Oscar Cox was also disappointed with the proposals about Reciprocal Aid and he and Morgenthau argued within the administration that the value of raw materials being offered would not be well received by Congress or the public[48]. Stettinius and Acheson began to waver; they then came to the conclusion that if the $1 billion limit on Britain's reserves was to be raised they might have to get some kind of Congressional blessing in which case larger amounts of raw materials from Reciprocal Aid were desirable. Their immediate aim thus coincided with Morgenthau's i.e. to expand Reciprocal Aid, though the latter's longer term aim was to do his best to keep the British balances down[49]. On the 18 August the State Department informed the British that their proposals were unduly restrictive, and that the US wanted to rescind the list of raw materials Stettinius had sent Phillips on 26 June and back-date the start of the new proposals to 1 July[50]. The British were now confronted with an open-ended commitment to Reciprocal Aid of a kind which they had striven to avoid in their talks with Stettinius because of its potential to drain their dollar reserves.

During the following weeks the US Treasury insisted that Britain's ability to pay had to be the limiting factor on Lend-Lease supplies, and as Reciprocal Aid now looked as if it would not significantly reduce Britain's reserves Morgenthau, White and Bernstein instigated moves to reduce civilian Lend-Lease to Britain. They argued for this with the British on the pretext that some Lend-Lease items were now vulnerable to political criticism.

Reserves, Exports and Reciprocal Aid

On 21 August Halifax, realising what was afoot, reported that if they could not convince American officials that Britain needed to increase her dollar reserves, and if they could not convince them that Congress would regard this as reasonable, then despite their assurances in January the Americans would continue with a unilateral policy of restricting Britain's reserves: they would do this by pressing for more Reciprocal Aid and by restricting Lend-Lease[51].

At the beginning of September Kingsley Wood wrote a strong letter to Morgenthau refusing to back-date the new Reciprocal Aid proposals to 1 July. He said the suggestion to do so raised the question of Britain's dollar balances and he enclosed a paper entitled, 'The Overseas Assets and Liabilities of the UK', which he thought would persuade Morgenthau that it was unreasonable that, 'a limit should be placed on our gold and dollar holdings which pays no regard to our liabilities and their growth'. This, and subsequent explanations in Washington of Britain's financial difficulties, while reinforcing the convinctions of Stettinius and Acheson, failed to move the US Treasury[52].

Unfortunately for the British the political climate in the US was moving against them. The mid-term elections in November 1942 had seen significant Republican gains and as the presidential election year of 1944 got closer Roosevelt and his administration became more sensitive to political pressures in Washington, which by late 1943 were more conservative, more anti-British, and more business orientated than they had been. As the war progressed production and efficient administration had replaced social and economic reform as Roosevelt's main priorities. Some of the New Dealers now began to leave government service as the administration absorbed more and more talent from the business world to meet its new goals. Gradually the prevailing ethos in Washington began to change and in September 1943 there were two important developments which reflected this.

On 7 September Roosevelt felt obliged to correct a statement, which he had not personally authorised but which had been included in his quarterly report to Congress on Lend-Lease. The original phrase read as follows: 'Victory and a secure peace are the only coin in which we can be paid'. Roosevelt now qualified this by saying that, 'There were all kinds of coin whether or not they jingled'. This raised the spectre of postwar debts, damaged the idea of pooling resources and, as one State Department official noted, gave the British further grounds for wanting to build up their dollar reserves[53].

The second development occurred towards the end of the month and it also adversely affected British interests. In July 1943 a dispute between Wallace and Secretary of Commerce Jesse Jones had resulted in their responsibilities for foreign economic policy being largely transferred to Leo Crowley, head of the Organisation for Economic Warfare. In September Crowley's star continued to rise: Sumner Welles had to resign from the State Department because of rumours of a sexual indiscretion and Stettinius was appointed in his stead as Undersecretary of State. The OLLA was now given to Crowley and a new agency came into being under him called the Foreign Economic Administration (FEA). It soon reflected his business values and his anti-British sentiments. Within days Acheson was looking 'pretty blue' about the new organisation and before long officials friendly to Britain were demoted or shunted sideways. Keynes wrote that the only powerful friendly face in the FEA was that of Oscar Cox, but in fact, even he was not as friendly as Keynes thought. The new regime in charge of Lend-Lease showed its colours at the end of the month when Phil Young, Deputy Administrator in the FEA, strongly recommended that progress towards a joint declaration to supersede the Export White Paper should be held up because talks so far had produced unsatisfactory results which were at odds with the recommendations of the Steven's Committee Report[54].

The unfavourable trend of events for Britain continued in October when much publicity was given to criticisms of Lend-Lease made by five senators who had been on a tour of the war zones in Europe and the Mediterranean. These criticisms led to a Congressional investigation into Lend-Lease, a State Department request - to which the British acquiesced - for a further postponement of the announcement about the extension of Reciprocal Aid, and a letter from Oscar Cox to Knollenberg on 11 October suggesting that the replacement of the Export White Paper by a new agreement should be postponed for a while in the light of recent criticisms of UK policies[55]. The FEA was also now giving strong support to the US Treasury in its attempts to reduce civilian Lend-Lease to Britain. At a meeting on 16 September David Waley, who had assumed some of

Reserves, Exports and Reciprocal Aid

Phillips' responsibilities after his sad death during the summer, had tried to reassure the Americans that even though the British would not back-date the proposed Reciprocal Aid arrangements to 1 July that they did intend to provide substantial amounts of raw materials, but the US Treasury and the FEA remained dissatisfied and were now convinced that the only effective way to reduce Britain's dollar balances was by reducing Lend-Lease supplies to her.

At a Treasury meeting on 29 September White pointed out that Britain's dollar reserves would be above $1.5 billion at the end of the year, and he recommended that, 'the time had come to take a strong line to reduce the lend-leasing of non-military goods'. On 11 October a draft memorandum to the same effect was circulated to the FEA and plans to implement this proceeded apace[56]. From the point of view of avoiding political criticism even Denby and Knollenberg could see advantages of removing certain items from Lend-Lease, but in comparing Britain's treatment with that of the Soviet Union and China, which did not have their dollar balances monitored, and which were not about to have things such as capital equipment removed from their Lend-Lease supplies, Knollenberg wryly commented that the real, 'the deeper' reason as he put it for Britain's different treatment was that neither the Soviet Union nor China, 'is a great traditional competitor of ours in international trade'[57].

The likelihood of a satisfactory resolution for Britain of the issues connected with Lend-Lease was rapidly diminishing. The report of the five senators had stirred up what many in the US Administration saw as dangerous congressional interest. Cox wrote to Hopkins on 16 October that, 'The President's conduct of the war and the handling of our foreign economic affairs are definitely going to be included in the open season'[58]. And with Crowley having taken over Lend-Lease from Stettinius there only remained the State Department, with intermittent help from Harry Hopkins, to champion the British cause on dollar balances and Reciprocal Aid. In a meeting in the State Department on 18 October that is exactly what Acheson set about doing.

He presented a paper entitled 'Imminent Problems in British American Relations Growing Out of Lend-Lease', and in the ensuing discussion reviewed Britain's attitudes, her economic problems,

Reserves, Exports and Reciprocal Aid

and her difficulties with the FEA and the US Treasury. The account of this meeting which follows also includes some references to later developments which can appropriately and conveniently be mentioned here. It was clear to the officials at the meeting that the British were frustrated and defensive: they were being prevented from announcing the proposed extension of Rciprocal Aid which they thought would improve their public standing in the US, and contrary to their expectations they had become involved in interminable wranglings with the FEA and the US Treasury. They desperately wanted relief from the Export White Paper restrictions and, trying to drive home the injustice of them, they had suggested that they should be applied to Reciprocal Aid. Acheson knew this was simply a tactic to try to get a joint declaration on exports, but officials in the FEA were distinctly unimpressed. They wanted to maintain the Export White Paper and viewed Reciprocal Aid solely as a means of reducing Britain's dollar balances. However, by mid-October the FEA thought that Reciprocal Aid was not worth the trouble that it was causing, and instead they favoured White's proposals to reduce civilian Lend-Lease to the UK. Given this fact it is not surprising that later in the month when Llewellin, thinking that the joint export proposals were slipping though his fingers, tried to make the extension of Reciprocal Aid dependent upon the supersession of the Export White Paper by a new agreement, that Acheson quickly managed to get him to abandon this tactic, presumably by pointing out that it had no leverage in the FEA[59].

The State Department officials were worried by recent developments and so they decided that firstly, the British should announce their figures for Reciprocal Aid and its extension to include raw materials as soon as the congressional investigation was out of the way, and that secondly, regarding the extension to raw materials, 'any suggestion that might be made by FEA that the idea be given up should be resisted vigorously by the Department', for otherwise their plans for preparing a political atmosphere which would permit larger dollar reserves for Britain would be set back. Also, thirdly, they decided that the time was inauspicious for the replacement of the Export White Paper though the British should be told that a joint export declaration could be made at a later date, and finally they thought that Britain's dollar reserves required further discussion. Ironically, the following day Churchill gave a statement of principles to the British Cabinet for guiding the transitional policy to peacetime conditions. In it he identified the resumption of exports as one of three overriding priorities. Little did he know how difficult to achieve that priority was now likely to be[60].

After the meeting on 18 October Acheson and his colleagues reconsidered Britain's dollar situation in the expectation of early progress in planning a liberal postwar economy. During September and October Richard Law, recently promoted to Minister of State with special responsibility for coordinating postwar economic policy, had led a mission to Washington which had belatedly - but apparently successfully - begun commercial and trade talks with the State Department of a kind which both countries had committed themselves to in the Mutual Aid Agreement. Bearing in mind Britain's need for reserves if she was to participate in a system of freer trade Acheson proposed that Congress should be approached to approve a policy which would allow Britain's dollar reserves to rise in a fixed proportion to her liabilities, such as 1:6[61].

As soon as this plan had taken shape it was threatened when the US Treasury and the FEA moved to reduce Britain's dollar balances by stopping some civilian items of Lend-Lease supply without seeking the concurrence of the State Department. Acheson reacted quickly with a suggestion that Morgenthau, who was in Algiers at the time, should stop off in London on his way home to discuss matters with Sir John Anderson, who had succeeded Kingsley Wood on his death on 21 September. Acheson's initiative had the desired effect of holding up the take-out of Lend-Lease items, but it also pushed this issue to the highest government level and as we shall see in the next chapter, when we resume this part of the story, it angered Morgenthau who suspected Acheson of trying to set him up for what would have been an embarrassing and difficult meeting with Anderson[62]. It also helped to confirm his beliefs that Stettinius and Acheson were colluding with the British to defy the US Treasury and the Lend-Lease Act, and that they were undermining the economic interests of the US.

While these developments were taking place in Washington Anderson, Dalton, Law and Keynes were dolefully ruminating on the way the Reciprocal Aid proposals had gone awry. Anderson wanted to announce the proposals before the US Senate Report on Lend-Lease was made for otherwise the British would look as if they were acting under pressure. He complained of the shabby treatment that they had received, particularly with regard to Morgenthau's veto in early August and the lack of repsonse to Wood's letter of 3 September about Britain's dollar balances. Dalton thought it was essential to get the export restrictions removed and Law, just back from his talks in Washington, was worried about the re-emergence of the idea of war debts in the US. Keynes was so angry he said that they should insist that Reciprocal Aid was subjected to the same controls as Lend-Lease. He cavalierly added that the Americans could always refuse it if they wanted to[63].

Then suddenly the situation changed, partly because of State Department pressure and partly because the Congressional investigation did not develop in the manner expected. The Americans now said that Britain could go ahead with its announcement about Reciprocal Aid. The State Department also informed the British Embassy in Washington that removal of the White Paper could not be closely connected with Reciprocal Aid for political reasons and would thus have to wait for a while. This dampened British spirits somewhat but Stettinius softened the blow by helping to persuade Roosevelt to make a statement in praise of Reciprocal Aid simultaneously with the announcement of its extension. Anderson was delighted and got Churchill to support the idea by writing to Harry Hopkins about how helpful this would be - clearly in the hope that he would convey these sentiments to Roosevelt[64].

Dalton announced the figures and new proposals for Reciprocal Aid on 11 November, and he included references to the negotiations which were seeking to replace the Export White Paper with a joint declaration[65]. The President issued his statement as promised, but it was muted in its praise and was poor consolation for the adverse developments of the previous three months. The hopes that the British had had in July now lay in tatters. The Export White Paper was still in force and Whitney was pushing for stricter observance of it; the FEA, Congress and the US Treasury had become more hostile, not more friendly as expected; procedures for Reciprocal Aid and negotiations with India and the Dominions had not been completed and were still causing trouble; the issue of Britain's dollar reserves was still unresolved and now more controversial than ever; Britain's economic position had become weaker; and the FEA and the US Treasury were poised to mount an offensive to reduce Britain's dollar reserves to $1 billion by contracting Lend-Lease.

NOTES

1. See: R. G. D. Allen, 'Mutual Aid Between The US and the British Empire', *Journal of the Royal Statistical Society*, *109* (1946) pp.243-271; draft telegram by H. Dalton, 6 July 1944, UE234/5/71, F0371/41012; and J. E. Coulson, 'The Effect of Our External Financial Position on Our Foreign Policy', 30 March 1945, UE813/813/53, F0371/45694.
2. H.M. Diary, 493, pp.53-56, 6 Feb. 1942.
3. Ibid, 344, pp.238-242, 3 Jan. 1941.
4. Ibid, 405, pp.49-50.
5. Ibid, 383, pp.99 and 121-122, 18 March 1941; 405, pp.49-50, 19 March 1941.
6. Ibid, 397, p.221, 13 May 1941.
7. Keynes to Wood, 7 July 1941, T160/1105/F17660/02/1; and for RFC loan see: Washington to FO, 18 July 1941, W8780/37/49, F0371/28802.
8. See: H.M. Diary, 410, pp.53-57 and 103-112, 17 and 19 June 1941 respectively; and Waley to Keynes, Catto and Hopkins, 13 Feb. 1942, T160/1105/F17660/02/4.
9. H.M. Diary, 493, pp.53-56, 6 Feb. 1942.
10. Welles (from Hopkins) to Winant, 9 July 1941, 841.24/6176.
11. See: Winant to Hull (personal for Welles), 31 July 1941, 841.5081/714; Hull (from Cox) to Winant, 15 Aug. 1941, 841.24/688; Winant to Hull (for Cox) 19 Aug. 1941, 841.24/689; Cox Diary, 20 and 22 Aug. 1941, Cox Papers, box 145; and Winant to Hull, 3 and 7 Sept. 1941, 841.24/720 and 841.24/741 respectively. For a more detailed account see: A. P. Dobson, 'The Export White Paper, 10 September 1941', *Economic History Review*, forthcoming February 1986.
12. Cmd. 6311, 'The Export White Paper', 10 Sept. 1941.
13. Sir A. Cairncross (Ed.), *Anglo-American Economic Collaboration in War and Peace 1942-49: The Papers of Sir Richard Clarke* (Oxford University Press, Oxford, 1982), p.xiii.

14. See: Stevens Committee Report on White Paper Policy, July 1943, Cox Papers, box 102, folder: Reverse Lend-Lease.
15. See: Long Diary, 29 Jan. 1942, Long Papers box 5; and Wickard Diary, 13 Feb. 1942, Wickard Papers.
16. See: Lyttleton to Harriman, 7 March 1942, 841.24/1465; and Deputy Lend-Lease Administrator to Chalkley, 20 April 1942, 841.24/1465.
17. Treasury to Phillips, T160/1105/F17660/02/4.
18. Cmd. 6391, 'Principles Applying to Mutual Aid', 23 Feb. 1942.
19. Memo. by Acheson, 19 Feb. 1942, 841.24/1227 and minutes of meeting with treasury officials H.M. Diary, 503, pp.127-136, 28 Feb. 1942.
20. H.M. Diary, 508, pp.225-48, 17 March 1942.
21. Ibid, 523, pp.163-167, 'Memorandum on the British Financial Position', 18 April 1942.
22. Ibid, 526, pp.333-334, 8 May 1942; 533, pp.78-117, 28 May 1942; and 534, p.36, 29 May 1942.
23. Cmd. 6389, 'Reciprocal Aid Agreement', 3 Sept. 1942.
24. See: Stettinius and Harriman to Acheson and his reply, 29 July and 6 Oct. 1942, 841.24/1459; and Stettinius to McCabe, 29 July 1942, 841.24/1460.
25. Shirer and Hyde to Stettinius, 4 Sept. 1942, RG169, box 140, folder: Conference Committee Meetings.
26. See: H. L. Whitney, 'History of the Administration of the British White Paper of 10 September 1941', RG169, box 795, folder: Lend-Lease 9; and draft by Whitney 13 Nov. 1942, and Stettinius to Raynor 22 Nov. 1942, RG169, box 165, folder: British White Paper.
27. H.M. Diary, 592, p.292.
28. See: H.M. Diary, 597, pp.110 and 150-178, 17 and 18 Dec. 1942 respectively; minutes of Dollar Position Committee, 29 Dec. 1942, RG169, box 163; and BEW board meeting, 29 Dec. 1942, RG169, box 721.
29. Ronald to Campbell, 18 Feb. 1943, U671/47/70, FO371/35330.
30. H.M. Diary, 604, p.5, 13 Jan. 1943.
31. See: Knollenberg to Stettinius, 16 Jan. and 14 April 1943, RG169, box 163, folder: Dollar Position More Important Papers; and H.M. Diary, 607, p.99, 8 Feb. 1943.
32. H.M. Diary, 607, p.106, Wood to Morgenthau, 19 Jan. 1943; concerning memoranda from Phillips to Bell, RG169, box 163, folder: British Reverse Lend-Lease.

Reserves, Exports and Reciprocal Aid

33. See: H.M. Diary 623, pp.239-41, memo., by White, 30 March 1943; 'History of Negotiations During 1943 with British Concerning Obtaining of Raw Materials as Reverse Lend-Lease' 18 September (sic October?) 1943, RG169, box 165, folder: British Reverse Lend-Lease; 'History of Negotiations', RG169, box 165, folder: British Reverse Lend-Lease; H.M. Diary, 623, p.292, telephone conversation between Morgenthau and Welles, 8 April 1943.

34. Hopkins to Stettinius, 6 April 1943; Cox to Stettinius, 13 April 1943; Stettinius to Cox 14 April 1943; Stettinius to Hopkins, 14 April 1943, RG169, box 162, folder: British Cash Reimbursements.

35. Denby to Knollenberg, 20 April 1943, RG169, box 163, folder: Dollar Position More Important Papers.

36. H.M. Diary, 632, p.117, Stettinius to Morgenthau, 29 April 1943.

37. New York Herald Tribune, Morgenthau to Truman, 31 March 1946.

38. Denby to Knollenberg, 1 May 1943, RG169, box 163, folder: Dollar Position More Important Papers.

39. White to Phillips, 27 May 1943, Cox Papers, box 102, folder: Reverse Lend-Lease.

40. See: Whitney to Stettinius, 9 June 1943, RG169, box 165, folder: British White Paper; H.S. Fullerton, Division of European Affairs, State Department, commenting on 'Postwar Position of British Balance of International Payments', 10 June 1943, 841.24/6-1043; Cowles to Stettinius 16 and 17 June 1943, RG169, box 165, folder: British White Paper, and box 163, folder: British Dollar Position, respectively; and memo. 12 July 1943, 841.24/7-1243.

41. Memo. 19 June 1943, T160/F17660/024/043/1; and memo., for Waley, 25 June 1943, T160/1243/F17660/039/1.

42. See: memo. of conversation between Phillips, Opie, Stettinius, Acheson and Feis, 25 June 1943, RG169, box 165, folder: British Reverse Lend-Lease.

43. Memo. 10 July 1943, T160/1244/F17660/024/043/1.

44. Memo. by Achilles, 29 June 1943, 841.24/2097.

45. 'Stevens' Committee Report', RG169, box 165, Folder: British White Paper.

46. Memo. by Eden, Wood and Dalton, 22 July 1943, WP(43)329, CAB 66.

Reserves, Exports and Reciprocal Aid

47. H.M. Diary, 653, pp.187-99, meeting in the Treasury, 4 Aug. 1943, and pp.260-261, memo. by Bernstein, 4 Aug. 1943.
48. Waley to Playfair, 10 Aug. 1943, T160/1244/F17660/024/043/1.
49. H.M. Diary, 656, pp.50-52, memo. of conversation between Morgenthau and White, 16 Aug. 1943.
50. Ibid, 657, pp.107-110, memo. by State Department, 18 Aug. 1943.
51. Halifax to FO, 21 Aug. 1943, T160/1244/F17660/024/043/1.
52. Wood to Morgenthau, 3 Sept. 1943, T177/58; and 'The Overseas Assets and Liabilities of the UK', 2 Sept. 1943, AD(43)2, U4500/251/70, FO371/35355.
53. I. S. Rosenman (Ed.) The Public Papers and Addresses of Franklin D. Roosevelt 13 Vols. (Harper, New York, 1938-50), Vol. XII, pp.374-375; and Kermit Roosevelt to Ted Acheson, 9 Sept. 1943, 841.24/2093.
54. See: Cox Diary, 27 Sept. 1943, Cox Papers, box 148; H. G. Nicholas (Ed.) Washington Dispatches 1941-45 (Weidenfeld and Nicolson, London, 1981), 31 Oct. 1943; Keynes to Waley, 1 Nov. 1943, T160/1234/F17660/024/039/3; memo. by Young, 30 Sept. 1943, RG169, box 165, folder: British White Paper.
55. Cox to Knollenberg, 11 Oct. 1943, RG169, box 165, folder: British White Paper.
56. See: memo.'s 16 Sept. 1943 at, 841.24/2046B, RG169, box 165, folder: British Reverse Lend-Lease including 'History of Negotiations'. The British paper AD(43)2, on Britain's finances, was presented to FEA that afternoon; H.M. Diary 668, pp.68-69, memo. of meeting in Morgenthau's office, 29 Sept. 1943; and H.M. Diary, 670, pp.186-187 draft Treasury memo., by White, from Morgenthau to Crowley, 11 Oct. 1943.
57. Knollenberg to Crowley, 15 Oct. 1943, RG169, box 163, folder: British Capital Goods.
58. Cox Diary, Cox to Hopkins, 16 Oct. 1943, Cox Papers, box 148.
59. See: minutes of meeting in the Undersecretary of State's office, 18 Oct. 1943, 841.24/2124; memo. on conversation between Jopson, Commercial Secretary British Embassy, and Achilles, 29 Oct. 1943, 841.24/2148; memo. by Keynes, 1 Nov. 1943, T160/F17660/024/039/3; and Cox's comments at US Treasury meeting, 2 Nov. 1943, H.M. Diary, 672, pp.190-193.

60. Memo. by Churchill, 19 Oct. 1943, WP(43)467, CAB 66.

61. See: memo. 'The Question of The British Gold and Dollar Balances', 26 Oct. 1943, Hopkins Papers, box 314, folder: Financing the War; and H.M. Diary, 673, pp.295-297, meeting in White's room, 4 Nov. 1943.

62. See: Roosevelt to Morgenthau, 22 Oct. 1943, 841.24/2120; Crowley to Reed, 22 Oct. 1943, Cox Papers, box 102, folder: Reverse Lend-Lease; Morgenthau to Roosevelt, 23 Oct. 1943, Roosevelt PSF, Box 101; memo. by Gaston of US Treasury for Morgenthau, 25 Oct. 1943, H.M. Diary, 671, pp.101-102; ibid, 672, pp.173-209, minutes of meeting between Morgenthau, Bell, Crowley, Currie, Cox, White and Kistler, 2 Nov. 1943, particularly p.195, where it becomes clear that no state Department personnel were in the meeting when the decision to remove items from Lend-Lease supplies to Britain was taken.

63. See: memo. by Anderson, 'Reciprocal Aid to the US', 25 Oct. 1943, WP(43)77, CAB 66; memo. by Law, WP(43) 478, CAB 66; and memo. by Keynes, 1 Nov. 1943, T160/F17660/024/039/2.

64. See: memo. to Hopkins concerning Crowley's interview by Senate Overseas sub-committee of the Truman Committee, 20 Oct. 1943, Cox Papers, box 148, Cox Diary, and Cox to Eady, 6 Nov. 1943, box 111; Washington to FO, 2 Nov. 1943, T160/1234/F17660/024/039/3; and Churchill to Hopkins, 2 Nov. 1943, Hopkins Papers, box 314, folder: Quadrant Conference.

65. Cmd. 6483, 11 Nov. 1943.

Chapter Six

LEND-LEASE TAKE-OUTS AND EXPORT RESTRICTIONS

The most ominous aspect of the 1943 Reciprocal Aid Talks was the extent to which the US Treasury and the FEA repudiated the idea of pooling resources. These departments argued that Lend-Lease had been introduced to keep supplies going to Britain when she could no longer afford them, and that that criterion, often referred to as the marginal principle, should continue in effect. There was an element of casuistry involved in this, because the marginal principle suited both Crowley's and Morgenthau's wider economic aims. The British, and the State Department, which still thought it had got an adequate quid pro quo for Lend-Lease, argued that America's entry into the war, and the idea of pooling resources, had altered the character of the relationship which had originally been created by the Lend-Lease Act, but in the Reciprocal Aid Talks this view did not prevail.

The British had tried to make Reciprocal Aid approximate to Lend-Lease as far as they could in the hope that unilateral restrictions on their economic activities would be replaced by rules which would create a symmetry in Anglo-American economic relations. In the 11 November announcement Dalton stated, with what proved to be a futile sense of equity, that Reciprocal Aid would be extended on terms analogous to Lend-Lease. Lauchlin Currie, who was a White House aid recently appointed Deputy Administrator in the FEA, gave an indication of how unrealistic this declaration of intent was when he said that the Americans would not go through the procurement hoops, that the British had had to for Lend-Lease, and nor would they accept the policing of their exports[1]. In short if the British wanted to reduce the asymmetry of their economic relations with the US they would have to do it by removing existing controls rather than by getting the US to accept restrictions similar to those the British now laboured under. The main questions in November 1943 were whether Britain could do this, and the extent to which the FEA and the US Treasury were going to undermine the idea of pooling resources further by insisting on the marginal theory.

Discussions between Britain and the US about Reciprocal Aid continued for some months after the announcement of its extension on 11 November. The main disagreements concerned methods of procurement, supplies from Australia and India, and the extent to which the new arrangements were to be applied retrospectively. As we saw in the last chapter the FEA thought that the extension of Reciprocal Aid to raw materials was not worth the trouble it was causing, but nevertheless, on 7 December Crowley did suggest that a further addition should be made to Reciprocal Aid by Britain transferring ownership of her war plants in the US to the American Government. He made this gesture to protect himself from the possibility of domestic political criticisms concerning Britain's assets in the US and her large dollar balances while she was still receiving Lend-Lease supplies, so when Hull firmly rejected the idea, thus effectively absolving him from responsibility for not getting the transfers, nothing else was heard of the matter[2]. In the end the troublesome issues connected with Reciprocal Aid faded into the background, partly because Britain made some concessions - particularly on procurement, partly because India (though not Australia) eventually came to an agreement on raw materials, but mainly because the US Treasury and the FEA did not think that Reciprocal Aid was an effective means of reducing Britain's dollar balances and so directed their energies elsewhere.

The talks about a joint declaration to replace the Export White Paper continued after 11 November in a low key, which was in accordance with State Department wishes that a close connection between them and the new Reciprocal Aid provisions should not be made by the American public. It was not until early 1944 that serious problems arose again in the Export White Paper Talks; for the time being the attention of both the Americans and the British was devoted to Britain's dollar balances and the possibilities for reducing Lend-Lease.

The British exerted pressure on the Americans during October and November 1943 to expedite matters concerning their dollar balances, and the favourable

Lend-Lease Take-outs and Export Restrictions

reaction in the US to the announcement about the extension of Reciprocal Aid revived hopes that a satisfactory solution could be achieved. Ever since Charles Denby had disclosed the US Treasury position to Waley in early August, the British had felt that they ought to resolve the problem of dollar balances through negotiations, because they believed that they could make a strong case for accumulating larger reserves. They worked mainly through Stettinius, Acheson and Harry Hopkins; the last two for example were provided with briefs, especially prepared for them by Keynes, to help them to explain the British financial position to colleagues of theirs who were less well disposed to Britain. These tactics had mixed results: Roosevelt did ask Morgenthau to get a clear decision and policy on the question of Britain's reserves from the Cabinet Dollar Committee; however, the manoeuvrings of Stettinius and Acheson angered Morgenthau and helped to confirm his supicions of their collusion with the British[3].

After returning from his trip to North Africa Morgenthau wanted to meet with Crowley, before seeing Roosevelt, to discuss both the position of Britain's dollar balances and, as he put it, Lend-Lease going sour. They met on 2 November with Currie and Cox accompanying Crowley, and Bell and White there for the Treasury. Morgenthau gave vent to his feelings about the way he believed that Stettinius and the State Department had colluded with the British and had frustrated his attempts to reduce Britain's dollar balances. He complained of major abuses of Lend-Lease in North Africa and the Mediterranean area. He was angered by British and French exploitation of Lend-Lease and he was worried about congressional reactions if it became aware of what was happening. Referring to the abuses of Lend-Lease he said, 'I don't see how Ed. Stettinius can ever explain that stuff'; he went on, 'If the Congress got hold of these cases they would just raise bloody hell! There are so many anti-English up there'. He said that the abuses could lead to the destruction of Lend-Lease, that they could undermine the President's position and that they could strengthen the Isolationists[4]. One might add that other Treasury meetings at the time reveal that he also wanted to protect his own reputation from charges of complicity in the misuse of Lend-Lease. Crowley was equally concerned to avoid public criticisms and he suggested that the best and the most discreet way of correcting things would be

Lend-Lease Take-outs and Export Restrictions

by administrative action; he proposed that screening of Lend-Lease should be done solely by American officials. For example the voluntary, unilateral declaration by Britain in the Export White Paper was now to be interpreted and enforced as far as possible by the Americans irrespective of whether the British agreed with them or not!! White commented that it was a question of either keeping to the President's directive concerning the $1 billion limit for Britain's balances or else getting him and the Congress to 'mortify it'. Crowley suggested that White, Currie and Cox should try to work something out between them which would effectively reduce Britain's balances, and after further discussion Morgenthau agreed to this. White, acting as something of a devil's advocate, pointed out that if the FEA and the Treasury pursued their present policy then they would be 'putting the screws on them [i.e. the British] in a way that is wholly unjustified by the President's policy of sharing resources'. Morgenthau responded by saying that if they did not reduce Britain's dollar balances then someone would have to go to Congress in order to get approval for a use of Lend-Lease which the act had not intended. He thought that this would be a futile exercise because the people in Congress did not 'give a damn' about the British dollar position, and despite the fact that the congressional investigations into Lend-Lease had so far not proved to be as hostile as expected, there was evidence from developments in Congress to support what Morgenthau said. For example on 5 November Harry Truman, the chairman of the Senate Committee to Investigate the National Defense Program, described the purpose of the Lend-Lease Act in terms of the marginal theory[5].

On 4 November Acheson put his department's position to Harry White saying that British arguments about their finances seemed valid, that the US was not imposing restrictions on Lend-Lease to the Soviet Union as they were with the British, and that while items should be removed from Lend-Lease if they were politically sensitive he said that the State Department thought that they had already gone far enough with proposals that had been put to the British. He went on to conclude that,

> It is recommended that the present policy, restricting British gold and dollar resources under a rigid ceiling, be abandoned in favour of a policy which will

Lend-Lease Take-outs and Export Restrictions

> permit those resources to increase in a given ratio to the short term liabilities against them[6]

Acheson proposed that a statement recommending this should be prepared for presentation to Congress.

No immediate decisions were taken on these proposals though the meeting did agree that the first step should be a memorandum for the President indicating what policy the US ought to pursue. Given the gulf separating the State Department from both the Treasury and the FEA, it is hardly surprising that in the weeks that followed they failed to reach an agreed policy. It is also important to note, however, that the cooperation between Morgenthau and Crowley was based on shaky foundations. For the moment their perceptions of their country's and of their departments' interests coincided, but there was not much else which brought the two men together; they had little personal rapport, and their political dispositions were very different: Morgenthau was a close friend of Roosevelt, a member of the eastern seaboard's aristocracy, and a New Deal progressive; Crowley supported Roosevelt politically but he was on the conservative wing of the Democratic Party with close ties and affinities with the business world. It was not long before irritating differences and suspicions began to arise in their temporary alliance. The first misunderstanding, however, was only minor and was soon cleared up.

In the evening of 5 November Morgenthau discovered from Roosevelt that Crowley had stayed behind after the Cabinet meeting earlier in the day to discuss Britain's reserves, and he was peeved that Crowley had done this without him. By 8 November Crowley and Morgenthau had sorted things out and they were united again by a common concern over the President's having said that Britain's balances should be kept where they were then, and by his having mentioned $2 billion as an acceptable limit. They held Stettinius responsible for having put this figure into the President's head and Morgenthau, who still wanted a $1 billion limit to be adhered to, thought that it was now time to take the State Department 'head on'. This meant going to Hull, whom he thought would be straight with them, and with whom he clearly thought he could get his way over the British dollar balances[7]. The US Treasury and the FEA now steamed ahead with making sure that their own records on Lend-Lease were defensible in Congress, and with work on a document to recommend their policy to the President.

On the 14 November, in what must have been an extraordinary meeting for Halifax, Morgenthau also took the British head on. He reprimanded Halifax for lobbying in Washington over the dollar balances, 'for fighting me with Stettinius', and for taking advantage of American innocence in international affairs. He went on to say that,

> After all, if you people would only agree with me that your balances should be cut down, I would be glad to tackle your other post-war problem of what you're going to do with your big sterling balances. I don't know whether I can be helpful, but at least we would look at it as a separate matter, and not try to use lend-lease to solve a post-war English problem when lend-lease was never designed for that.

On 17 November, when Waley and Halifax came to give John Anderson's response to Morgenthau's offer of help, the latter disclosed just how unsubstantial it was - he said that, 'quite obviously he could not make any specific promises inasmuch as he could not bind the Government, especially the government that might exist in the post-war period'. Waley conveyed Anderson's gratitude for Morgenthau's kind offer but he said that 'the British Treasury could not be expected to take action and make recommendations to reduce their vitally necessary balances with no definite knowledge or prospect of being able to rebuild them in the near future'. When Waley and Halifax suggested that Congress might be persuaded to accept Britain's dollar position in the light of the changed circumstances since the passage of the Lend-Lease Bill Morgenthau's and White's responses were that this would be more likely if the British first reduced their balances to show their good faith with regard to the existing intention of the Lend-Lease Act[8]. The British arguments did not alter the policy of the US Treasury, which was now more strongly committed than ever to the reduction of Britain's balances.

After the consultations suggested by Crowley had taken place between Currie, Cox and White, these three had a lunch-time meeting with Crowley and Morgenthau on 23 November. Cox proposed that the best way to reduce Britain's reserves would be to remove supplies from Lend-Lease item by item on the pretext of their political sensitivity. He said this would avoid the danger of Churchill's intervening and appealing to Roosevelt which he suspected he would do if a clear general policy for reducing the balances were formulated and pressed upon the British. White was unsure if this piecemeal administrative kind of policy would yield sufficient results, but Cox claimed that savings would run to hundreds of millions of dollars and after Crowley had declared his support for Cox's idea White and then Morgenthau 'agreed and it was decided to pursue that course as quickly as possible'[9].

During the next few weeks the US Treasury and the FEA pushed ahead on two fronts. Firstly, they speeded up discussions with the British, which had now been going on for several weeks, concerning the removal of capital equipment from Lend-Lease. By 16 December they had told the British that the decision to stop large supplies of capital equipment for civilian end use as of 15 November was 'irrevocable'. 'Consequently', as a British memorandum stoically put it, 'our chief concern will be centred in the interpretations and applications of the decision' and in contesting dubious FEA decisions[10]. Secondly, a joint memorandum by the two departments gradually emerged during November and early December which took a swipe at State Department officials and Stettinius for their handling of policy on Britain's reserves, and then went on to call for the following to be removed from Lend-Lease: (i) long-term capital installations, (ii) off-shore purchases, e.g. Icelandic fish and Caribbean sugar; (iii) civilian goods for the Middle East; (iv) small requisitions; and (v) controversial items. Much of this was acceptable to the State Department, but the sting came in the tail, and it was a sting that the State Department could not accept: these proposed reductions in Lend-Lease, the memorandum stated, were, 'to help reduce the British Government's gold and dollar holdings to, and keep them at, about $1 billion'[11].

While the FEA and the US Treasury were preparing their onslaught on Lend-Lease and Britain's dollar balances a counter-attack was being prepared in London by the Paymaster General, Lord Cherwell, who was one of Churchill's advisers and a close personal friend. Cherwell played a ubiquitous role during the war, advising on everything from the ill-fated Churchill Tank to economic policy. In December

Lend-Lease Take-outs and Export Restrictions

1941, before Churchill left to confer with Roosevelt in Washington, Cherwell had urged him, unsuccessfully as it transpired, to accept article seven of the Mutual Aid Agreement because of his desire for cooperation with the US in setting up a freer world economy. He now began to take an interest in the question of Britain's balances for similar reasons, and prior to the Cairo and Teheran Conferences, 22 to 28 November and 28 November to 1 December respectively, he briefed Churchill fully on the background and likely consequences of a continuation of America's policy of restricting the growth of Britain's reserves. At Cairo Churchill gave memoranda on Britain's financial plight to Harry Hopkins and talked things over with the President who said that Britain should not be treated differently from the Soviet Union. This gave some ammunition to the British and their friends in Washington for use against the FEA and the US Treasury, but it turned out not to be a statement that Roosevelt stood by for long[12].

On the 16 December Morgenthau and Crowley put the joint recommendations that they had prepared for the President to Acheson and Stettinius, and the arguments that followed fell into what was now a familiar pattern: they wanted to manipulate Lend-Lease to reduce Britain's dollar balances whereas the State Department, while agreeing that Lend-Lease ought to be reduced, insisted that this should be done on the grounds of items being politically sensitive. Acheson and Stettinius were still motivated by the idea of creating a favourable political atmosphere in the US which would permit Britain's dollar balances to rise in proportion to the growth of her sterling liabilities[13].

After the meeting State Department officials, realising that the disagreements would have to be resolved at the highest level, began to produce a number of memoranda for Hull. In one Acheson argued that the legalistic position of Crowley and Morgenthau, which insisted on narrowly restricting the use of Lend-Lease, did not seem convincing in the light of the actual wording of the Lend-Lease Act and the President's avowed policy of pooling resources. He said that the State Department agreed with the idea of reducing Lend-Lease on political grounds and that the British accepted this as well, but that they could not understand, 'the political necessity of so conducting the lend-lease program as to bankrupt Britain, or keep the British at the edge of bankruptcy indefinitely'[14]. Kermit Roosevelt

Lend-Lease Take-outs and Export Restrictions

and other State Department officials also pointed out in a paper for Stettinius, that if the recommendations of the FEA and the US Treasury were accepted that they would make it difficult for Britain to participate in a liberal world economy, that they would damage Britain's war finances, and that they would undoubtedly cause Anglo-American friction[15].

In the light of the feelings in his department Hull could not go along entirely with the joint recommendation that Crowley and Morgenthau sent to the President. On 31 December he wrote to Roosevelt that he agreed that Britain's dollar balances should be brought to the President's attention, and that specific items of Lend-Lease should be discontinued on political grounds, but he continued: 'If in your judgement it is still practicable and wise to attempt to hold Britain's balances to a fixed amount, I respectfully suggest that this policy should be made clear to the British'[16]. Hull was proposing the very thing that Morgenthau and Crowley had wished to avoid because of the danger of an intervention by Churchill which might upset their plans. The President's response was very much in character; he agreed with the memorandum from Crowley and Morgenthau, but in deference to the State Department he asked them to take up the question of Britain's dollar balances with the British once again, though with a deadline of 7 February for a decision in order to prevent the kind of procrastination by the British of which Morgenthau and Crowley had already bitterly complained. In fact the FEA had become so impatient with the British that, in pursuance of the decision by Treasury and FEA officials on 23 November, it had unilaterally produced a list of items to be removed from Lend-Lease and had presented it to the British early in the New Year. The British were incensed by this high-handed behaviour and when talks were renewed in accordance with the President's directive the atmosphere between the British and the Americans was very strained[17].

Before talking with the British on 7 January Hull, Morgenthau and Crowley, accompanied by their senior assistants, met to agree a common policy. They accepted that the list of items drawn up by Crowley and Morgenthau should be pressed upon the British: it consisted of capital equipment except that for military use, off-shore purchases, civilian goods for the Caribbean, Southern Rhodesia and the Middle East, pulp and paper, tobacco for the armed

Lend-Lease Take-outs and Export Restrictions

forces, and certain other controversial items. Acheson now broached the crucial question of what would happen if these take-outs failed to reduce Britain's balances to the level the FEA and the Treasury desired. On this occasion, he got a significant concession from Morgenthau, who said that this was all the action that they intended to take for the moment, though he would not tie his hands for the indefinite future. When Halifax, Waley and Ben Smith, the British Resident Minister for Supply, entered the meeting, it soon became clear that they were unhappy with recent developments, and Crowley's arrogant assertion that he was under no legal obligations to consult with the British about removing items from Lend-Lease did not help matters, though he quickly qualified this by saying that of course he was more than willing to discuss things.

Waley took the lead on the British side saying that as he was about to end his tour of service in Washington he was especially saddened by the recent turn of events. He said that there seemed to be a move away from the previous mood of cooperation which he had experienced with Stettinius when discussing the extension of Reciprocal Aid, and that the idea of pooling resources was receding into the background. He felt deep concern that, 'steps were contemplated purportedly on political grounds when the effect sought for was to keep down British gold and dollar balances. He said that if the measures proposed were designed chiefly to curtail British dollar and gold assets that the procedure would "not be very tasty", to his colleagues and members of Parliament'. At the end of the meeting Waley was given some comfort by Morgenthau, who, although refusing to give a written acceptance of Britain's case about her dollar balances, which as Halifax later reported was 'profoundly unsatisfactory', did repeat the position he had outlined to Acheson, before the British had entered the room, that no further action was presently contemplated though, 'this list did not preclude reopening the question [of the balances] at some future time if the circumstances seemed to warrant it'. With that, and an understanding that the FEA and the British were to proceed with talks about the list of Lend-Lease take-outs, the meeting ended[18].

The British were still unhappy, but given the increased congressional interest in Lend-Lease, Keynes and others thought that the compromise whereby the Americans, 'have agreed to avert their

Lend-Lease Take-outs and Export Restrictions

eyes from the size of the balances, but not to avert their eyes from the politically difficult items of Lend-Lease' was the best that they could expect, and that it was probably a result of Churchill's discussion with Roosevelt at Cairo[19]. Even more consoling was the estimate that dollar income from GI pay in the Sterling Area would continue to enlarge Britain's reserves, at least for a while, despite the contraction of Lend-Lease. The future was seen by London to depend greatly upon how the FEA behaved, in the weeks that followed satisfactory progress was made and the issue of Lend-Lease take-outs was more or less settled during February with $145 million worth being agreed upon and with negotiations continuing amicably on a second category of items[20]. Morgenthau was a little disappointed with the overall savings but not to the extent of wishing to re-open the Pandora's Box of Britain's balances.

Feelings of relief about the compromise over these were not universal in London, Nigel Ronald writing bitterly on 24 January that,

> The American Administration are attempting to reduce lend-lease to the lowest possible figure, that is to say they bleed us as near as possible white and just contribute enough to prevent our passing out of existence. They never refuse lend-lease on the ground that America is unable to afford it, but on the ground that we are getting all we need to keep going and anything further will be unacceptable to American public opinion.[21]

We shall see later in this chapter that there were also worries in Whitehall about developments in the application of the Export White Paper restrictions by FEA officials; nevertheless, the British took comfort from the thought that they had averted a concerted American move to reduce Britain's balances to the arbitrary level of $1 billion, though they were soon horrified when they discovered that they had had no such success in fact.

Crowley was more dissatisfied than Morgenthau with the dollar savings from the Lend-Lease take-outs and it appears that he tried to persuade Roosevelt to take further action. At a Cabinet meeting on 19 February from which, significantly, Morgenthau was absent, Crowley made some general

Lend-Lease Take-outs and Export Restrictions

comments about FEA operations and then, according to Daniel Bell, Roosevelt said something like the following: 'You all prepare a message for my signature to the Prime Minister telling him that for political reasons they ought to do what they can to bring the dollar and gold balances down to about $1 billion'. This was contrary to what Morgenthau and Crowley had promised Halifax and Waley on 7 January, and contrary to what Roosevelt had told Churchill at the Cairo Conference. Several factors, in addition to Crowley's lobbying, seem to have been instrumental in bringing Roosevelt to this momentous decision; these were his sensitivity to congressional criticisms, and economic difficulties with the British over their commercial relations with Argentina, over oil and aviation rights, and over the approaching conference which eventually led to the establishment of the IMF.

Ironically the man who responded most quickly to the President's request for a draft letter to Churchill was Stettinius, who favoured a generous Lend-Lease policy towards Britain. Morgenthau later suspected Stettinius of trying to contrive an embarrassing show-down on the dollar balances but the truth of the matter appears to be that Stettinius acted in accordance with what he took to be a direct order from the President. He gave the job of drafting the letter to Acheson, who did so, but who insisted on appending a memorandum for the President which strongly advised that the letter be not sent. He rehearsed yet again the State Department's arguments against reducing Britain's balances and pointed out that the letter would be contrary to the understanding reached with the British on 7 January. Stettinius later told Acheson that after the President had read his memorandum he said that, 'the domestic political aspect of the situation was great enough to be controlling'. The President then, without clearing the letter first with Morgenthau, wrote to Churchill that,

> I have been wondering whether it would be feasible for you to consider so ordering your financial affairs as to reduce your gold and dollar holdings available in this country to the neighbourhood of about $1 billion.[22]

Sir John Anderson was flabbergasted. He presented Churchill with a brief history of the negotiations relating to Britain's dollar balances

Lend-Lease Take-outs and Export Restrictions

which included the crucial things said at the Cairo Conference and on 7 January. He added that,

> If we were to accept the President's proposal, we should have lost our financial independence, in any case precarious, as soon as lend-lease comes to an end, and would emerge from the war, victorious indeed, but quite helpless financially with reserves far inferior not only to Russia but even to France and to Holland.[23]

He was so angry that he suggested that Britain should reconsider the Lend-Lease take-outs she had agreed to if Roosevelt did not abandon his aim of reducing Britain's balances to $1 billion. Churchill did not use this threat in his reply, but he did protest vehemently to Roosevelt about his proposal, and in the days that followed a sort of apology was forthcoming. Roosevelt did not completely retract what he had said, but with Morgenthau unwilling to support the President's letter of 22 February because of the promises to Waley and Halifax on 7 January, and with the State Department strongly opposed to further reductions of Britain's reserves, Roosevelt decided that it would be diplomatic to give way to Churchill on this occasion. Thus the question of the dollar balances was left alone for the time being, though in his letter of 24 March, which was cleared by Hull, Crowley and Morgenthau, the President repeated the caution which the Treasury Secretary had given Waley on 7 January that the understanding on Lend-Lease take-outs did not preclude re-opening the question of Britain's dollar balances in the future if the circumstances warranted it[24].

Apart from causing the British further anxiety the episode concerning Roosevelt's letter of 22 February also had some important consequences in Washington. Morgenthau was upset by the letter because it made it look as if he had broken faith with the British, which was something he was particularly sensitive about since he had criticised them in the past for duplicity. He was unhappy with the Lend-Lease take-outs and with the level of Britain's balances, but as he said on 13 March, he was not so dissatisfied that, 'I want to re-examine the whole thing'[25]. From a flurry of meetings in March, attempting to sort things out, two important points emerged. Firstly, after Morgenthau's suspecting that the State Department was responsible for deliberately engineering a show-down on the dollar balances, it gradually became clear that the responsibility lay more with Crowley, though his intention, unlike that of the State Department, was to reduce Britain's balances. Morgenthau received a report which claimed that Crowley was even trying to cause a breach between Roosevelt and Churchill to achieve this goal. Furthermore, in conversation with Halifax, Morgenthau discovered that after the FEA had stirred things up, it had tried to put the blame on the Treasury. Halifax told Morgenthau a 'weird' story that Crowley's number two had been to see him and said that, 'Mr. Crowley wants you to know, don't worry about the dollar balances'. Morgenthau's comment to Halifax about this was that, 'Well, I guess the only way to explain it is that Mr. Crowley was trying to curry favour with you and leave me as the prize S.O.B.'. The political and personal differences between Morgenthau and Crowley were beginning to show, and it is interesting to note that from now on Morgenthau's Treasury and the FEA did not collaborate so closely as they had done from November 1943 to March 1944[26].

The second development was that Morgenthau succeeded in getting primary authority over Britain's balances by arguing that this would prevent administrative confusion of the kind they had recently experienced. In a meeting on 13 March, with Hull and Crowley present, Morgenthau cornered Acheson - the main champion of Britain's dollar balances - and forced him to speak frankly about the Treasury having final authority in this area. Acheson could do nothing but mutter that, 'I think that is all right. I think it should be the Treasury's responsibility'. This decision was conveyed to Churchill by Roosevelt, and one immediate consequence of it was that Stettinius, who was about to leave for talks in London, was prohibited from discussing policy connected with the dollar balances[27]. In the light of Morgenthau's behaviour during the preceding fifteen months (notwithstanding his refusal to support the President's letter of 22 February) this jurisdictional decision looked ominous for Britain, but in fact, over the following six months Morgenthau's attitude towards both Britain's financial position and Lend-Lease changed and once again, as in 1940, he became a leading advocate of aid for Britain.

Lend-Lease Take-outs and Export Restrictions

Rather perversely, just at the time when Morgenthau was undergoing a change of heart, people in the State Department began to have renewed doubts about Britain's commitment to a liberal world economy, and in the autumn of 1944 a more demanding attitude towards Britain on economic policy became evident on their part. A number of developments in Britain were responsible for this. All political parties there had become more concerned with postwar policies, and with economic and social reform following the Beveridge Report on Social Security in December 1942. On 22 March 1943 Churchill made an important broadcast proposing a four year programme of postwar reconstruction and domestic policy in line with the Beveridge Report, and later in the year he earmarked full employment, better food, and an expansion of British exports as overriding priorities after the war[28]. The increased emphasis on social reform and full employment highlighted the necessity of not entering a free-market world-economy prematurely in case it destroyed British industries - already weakened by the war - and in case it led to an imbalance in Britain's international payments requiring deflationary policies, and therefore unemployment, in order to force out more exports.

In December 1943, and during the early months of 1944, such considerations in conjunction with desires to protect British farming and Imperial Preference led Hudson, Amery and Beaverbrook, with widespread Labour support, to send a spate of papers to the Cabinet and to Churchill opposing British entry into commercial talks with the State Department of the kind which had been envisaged in the Law Mission Talks of September and October 1943. Even the projected IMF, where great progress had been made, was now causing serious worries. Its critics argued, with some cogency, that it would create a rigid system similar to the gold standard, that Britain would not have sufficient discretion to alter her exchange rate, and that the US would be firmly in the driving seat. Keynes and its other defenders had reservations as well but they thought the alternatives were worse. In other areas of economic discussion between Britain and America such as oil rights, aviation rights, and commercial links with Argentina there were also heated disputes, and finally of course there was the distressing story of Britain's dollar balances and the suppression of her export trade. In the light of these difficulties the Cabinet ordered a halt to macro-economic planning talks with the US except for those to do with the IMF. The Americans were not fully informed of this decision but they soon became aware of the drift in thinking in London, especially when Churchill stated in the House of Commons that article seven of the Mutual Aid Agreement no more committed Britain to the abandonment of Imperial Preference than it committed the US to the abandonment of her high protective tariff. The supports for State Department beliefs that the Consideration Agreement had got a sound commitment from Britain to cooperate in the promotion of liberal economic policies were being hacked away[29].

On 16 July Law wrote to Anderson, Dalton and Eden about the ill feeling that had developed in the State Department during the course of the year. He explained that it was not so much because Britain had not undertaken to renounce Imperial Preference or to open up her agriculture to the wind of competition so much as her refusal, 'to discuss these matters with them' and the fact that they had, 'not even had the courtesy to explain [their] difficulties and grounds of [their] refusal'[30].

It was against this backcloth that renewed attempts were made to replace the Export White Paper with a joint declaration and that the British, first with Stettinius and then with Hopkins and Morgenthau, began to consider Lend-Lease Stage II - the period between VE-day and VJ-day - in relation to the problems of reconverting the British economy back to peacetime production.

The decision by Crowley and Morgenthau in November 1943 to tighten up Lend-Lease was being vigorously put into effect in the New Year. Morgenthau's tales of Lend-Lease abuse after his trip to North Africa encouraged the FEA even more in their adherence to the marginal theory of Lend-Lease. After the exchange of letters between Roosevelt and Churchill about Britain's reserves, an American frontal assault to reduce them was out of the question for the time being, which gave the FEA yet another reason for tightening Lend-Lease controls and for Whitney in particular to urge the need for a stricter observance of the Export White Paper restrictions[31].

By 17 January the State Department and the FEA had drawn up a joint declaration to replace the White Paper, though the former wanted to emphasise Britain's right to gain export freedom by paying for materials (except for those in short supply),

Lend-Lease Take-outs and Export Restrictions

whereas the FEA wanted to maintain screening and controls in a way the British could not accept. They were prepared to undertake some policing of exports in a joint Anglo-American export programme but as the British Treasury commented the American draft, 'appears to involve joint agreement in advance on exports containing materials which are not scarce and notwithstanding that we should have payed for them. We could not possibly accept such a provision'. On 25 February Stettinius tried to pierce the FEA's obsession with controls by suggesting a move back to private channels of trade, but Scheuer, the Executive Director of the Bureau of Supplies in the FEA, firmly opposed this by saying that the government needed to support American companies in order to counteract the assistance foreign companies were receiving from their own governments. On 10 March Stettinius conceded defeat and withdrew his proposals[32].

The British knew how serious the situation had become. In February they noted that FEA officials in North Africa were claiming the exclusive right to interpret Britain's own Export White Paper, and they knew that this was only one symptom of a new dispensation[33]. In an attempt to halt these developments and to resolve the difficulties which existed in the new American draft of the export declaration Sir Samuel Beale and Stirling were sent to Washington, but despite valiant efforts and a willingness to compromise agreement proved elusive. Then, rather surprisingly, Whitney withdrew his objection to Britain exporting goods which she had payed for. He did so on the understanding that the US could intervene at the point of allocation if this resulted in inequities for American exporters, but in the weeks that followed there were more concessions. The Americans agreed that no advance clearance would be required for exports which were not scarce and which had not been supplied on Lend-Lease, or which had been removed from Lend-Lease for six months, or which the British had payed for during the previous three months. This brought the two sides to the verge of an agreement and on 17 April Dalton recommended acceptance of the extant proposals[34].

Fortunately for the British Dalton also suggested that Beale should gently ask for clarification of certain parts of the proposals. When he did so it became clear that the export restrictions applicable to items similar to those supplied on Lend-Lease included military Lend-Lease,

Lend-Lease Take-outs and Export Restrictions

which covered such a broad category that it would be almost impossible to monitor exports properly, and it could also give the FEA grounds for even tighter regulation of Britain's exports. The British thought of voluntarily removing items from Lend-Lease to facilitate the expansion of their exports but they concluded that they could not afford to do this, and that given the attitude of FEA officials, it would not appease them or ease Britain's export problems. In fact Dalton explained to his colleagues on 6 July that, despite the American refusal to clarify matters associated with military Lend-Lease, they might still have been willing to accept the proposals except for an even more intractable problem, which showed that the Americans would not accept a truly reciprocal agreement on exports[35].

There was a phrase in the American draft which referred to Lend-Lease and Reciprocal Aid being imported into the UK and the US respectively, and that the export controls would only apply to such supplies. As most of Reciprocal Aid did not enter the US because it was supplied at the points of use in the theatres of war and in the UK, and as virtually all Lend-Lease to Britain was imported into the UK, then clearly the export restrictions would be very one sided.

By July Dalton, despite reluctant advice to the contrary from Halifax and the British missions in Washington, decided he could not accept the American draft. On the 28 June, in a memorandum for Attlee's Lord President's Committee, he bemoaned the American return to the Landis or marginal theory according to which he said that for Britain to receive any type of Lend-Lease material she had to, 'have reduced the civilian population to siege levels and given up all export trade in that particular commodity'. He recommended that the White Paper Supersession Talks should be postponed in case they prejudiced the possibility of a beneficial outcome to the high level talks between Britain and the US which were then under consideration[36]. So it was not just the objectionable nature of the American draft and evidence of what the British took to be as bad faith that caused them to pause; there was also the fact that encouraging conversations had taken place between Stettinius and various British officials about future American aid for Britain.

At a rather conspiratorial secret meeting 'some miles' from Bretton Woods, where the final details of the IMF were being hammered out, Keynes, Eady,

Lend-Lease Take-outs and Export Restrictions

Ronald, Opie and Brand, who was the new British Treasury representative in Washington, 'agreed to suspend the discussions on the Export White Paper until we have made some progress with [Lend-Lease] stage two'. Law added that they had to get the Americans to agree that, 'during stage 2, lend lease on a full scale or some other dodge and a British export drive (not merely some slight relaxation of existing limitations on British exports) must be continued side by side'[37].

The Americans agreed to the suspension of the talks. The FEA had wondered for some time about whether a joint declaration would be preferable to the White Paper and about the wisdom of continuing talks on such a controversial subject when the presidential election was so near. Stettinius was also happy to suspend the talks, though for rather different reasons. He thought that the issues were now so important that they needed to be taken up at the highest level. He was motivated by a desire to help the British and when Law told him that the FEA had been 'putting the screws on' recently, and that a moratorium on Lend-Lease policy was necessary to accompany the suspension of the White Paper Talks, he was at first surprised at the behaviour of the FEA but then promised to do all he could to help[38]. As we shall see further high level moves were necessary before a moratorium was actually imposed, because Whitney and others continued to criticise British export policy and to support the application of the marginal theory through the summer[39]. However, things began to move on the highest political plane which were soon to alter things. To see how this happened we must go back to April 1944 for a brief account of developments involving Stettinius, Hopkins, Morgenthau and the British.

Stettinius was ordered by Hull, on Morgenthau's request, not to talk about Britain's dollar balances when he went to London in April, but he was allowed to listen to what Churchill and Anderson had to say[40]. The Prime Minister, despite Britain's financial difficulties, said little because of the Cabinet decision not to proceed with macro-economic talks with the US; the British were able to camouflage that decision for some time by arguing that they were too preoccupied with the imminent invasion of Europe to discuss economic policies. The talks with Anderson were more fruitful. Stettinius did warn him at their final meeting that a Kansas farmer might think that Britain was rich

177

after all the Lend-Lease she had received, but he was sympathetic toward Britain's financial plight and tried both to make the British aware of the political difficulties in Washington and later to educate Crowley and Morgenthau about the precarious financial situation that Anderson had outlined to him. He also reported to Hull that he thought Britain would still go a long way to meet them over liberal economic policies, which must have helped allay Hull's apprehension after Churchill's statement about Britain not being committed to the abandonment of Imperial Preference[41].

Stettinius' efforts at building bridges became even more valuable in May because of amendments to the renewal of the Lend-Lease Act in Congress by Wadsworth and Senator Vandenberg which made it clear that Lend-Lease would end when hostilities did and that it was not to be used for any postwar purposes. Stettinius, Denby and Cox now began to suggest the possibility of credits or low interest loans for Britain, including a '3(c) Agreement' under the auspices of the Lend-Lease Act which would allow American supplies to continue to Britain after the war on favourable financial terms. Stettinius pointed out to Halifax that Lend-Lease was likely to contract after VE-day, and he suggested that matters were so serious that Anderson should come to Washington for talks with Morgenthau[42]. On 10 June Anderson explained to Halifax that Britain would need more help, not less, in Stage II, and that it would be very difficult for Britain to accept any help involving dollar liabilities. In the middle of June the domestic political situation in the US became even more sensitive with the Democrats losing their overall majority in the House of Representatives for the first time since 1933 because of two by-election defeats. Stettinius now urged the British to consider approaching Hull and Roosevelt, who he thought would have more sympathetic ears than Morgenthau, for a 25 year loan at two and a half per cent interest[43].

The British were not prepared to do this but with the problems of reconversion raised by Lend-Lease Stage II and exports merging into each other, the British did begin to consider a high level meeting to sort out her economic problems, and as we have seen this was one of the reasons why they suspended the White Paper Talks.

In mid-summer 1944 allied successes in Europe made it important that Churchill and Roosevelt should meet to discuss the problems raised by the

Lend-Lease Take-outs and Export Restrictions

occupation of Germany and Britain's part in the war against Japan. There were also two important developments on the economic front, which were also on the agenda for the meeting that took place in September, and which became known as the Second Quebec Conference. Firstly, although a visit by Anderson to Washington never materialised, Morgenthau crossed the Atlantic in August to discuss the currency problems of liberated France, and while he was in London he also had discussions with Anderson about Britain's financial problems. When he returned to Washington he told Roosevelt that Britain really was broke, and although he was still reluctant to use Lend-Lease to alleviate Britain's reconversion problems he was now much more sympathetic. Morgenthau now began to cooperate with Harry Hopkins who, as we shall see in a moment, was already busy trying to help the British, and on 24 August he began to review Britain's finances, on the basis of a report from Brand, in preparation for a top level meeting with them[44]. This change of heart was partly because he got on well with Anderson and partly because he was basically Anglophile, but there was also another more important reason which was that the Bretton Woods Conference had agreed upon on IMF that realised most of the goals that Morgenthau had set himself for the international monetary system. There now seemed little chance of British monetary power thwarting his ambitions.

The second development began at the end of July when Harry Hopkins declared his intention to help Britain with her economic problems, because the US would need her as a strong ally after the war[45]. Hopkins was not always the friend of Britain that Churchill and others took him to be, but on this occasion he did much to oil the machinery before the Quebec Conference.

Close cooperation in the preparations for the meeting began in July between Campbell, Brand and Hopkins, and then later between Denby (who was a member of the American briefing committee that was set up to prepare papers for Roosevelt on Britain's economic circumstances) and Frank Lee, a member of the British Treasury delegation in Washington. At first Hopkins wanted to circumvent Morgenthau's influence because of his hard line on Lend-Lease, but after the latter's trip to London Hopkins realised that it would be prudent and helpful to include him in the preparations and to involve him in the conference[46]. Hopkins was also active in helping the British to get the moratorium they desired on Lend-Lease administrative policy. After correspondence about this between Churchill and Hopkins in August, Roosevelt issued a directive in which he ordered that there was to be no change in Lend-Lease until after his meeting with Churchill[47].

The situation now looked favourable, but in a way Hopkins and the British were too clever for their own good. Details of Britain's financial and economic difficulties were not fully revealed to the American briefing committee for fear that some of its members might use the information contrary to British interests. Instead information was secretly fed to Denby by Lee in order to correct the worst errors and attitudes of his colleagues, and Hopkins was also given fairly comprehensive details. A second unusual feature of the preparations for the Quebec Conference was that Roosevelt, Hopkins and Morgenthau arranged it so that although Morgenthau would not be named as an official participant in the conference he would be on call to attend at short notice[48]. The reasons for this are not entirely clear. One theory is that Roosevelt wanted the public to receive a vote-catching image of the President embroiled solely in war strategy at Quebec because of the impending election. Perhaps it was for similar reasons that he misleadingly claimed that no political decisions were going to be made at Quebec and thus excluded State Department officials from the meeting. Unfortunately this, and the way in which the British presented their case to only a narrow section of the American Administration, was to have serious consequences. At first the Quebec Conference seemed to be a great victory for the British on the economic front, but the way in which it was achieved and the growing suspicion in the State Department that the British were wavering in their commitment to a more liberal world economy after the war caused a reaction in Washington which turned it into a Pyrrhic Victory.

NOTES

1. See: Cmd.6483, 'Report on Mutual Aid', 11 Nov. 1943; and memo. by Keynes, 1 Nov. 1943, T160/1234/F17660/024/039/2.
2. Crowley to Hull, 7 Dec. 1943, Stettinius to Acheson, 10 Dec. 1943, and Hull to Crowley, 26 Jan. 1944, all at 841.24/2181.

Lend-Lease Take-outs and Export Restrictions

3. See: Cherwell to Churchill and accompanying memoranda of 26 Oct. and 11 Nov. 1943, all of which were handed to the Americans, Roosevelt PSF, box 49, folder: GB 1943; and H.M. Diary, 672, pp.173-209, 2 Nov. 1943.
4. H.M. Diary, 672, pp.173-209, 2 Nov. 1943.
5. Ibid, and J. M. Blum, *Roosevelt and Morgenthau: A Revision and Condensation of 'From the Morgenthau Diaries'* (Houghton Mifflin Company, Boston, 1970), p.145.
6. H.M. Diary, 673, pp.295-297, 4 Nov. 1943.
7. Ibid, 674, pp.70-74 and 213-216, telephone conversations between Morgenthau and White, and Morgenthau and Crowley, 6 and 8 Nov. 1943 respectively.
8. Ibid, 674, pp.34-36, 14 Nov. 1943 and 678, pp.43-45, 17 Nov. 1943.
9. Ibid, 679, pp.91-92, 23 Nov. 1943.
10. Minutes by T. W. Childs, chairman Lend-Lease Sub-committee, 16 Dec. 1943, on LL(43)40, CAB 92.
11. See: H.M. Diary, 684, pp.267-301, 16 Dec. 1943, and State Department minutes, 16 Dec. 1943, 841.5151/2005.
12. See copy of Cherwell to Churchill, 12 Nov. 1943 at Roosevelt PSF, box 49, folder: GB 1943, and Anderson to Churchill, 24 Feb. 1944, U1834/12/71, FO371/40881.
13. State Department minutes, 16 Dec. 1943, 841.5151/2005.
14. Acheson, 'Memorandum on Lend-Lease Policy and the British Gold and Dollar Balances', 17 Dec. 1943, 841.5151/2010.
15. 'US Policy on Limits of British Gold and Dollar Balances', 30 Dec. 1943, 841.51/1848.
16. Hull to Roosevelt, 31 Dec. 1943, Roosevelt PSF, box 20, folder: Lend-Lease, Jan.-Feb. 1944.
17. See: H.M. Diary, 691, p.132 Roosevelt to Hull, Morgenthau and Crowley, 5 Jan. 1944, and Washington to Whitehall, 4 Jan. 1944, U204/12/71, FO371/40880.
18. H.M. Diary, 692, pp.2-5, 7 Jan. 1944, State Department minutes, 7 Jan. 1944, 841.24/2176, British minutes 7 Jan. 1944, U145/12/71, FO371/40880, and the 'Crowley List of Take-outs' 7 Jan. 1944, U187/12/71, FO371/40880.
19. Keynes to Robertson, Waley and Catto, 12 Jan. 1944, T177/58.
20. Hull, Morgenthau and Crowley to Roosevelt, 4 Feb. 1944, Roosevelt PSF, box 20, folder: Lend-Lease, Jan.-Feb. 1944.

Lend-Lease Take-outs and Export Restrictions

21. Ronald to Campbell, 24 Jan. 1944, U145/12/71, FO371/40880.
22. See: Stettinius to Acheson, 19 Feb. 1944, 841.5151/2015; Bell's comments at, H.M. Diary, 709, pp.122-125, 13 March 1944; Stettinius' views on Lend-Lease at, Stettinius to Roosevelt, 21 Feb. 1944, Roosevelt: PSF, box 175, folder: Post-war; draft letter by FEA at Currie to Cox, 21 Feb. 1944, RG169, box 795, folder: Dollar Balances; draft letter and memo. by Acheson, 21 Feb. 1944 841.24/2197A; Stettinius to Acheson 23 Feb. 1944, 841.5151/2016; and Roosevelt to Churchill, 22 Feb. 1944, Roosevelt PSF, box 49, folder: GB 1944-45.
23. Anderson to Churchill, 24 Feb. 1944, U1834/12/71, FO371/40881.
24. W. F. Kimball, Churchill and Roosevelt: The Complete Correspondence, 3 Vols. (Princeton University Press, New Jersey, 1984), Vol. III, pp.35-36, and pp.65-66, Churchill to Roosevelt and his reply, 9 and 24 March 1944.
25. H.M. Diary, 709, p.109, 13 March 1944.
26. Ibid, 709, pp.1-13, 11 March 1944; 709, pp.122-125, 13 March 1944; 711, p.218, draft of letter for Roosevelt to send to Churchill, 18 March, 1944; 716, pp.240-244, 30 March 1944.
27. Ibid, 709, pp.122-125, 13 March 1944.
28. Churchill, 'Statement of Broad Principles', 19 Oct. 1944, WP(43)467, CAB 66.
29. See: memo. by Hudson, 14 Dec. 1943, WP(43)566, and memo. by Amery, 20 Dec. 1943, WP(43)576, both at CAB 66; The Earl of Birkenhead, The Prof in Two Worlds - The Official Life of Professor F. A. Lindemann Viscount Cherwell (Collins, London, 1961), p.266; A.J.P. Taylor, Beaverbrook (Hamish Hamilton, London 1972), pp.556-557; Lord Robbins, Autobiography of an Economist (Macmillan, London, 1971), p.203; Churchill, House of Commons Debates, April 1944, 399:579-580.
30. Law to Anderson, Eden and Dalton, 16 July 1944, T160/1418/F17660/072/5.
31. Whitney to Currie, 24 Feb. 1944, RG169, box 821, folder: UK Lend-Lease; and Whitney to Coe, 6 March 1944, RG169, box 744, folder: Politics and Propaganda.
32. See: 'Draft of Proposed Joint Statement of Policy', and Acheson to Stettinius, 17 Jan. 1944, 841.24/2190; FO, Treasury Extra to Washington, 3 Feb. 1944, U718/12/71, FO 371/40880; memo by Scheur, 1 March 1944, and J. L. McCamy, Executive Director of the Bureau of Areas in the FEA, to

Lend-Lease Take-outs and Export Restrictions

Sherwood, 6 March 1944, RG169, box 748, folder: Trade Relations; and Stettinius to Crowley, 10 March 1944, ibid.
33. FO, Treasury Extra to Washington, 3 Feb. 1944, U718/12/71, F0371/40880.
34. See: Whitney to Coe, 6 March 1944, RG169, box 744, folder: Politics and Propaganda; and memo. by Dalton, 17 April 1944, LP(44)69, U3609/12/71, F0371/40882.
35. See: FO, Treasury Special to Washington, 25 May 1944, U4172/12/71, F0371/40883; memo. by W. T. Childs, 10 June 1944, U5882/12/71, F0371/40883; draft telegram by Dalton (not sent), 6 July 1944, UE234/5/71, F0371/41012.
36. Memo. by Dalton, 'Supersession of the Export White Paper', 28 June 1944, U5853/12/71, F0371/40883. Dalton also asked his colleagues to support the continuation of exports to the Eastern Hemisphere – even if they involved scarce materials – without seeking US approval i.e. this was a continuation of Stettinius's Eastern Hemisphere waiver, though interpreted very broadly.
37. Law to Anderson, 19 July 1944, UE362/5/71, F0371/41012.
38. Law to FO, 19 July 1944, ibid.
39. See: Whitney to McCamy, 26 July 1944, RG169, box 772, folder: EPC Agenda 1944; Whitney's White Paper Committee to Currie, 9 Aug. 1944, RG169, box 820, folder: UK; and Whitney to McCamy, 26 July 1944, ibid.
40. Stettinius to Hull, 11 April 1944, 841.5151/2023; H.M. Diary 720, p.231, White to Morgenthau, 13 April 1944; Hull to Stettinius, 13 April 1944, 740.0011 Stettinius Mission/22a.
41. See: 'Notes for Discussion with Roosevelt in Conversations in London' by Stettinius, Roosevelt PSF, box 95; memo. of conversation between Stettinius and Anderson, 19 April 1944, 841.5151/2029.
42. Halifax to FO, 27 and 30 May 1944, U4806 and U4888/12/71, F0371/40883; and Halifax to F0, 1 June 1944, T160/1418/F17660/072/5.
43. See: Anderson to Halifax, 10 June 1944 T160/1418/F17660/072/5; H. G. Nicholas (Ed.), Washington Dispatches 1941-45 (Weidenfeld and Nicolson, London, 1981), 18 June 1944; and Brand to R. Hopkins, 29 June 1944, T160/1375/F179420/010/2.
44. Blum, Condensed Diaries, pp.547-549.
45. Campbell to F0, 25 July 1944, T160/1418/F17660/072/5.

46. Campbell to Anderson, 3 Aug. 1944; Campbell to FO, 3 Aug. 1944; Washington to FO, 8 and 13 Aug. 1944, all at ibid.

47. Churchill to Hopkins, 10 Aug. 1944; Washington to Churchill, Eden and Anderson, 20 Aug. 1944, ibid.

48. See: Halifax to FO, 25 Aug. 1944; Eady to Brand 30 Aug. 1944; Washington to FO, 30 Aug. 1944; Halifax to Anderson, 11 Sept. 1944; and Halifax to Churchill, Eden and Anderson, 20 Aug. 1944, all at ibid.

Chapter Seven

STAGE II LEND-LEASE AND THE QUEBEC CONFERENCE

When the Second Quebec Conference convened on 11 September 1944 the Allies expected a German collapse within four months, followed by the defeat of Japan twelve to eighteen months later. Confronted with this timetable it became more vital than ever for the British to begin the difficult task of reconverting their economy to peacetime production. The riddle that the British Government had to solve was how to get America's help without incurring dollar liabilities and becoming more vulnerable to political and economic pressures from her.

Recent experience over Britain's dollar balances and the shift of policy within the FEA and the American service departments, which cut back Lend-Lease to Britain, caused great anxiety in the British Treasury where the first object of financial policy was, 'to avoid indebtedness to the United States'. Thus Stettinius' suggestions, in the spring and summer of 1944, of dollar credits and loans for Britain were unacceptable to Anderson, who asserted in a letter to Halifax on 10 June that, 'If in any single instance, we accept the proposal that we should obtain American supplies by being granted a loan, instead of obtaining Lend-Lease aid, we may be sure that this principle will be gradually applied over a wider and wider field'. In the same letter Anderson went on to explain how they should try to solve their economic reconversion problems. He wanted the Americans to abandon the marginal theory, allowing Lend-Lease to help Britain to begin both to reconvert her economy and to re-establish her export trade. He wanted civilian Lend-Lease to continue at about the 1944 level, and military Lend-Lease to be decreased only by the same proportion as Britain decreased her war production. He explained

Stage II Lend-Lease and the Quebec Conference

that the government expected to pay for food and raw materials that were required for exports but that, 'we cannot pay cash for food and raw materials required for United Kingdom domestic purposes during Stage II'[1].

In the period intervening between 10 June and the start of the conference at Quebec British aims did not change. To understand what happened to British hopes and plans at the conference, and the subsequent reaction in Washington to its outcome, it is necessary to explain the different attitudes in the American Administration concerning economic assistance for Britain. We must also consider how these attitudes interacted with discussions about the now infamous Morgenthau Plan, proposing the partition and de-industrialisation of postwar Germany, which was also one of the main issues at Quebec.

On 11 August Morgenthau, amply demonstrating the changed attitude which was explained in the previous chapter, promised Anderson that he would help to give Britain the economic help which was due to her because of her war effort and he commented that, 'But for England there would be no United States today'[2]. Anderson was delighted by his change of heart, but it was still unclear how he would actually deliver the goods. Two days later at their final meeting in London Anderson painted Britain's bleak economic picture: she needed to increase her present level of exports by five hundred per cent, and she needed Lend-Lease help for her balance of payments, for reconversion, and to help to meet the legitimate dollar demands of the Sterling Area. Morgenthau said that it might be difficult to stretch Lend-Lease in this way but that he would help providing that he was in charge of arranging economic assistance for Britain and on condition that the British did not lobby in Washington as they had done over the dollar balances with Acheson and Stettinius[3].

When Morgenthau returned to Washington and began to discuss preliminary details of Britain's economic requirements with Brand, he reiterated his determination to be in charge on the American side. On 19 August he tried to get Roosevelt to give him a commanding position over all American foreign economic policy, and although the President would not formally grant his request, this did not prevent Morgenthau from playing the major role for the US in the Stage II discussions during the following four months[4].

Stage II Lend-Lease and the Quebec Conference

The jurisdictional authority that Morgenthau sought proved to be an important matter. In early August, before Morgenthau's attitude towards economic assistance for Britain had changed, Keynes and others warned London about the inadvisability of concentrating on him for help in Stage II, not only because of his recent attitude on the dollar balances, but also because Lend-Lease and export policy were the preserves of the FEA and the State Department. The British asked Hopkins for advice about whether they should work closely with Morgenthau on Stage II; he prevaricated, saying that a committee chaired by Morgenthau with Crowley and Hull as members - the latter in his opinion being indispensable - might work, but that the British ought to await the outcome of the Quebec Conference before deciding whether or not to rely mainly on Morgenthau[5]. Despite the cautions from Keynes and Hopkins the British did move decisively towards close cooperation with Morgenthau during the weeks immediately preceding the Quebec Conference and this was to have very important consequences.

As Morgenthau talked with Brand and Campbell, the British Resident Minister in Washington, he became even more convinced of Britain's need for economic help. By the eve of the Quebec Conference he was in general agreement with the arguments contained in memoranda submitted to him by the British concerning the need for substantial Lend-Lease help in the reconversion of the British economy, and of the necessity of expanding Britain's export trade. Furthermore, he was prepared to make firm commitments to the British about Stage II, though, rather surprisingly as it transpired at Quebec, not as firm or as specific as the President was then prepared to make himself.

One question which remains to be asked about Morgenthau's attitude prior to the conference concerns what he wanted from Britain in return for American help. His comments to Anderson on 11 August suggest that he thought that Britain had paid her quid pro quo in advance through her war effort, but he also thought that it was in America's political and economic interests that Britain should have a viable economy. There is also some evidence which suggests that Morgenthau regarded British support for his plan for the pacification of Germany as part of their quid pro quo.

The State Department's position on the need for assisting Britain in Stage II was similar to that of

Stage II Lend-Lease and the Quebec Conference

the US Treasury, except that it was much more specific about conditions.

On 15 July Winant explained to Hull that Britain had failed to proceed with the article seven economic talks because of a split within the British Cabinet over what the Americans wanted them to do with Imperial Preference and British agriculture[6]. It had been obvious to the Americans for some time that the British were stalling on postwar economic planning talks; Churchill's statement that Britain was not committed to the abolition of Imperial Preference, and trouble over British meat supplies from Argentina, over oil rights in the Middle East and over civil aviation rights all contributed to renewing the State Department's interest in getting a firm British commitment to a liberal world economy. The 'commitment' in the Mutual Aid Agreement was now clearly seen to be inadequate for their purposes.

John E. Orchard, a State Department official, drew up a number of memoranda which advocated both Lend-Lease help and loans for Britain, 'in America's enlightened self-interest'. On 15 August he recommended that Lend-Lease should be continued for the war against Japan, and that the Combined Boards should take a liberal line on Britain's need to reconvert to peacetime production because of the hardships that she had endured and because of the particular economic difficulties that she had, however, there were to be conditions. In return for economic assistance Britain should be required to participate fully in the war against Japan and to commit herself to economic cooperation with the US[7]. By September these views had become accepted State Department policy.

On 2 September Hull asked Roosevelt to try to persuade Churchill to renew the article seven economic talks, and a week later he laid before the President his department's views about Stage II. The memorandum began by saying that, 'The most important international economic problem of the transition and post-war periods, will be the position of the United Kingdom': Hull went on to express his fears about the British adopting restrictive economic policies after the war and he argued that it was of paramount importance to prevent them from doing this. He mentioned the possibility of a loan to help the British with their economic difficulties and to bring them into a liberal economic system, but he added that much could first be done through Stage II Lend-Lease. He

Stage II Lend-Lease and the Quebec Conference

thought that this could be politically justified and made defensible by Britain's full participation in the war against Japan after Hitler had been defeated. He argued for a reasonable degree of coordinated British and American reconversion to civilian production, with Lend-Lease helping the British by being maintained at about two-thirds of its then current level, but - and this was a crucial 'but' - this help had to be tied to the renewal of article seven talks and a pledge from Britain to cooperate with the US in economic policy[8].

The position of Harry Hopkins was similar to Hull's; he was more cautious than Morgenthau and one gets the impression that he was more influenced by cold calculations of American self-interest. On 4 August, shortly after declaring his intention to Campbell of helping with Britain's economic difficulties, his friend and assistant the White House statistician Isador Lubin, sent him a memorandum which recommended that the US should help Britain to reconvert her economy with Lend-Lease and possibly with a loan, despite the fact that these recommendations were contrary to what the FEA was then thinking. Lubin went on with an anecdote which must surely have appealed to the worldly-wise Hopkins: 'Marlborough once remarked that in every alliance one party wears the boots and the spurs and the other the saddle...we are obviously wearing the boots in the Anglo-American Alliance. If we want to stay in this fortunate position, we have to find some way to feed the horse'[9].

Hopkins agreed and, despite his health failing once again, he busied himself in the preparations for the Quebec Conference by corresponding with Churchill, by reading British memoranda and by discussing things with Roosevelt. On 14 August he received a memorandum from Brand which made it clear that the British wanted military and civilian Lend-Lease on a large scale in Stage II to help reconvert their economy even though, as Brand commented, they knew that this was, 'a hard political doctrine for the President to put across'. After reading this Hopkins had a lengthy talk with the President, and they decided that it would be imprudent to accept requests for military Lend-Lease before deciding what part Britain would take in the war against Japan. Roosevelt even went so far as to say that, 'it would be unwise to make formal commitments' because the 'Japanese might collapse after V.E.'[10]. Roosevelt may have had the atom bomb in mind when he said this; however, by the

Stage II Lend-Lease and the Quebec Conference

time that he and Churchill came to discuss Stage II at Quebec he had changed his mind about making commitments to the British. After the conversation between Hopkins and Roosevelt the Americans told the British that the US military had not completed their plans for the war against Japan and therefore British military Lend-Lease estimates would have to be shelved for a while. However, they said that they hoped that a new broad military and Lend-Lease approach could be hammered out at Quebec, and, to reassure the British who had detected a growing tendency in the US service departments to be less forthcoming with Lend-Lease supplies, London was told that the military Lend-Lease programme would continue unchanged until after Quebec[11].

Apart from helping the President to work out his ideas for the Stage II discussions Hopkins also acted as a link-man between the White House and Churchill in arranging who was to attend the conference. The Prime Minister originally wanted to take a high-powered ministerial delegation to Quebec, but Hopkins and Roosevelt opposed this. Roosevelt wanted to avoid being seen to be involved in political issues so near an election; he wanted the vote-catching image of a President embroiled in the military strategy for victory to be projected from Quebec[12]. At this time he was also unsure about the wisdom of making firm commitments to the British about Stage II, which was another reason for deciding to keep the conference in a low political key. This decision was important; firstly, because it enabled Roosevelt to exclude the State Department from the conference on the grounds that no political decisions were going to be made there. (It was also well-known that Roosevelt disliked working with the dinosaurian State Department and the 'striped-pants boys' there, and their exclusion from Quebec was probably also to do with the fact that he preferred to work with his friend Morgenthau who on this occasion had views on foreign economic policy and on Germany that were more in tune than the State Department's with the President's own.) Secondly, although Churchill agreed to exclude Anderson and the Minister of Supply, Lyttleton, from his party, he insisted on taking Lord Cherwell as a statistical and economic adviser. Thirdly, in a letter to Roosevelt on 12 September Churchill more or less ensured that Morgenthau, in whom the British had now decided to place their hopes for Stage II, would attend at Quebec; he wrote to Roosevelt that, 'One of the most important things I have to discuss with

Stage II Lend-Lease and the Quebec Conference

you is Stage II. Would Thursday, 14th, do for that? - in which case I hope that you could have Morgenthau present'[13].

Given the fact that Roosevelt excluded State Department officials from the Quebec Conference Morgenthau's presence was to prove even more influential than it might otherwise have been. Morgenthau was able to work well with Cherwell and in fact they were crucial figures at Quebec: they both wanted Stage II Lend-Lease help for Britain and harsh treatment for postwar Germany, and they were the catalyst which helped with the reaching of agreements on these issues.

Sadly, Hopkins, as he informed Churchill on 28 August, was too ill to attend at Quebec, but he was active in the preparations right up to the last minute. On 8 September, echoing and reinforcing Hull's position, he advised Roosevelt to tell Churchill how strongly he felt, 'about knocking down some of the trade barriers', and to disabuse him of his delusion that such views were just the 'hobby horse' of Mr. Hull. And on the eve of the conference the British were still funnelling information to the President through Hopkins. In a memorandum dated 10 September the British explained that they wanted the US to move away from the marginal theory and to guarantee Britain Lend-Lease supplies in Stage II, either in proportion to Britain's level of war mobilisation, or in terms of fixed quantities, so that Britain could plan her reconversion to civilian production. It stated that the President would be asked for specific commitments: it also suggested that an Anglo-American committee might be established to implement whatever agreements were made at Quebec, and it commented that there should be as little interference as possible with the revival of Britain's export trade[14]. There was to be no misunderstanding of what the British wanted from the Americans at Quebec.

Although the US Treasury, the State Department and Hopkins advised Roosevelt to help Britain rconvert her economy with Lend-Lease in Stage II, there were two powerful power bases in Washington which were opposed to doing this: one was the FEA - the prevailing attitude of which we are already familiar with - and the other was a lobby composed of the Secretary of State for the Navy James Forrestal, Stimson, Roosevelt's military Chief of Staff Admiral Leahy, and General Somervell who was in charge of the army Lend-Lease programme. Since

Stage II Lend-Lease and the Quebec Conference

April 1944 Somervell in particular had been straining at the leash in his attempts to curb the flow of supplies to Britain, and by mid August relations were so tense in the Anglo-American military supply field that Brand vehemently told Hopkins that specific directives would be necessary to get the US service departments to continue with Lend-Lease at a level which would help Britain to reconvert to peacetime production. Brand was right to be apprehensive. On 7 September Somervell in a memorandum for the US Joint Chiefs of Staff argued for an extremely tight policy for Lend-Lease in Stage II: supplies were to be solely for the war against Japan; all civilian Lend-Lease was to be stopped and Britain, 'thrown upon its own resources'; he wanted bases, commercial rights, Lend-Lease articles returned, and repayment of the remaining debit balance on the Lend-Lease account. Hopkins advised Leahy that the Joint Chiefs should not accept Somervell's proposals and Leahy had to agree because of the holding order on Lend-Lease policy issued by the President[15]. However, the military and the service departments were to play an important role in Stage II and this episode was only a foretaste of what was to come.

There was another perspective to the opposition of the US military to helping Britain through Lend-Lease in Stage II. Unlike Hull, Hopkins, Morgenthau and eventually Roosevelt, who wanted an expansion of Britain's war effort against Japan, seeing it as essential if extensive Lend-Lease aid in Stage II was to be politically defensible, many US military leaders did not want more British help in the Pacific. There were a number of reasons for this; some US military leaders in the Pacific blamed the British for what they saw as the mistaken policy of giving priority to the war in the West and they did not want them to come in at the end of the day to take a share of the spoils and glory that were rightfully America's; many of the American military leaders had had disagreements with the British over other aspects of strategic policy, particularly with regard to the invasion of France, and there was a residue of ill-feeling which remained because of this; and finally Admiral King, the US Chief of Naval Operations, argued that the Americans already had more planes and ships in the Pacific than they could effectively use and thus there was no need for the British to be given a major part in the war against Japan[16].

Stage II Lend-Lease and the Quebec Conference

The final variables at Quebec in the equation of Stage II economic help for Britain were two issues concerning postwar policy on Germany.

Firstly, there was the matter of allied occupation zones. Roosevelt favoured Northern Germany because Leahy, who had been the US Ambassador to Vichy France, persuaded him that there would be a revolution in France after the war and the President wanted to avoid the possibility of getting involved there raised by the occupation of southern Germany which bordered that country. Stimson favoured the southern zone because otherwise there would have to be a geographical swop over of the British and American armies - the former were invading along the North German Plain and the latter were advancing further south - and because the northern zone would be contiguous with the Soviet area of occupation[17]. Morgenthau also favoured the southern zone for reasons connected with his plan for the pacification of Germany, which is the last variable in the equation.

On 23 August Roosevelt stated that all the German questions would be settled at Quebec, and at a Cabinet meeting the next day he set up a Germany Committee chaired by Hull, with Stimson and Morgenthau as members. Harry Hopkins joined the committee slightly later and Forrestal was on call if needed. Although Hull was the chairman it was obvious from the start that Roosevelt favoured Morgenthau's punitive approach to Germany and the plan which he had got Treasury officials to draw up. At the meeting of 24 August Roosevelt said that, 'the Germans should live on soup three times a day until they realised the errors of their ways' and in the following days he made numerous references to German soup kitchens. He directed the German Committee to draw up a plan for postwar Germany along the punitive lines he had indicated, and which were of course compatible with the Treasury plan[18].

The diaries of both Wickard and Morgenthau show that Hull went along with these harsh ideas for Germany but that Stimson, according to Morgenthau's diary, clearly did not. The division within the German Committee became very apparent when it met on 5 September. Stimson described it as the most unpleasant meeting he had had during his four years as Secretary of State for War, though he also commented that no personality issues were involved: the problem was over policy. Hull abandoned his liberal trade philosophy and supported Morgenthau as

Stage II Lend-Lease and the Quebec Conference

did Hopkins, at least to the extent of agreeing that the Ruhr should be de-industrialised. Stimson could not accept Morgenthau's views for humanitarian reasons: he could not accept the butchering of Germany into small parcels as Morgenthau proposed, nor the plan for an industrial 'ghost area', as he dubbed it, in the Ruhr[19].

In a telephone conversation the next day Stimson managed to ease Hull away from Morgenthau a little by getting him to agree that Assistant Secretary of War McCloy should draw up a compromise plan; however, Stimson's efforts to shift the administration towards a more charitable policy towards Germany met with little immediate success. At a Cabinet meeting on 9 September Roosevelt appeared to Stimson to be obsessed with German soup kitchens, and he was still inclined towards Morgenthau's plan, which had been slightly revised, and which now included arguments that Britain would gain economically from the de-industrialisation of Germany. No firm decision on policy was taken at the meeting, but by the start of the Quebec Conference two days later Roosevelt had been convinced by Morgenthau's arguments and he called him to Quebec to help to persuade the British to accept his plan for Germany[20].

At the opening session of the conference Roosevelt, following the advice of Hull and Hopkins, over-ruled his military advisers and accepted Churchill's offer of extensive naval and military assistance in the Pacific. Thus one of the necessary political preconditions for justifying Stage II economic assistance for Britain in the US was met early in the proceedings, but then Roosevelt doggedly avoided discussion of Stage II until matters pertaining to Germany had been dealt with[21].

In the evening of 12 September Churchill was presented with the Morgenthau Plan, and he promptly condemned it in a flood of rhetoric: 'un-Christian' was (given the semitic origins of Morgenthau and of White who assisted him at Quebec) one of the less sensitive of the epithets he used. After the Prime Minister's outburst matters were referred to Morgenthau and to the equally rabid anti-Nazi, Lord Cherwell. Within hours Cherwell was supporting the Morgenthau Plan not only because it inflicted suitable punishment on the Germans but also because of the potential economic gains for Britain and, according to Harry White, because Morgenthau and

Stage II Lend-Lease and the Quebec Conference

Cherwell struck a tacit oral agreement for generous Lend-Lease aid in Stage II.

After Cherwell explained the economic perspective to Churchill he decided to accept the Morgenthau Plan. Churchill recorded that he considered the disarmament argument was decisive, though this was largely because of the fact that, 'beneficial consequences to us follow naturally' with German de-industrialisation. It was mooted that Britain could take over export markets worth up to £400 million a year which had previously been supplied by Germany. The British records do not indicate that Cherwell linked acceptance of the Morgenthau Plan with a Lend-Lease agreement, but that connection was certainly in Churchill's mind. He wrote of the Morgenthau Plan later that, 'At first I violently opposed this idea, but the President, with Mr. Morgenthau - from whom we had so much to ask - was so insistent that in the end we agreed to consider it.' Churchill, in fact, did more than this: he dictated the final draft of the plan himself[22].

With the Morgenthau Plan now accepted, the President's determination that the US should occupy the industrial north-western part of Germany began to waver, and on the afternoon of 15 September he finally agreed to it being the British zone[23]. The reason for his change of mind is not documented, but Henry Stimson's speculation on 20 September that, 'It may have been a shrewd move by Roosevelt to avoid having the American army handle a thorny problem' i.e. de-industrialising the Ruhr, seems plausible[24]. It should be added that Roosevelt also secured supply lines through the British zone from the Baltic ports in case the more direct routes through France had to be closed in the event of the revolution he expected there.

The provisions for Stage II now fell into place with remarkable ease. As we have already seen Churchill saw a connection between his response to the Morgenthau Plan and Morgenthau's disposition to be helpful about Lend-Lease. There was no formal connection between the two issues, and it is more accurate to say that the discussions moved in tandem in the minds of the negotiators rather than to say that they proceeded separately though in parallel. There is still debate about the closeness of the connection between the two agreements and the evidence is inconclusive. When White and Morgenthau discussed this very matter on 18 October Morgenthau could neither remember whether he had linked the two

Stage II Lend-Lease and the Quebec Conference

issues together in talks with Cherwell nor whether he had reached a tacit agreement with him on Lend-Lease prior to the formal acceptance of the Morgenthau Plan. On both counts White, who generally had the more accurate recollection of things, was convinced that he had. The matter remained unresolved because Morgenthau was mainly concerned about whether or not he had told Stimson the truth when he reported that the Morgenthau Plan was signed before the Stage II Agreement, and as both he and White agreed that this was the case, they then stopped arguing about the relationship between the two agreements[25].

When Churchill put his needs to Roosevelt and Morgenthau on 14 September - the day after the Morgenthau Plan had been signed - there was an agreeable conversation in which, as Churchill put it, 'all our desires were met both on munitions and on non-munitions supplies'. Churchill suggested that it would be proper for Lend-Lease to continue at a level proportional to Britain's war mobilisation and Roosevelt was prepared to accept this, but Morgenthau intervened and suggested that they ought to work with actual figures. The British were suggesting $3½ billion and $3 billion for military and non-military supplies respectively and these were the base figures from which Morgenthau thought calculations ought to proceed. However, he commented that, 'The exact needs would have to be recalculated in the light of decisions on military matters reached at the conference', and the president agreed that this was the better course to take[26].

Roosevelt's willingness to give firm commitments to the British is surprising, seeing that he had told Hopkins that such commitments should not be made. He appears to have changed his mind, partly because of Britain's obvious need for help, and partly because of Churchill's persuasive pleas - at one point Churchill demanded to know if he was expected to beg like the President's dog, Fala, in order to get Lend-Lease help; also, according to Morgenthau, Roosevelt's main aim at Quebec was to sort out policy for Germany, and on this Churchill had been most accommodating[27]. Although there was no formal quid pro quo involved, Roosevelt must have felt some obligation to meet Churchill on Lend-Lease in the same spirit in which the Prime Minister had eventually accommodated him after the conversations between Cherwell and Morgenthau.

Stage II Lend-Lease and the Quebec Conference

With the substance of an agreement on Lend-Lease in Stage II having been made the Prime Minister turned the talks to Britain's export trade.

> if the United Kingdom was once more to pay its way [remarked Churchill] it was essential that the export trade, which had shrunk to a very small fraction, should be re-established. Naturally no articles obtained on Lend/Lease or identical thereto would be exported ['or sold for profit' was later added]; but it was essential that the United States should not attach any conditions to supplies delivered to Britain on Lend/Lease which would jeopardise the recovery of her export trade. The President thought this would be proper.[28]

After this the two leaders decided that an Anglo-American committee, chaired by Morgenthau, should hold discussions to decide how these broad guidelines were to be implemented and that until it reported there should be no change in Lend-Lease policy.

Given the context in which agreement was reached there is no doubt that the Americans meant to give the British considerably more freedom to export than they had done in the past, and that they had committed themselves to substantial Lend-Lease assistance for Britain to enable her to begin the reconversion of her economy. The British were delighted, but the reaction in Washington to the Stage II arrangements was very hostile.

Before the conference ended senior members of the administration were concerned about the proceedings at Quebec. Stimson was angry that Morgenthau and not Hull, the chairman of the German Committee, had been summoned to the conference to advise on Germany, and when news came through about the Lend-Lease talks Hull hastily sent Roosevelt a memorandum urging him to tell Churchill that any Lend-Lease in excess of requirements for the war against Japan would have to be conditional upon the, 'soundness of the economic policies adopted by Britain', but by then the agreement had already been reached. Also, Hull was livid when he discovered that no economic quid pro quo had been obtained from the British. At a tense meeting on 20 September at which Morgenthau gave a report about Quebec, Hull, with ill concealed bitterness, said that,

Stage II Lend-Lease and the Quebec Conference

> there were a number of matters with respect to commercial policy which we were trying to get from the British and which the British were running away from, and that they were delaying decisions on the lend-lease aid to Britain during Phase II in the hope of getting the other matters settled first. Now, however, the President had given away that bait.[29]

Morgenthau tried to put the best gloss on events that he could. In particular, he emphasised that the Morgenthau Plan had been signed prior to the Stage II Agreement to allay suspicions that he had traded his German Plan in return for what Hull viewed as a very unsatisfactory Lend-Lease accord (as we can see from earlier discussions in this chapter there was probably an element of duplicity in Morgenthau's account). He also explained how he had prevented the President from making even more generous commitments than had actually been made; later in the day he went so far as to tell FEA officials that Churchill knew that the President was, 'willing to give them the works'. Nevertheless, although Morgenthau was right insofar as he had managed to keep some discretion for the US, as Stimson commented, 'there may be some flexibility, but not much', and this view was shared by his deputy McCloy, and by officials in the State Department such as Breckinridge Long - at least for a while[30]. If the spirit of Quebec were carried out, and one should add that Morgenthau certainly intended to even though he had tried to make much of the flexibility he had retained for the Americans, then the British would get more or less what they had set out to get at Quebec. On the other hand, if the spirit of Quebec were not carried out, if a sufficiently powerful and persuasive coalition emerged in Washington capable of shifting the President's position on Lend-Lease, and capable of over-riding Morgenthau's influence, then it would be possible to manipulate the understandings reached at Quebec, both on exports and on the level of Lend-Lease help to Britain, to her detriment.

The British satisfaction with the agreement on Lend-Lease at Quebec although great was not without qualification. The Treasury was still worried that the Americans might reassert the marginal theory, and there was unease over export policy. Anderson wanted to proceed in an orderly and cautious way to ensure a successful follow-up to the achievements at

Stage II Lend-Lease and the Quebec Conference

Quebec. Instead of this Cherwell rushed head-long into talks with Morgenthau in Washington. Frank Lee, who was the secretary of the British negotiating team on Stage II, later reported that these talks were a shambles. Cherwell was under the delusion that given a few hours alone with Morgenthau that he could get $5 billion to $6 billion worth of Lend-Lease for Stage II, whereas, although Morgenthau was happy to countenance such figures, he wanted more details of Britain's economic position so that the Americans would know exactly what they were doing. After some cautions from Anderson and some misunderstanding between him and Cherwell the talks were suspended until the British supplied the Americans with more details of their economy and until Keynes arrived from London to give form and clear purpose to the discussions. Cherwell left Washington in a huff and embarked upon a 'scientific tour' of the US i.e. to find out about the progress on the development of the atom-bomb[31].

While the British were preparing for the Stage II discussions Morgenthau's position in Washington and the Commitment to Lend-Lease for Britain in Stage II came under attack.

Towards the end of September the Morgenthau Plan for Germany leaked to the press and it was roundly condemned. With a presidential election only weeks away, the plan was soon shelved by Roosevelt. On 3 October he said to Stimson that Morgenthau had 'pulled a boner' at Quebec, and during the following weeks Morgenthau was clearly in the political dog-house[32]. One consequence of this was that the State Department began to reassert its normal role in foreign policy, which meant that its criticisms of the Stage II Agreement became influential. By October Roosevelt was more receptive to such criticisms, possibly because he had regarded British support for the Morgenthau Plan as part of the quid pro quo for economic assistance, and as it had now been abandoned there were fewer grounds for keeping to the arrangements on Lend-Lease. However, there were other reasons why Roosevelt began to back away from the Quebec Agreement which are more firmly attested to by evidence.

The anger in the State Department over the Lend-Lease issue had not been assuaged by Morgenthau's account of the Quebec Conference. John Orchard in a series of memoranda for Stettinius reviewed the possibility of still asking the British

Stage II Lend-Lease and the Quebec Conference

for an economic quid pro quo; he concluded that it would be difficult, not only because of what had happened at Quebec, but also - and this was another source of friction between Morgenthau and Hull - because Morgenthau was trying to reserve the right to talk to the British about Lend-Lease to himself and to his department. The State Department began to think a little bit like the FEA had done in the past; on 21 September Stettinius told Roosevelt that commitments on Stage II Lend-Lease without restrictions on Britain's exports would be difficult to explain to Congress. On the following day Hull, bitter, disappointed and with his health failing rapidly, noted that the proposed extent of Lend-Lease for Britain in Stage II was far in excess of her war requirements and that it should therefore be conditional upon a British commitment to liberal trade policies. On 30 September he took the matter directly to Roosevelt and in the course of the conversation he handed the President a memorandum which advised that,

> we not proceed too rapidly with the implementation of plans for lend-lease aid in phase two beyond the direct strategic needs of the Pacific war until we are able to ascertain a little more clearly the attitude of the British on...commercial policy questions.[33]

Basically, he argued that it was no good giving Britain Lend-Lease and credits unless they could be sure that she would adopt the kind of open economic policies which would once again make her, 'the largest market for American goods'.

Having dealt with what he saw as the substance of the problem Hull approached Roosevelt again on 2 October to argue about jurisdictional matters. He told the President that Lend-Lease in Stage II involved such wide issues of foreign policy that the State Department ought to be given charge over the coming talks with the British. This was one of the last things Hull did as Secretary of State. October 2 1944 was his seventy-third birthday and he was now a frail man suffering from ill-health. He did not resign until after the presidential election, but from the beginning of October the reins of power were in the hands of Stettinius who eventually became the new Secretary of State when Hull formally left office. Roosevelt did not comply with Hull's request; Morgenthau continued as chairman of the US

Stage II Lend-Lease and the Quebec Conference

negotiating team for Stage II though he came under increasing pressure to cooperate closely with the State Department, the service departments and the FEA. For example, on 2 October Crowley wrote to him that, 'it might not be politic for us to supply six and one-half billion dollars worth of Lend-Lease' to Britain if the US contributed proportionally more of her production to the war against Japan than Britain did, and he suggested that the Treasury, the FEA and the State Department should get together to discuss this[34].

Hull and Crowley were not the only ones who opposed what Morgenthau had done at Quebec; Forrestal, Leahy and Somervell all thought that the understanding on Lend-Lease was a profound mistake. The influential War Department was also rumbling with discontent and by mid-October Undersecretary Patterson, McCloy and Stimson, while they all thought that the US ought to help Britain, they also believed it should be done by going through Congress. Stimson said that it would be a grave mistake to use Lend-Lease as the vehicle for helping Britain with her reconversion problems. At a Cabinet meeting on the 13 October he reiterated this view and, 'Crowley at once intervened and said that [that] was his opinion too'[35]. Thus by the time the talks with Keynes and Sir Robert Sinclair, the Chief Executive of the Ministry of Production and Keynes' deputy in the Washington discussions, got under way there had already been a major reaction within the American Government against the spirit and the substance of the understanding on Lend-Lease that Morgenthau had negotiated at Quebec. And although Morgenthau still wanted to uphold the commitments he had helped to give to the British at Quebec his prestige had been undermined because of the fiasco over his plan for Germany, and it was also now obious that the FEA, the State Department, and the service departments, all of which opposed the understanding on Lend-Lease, would have to be given an important say in the coming negotiations with the British.

There was one bright spot for Britain in the gloomy prospect for the Stage II discussions that was developing in Washington. At a meeting with State Department and FEA officials on 6 October Morgenthau told Acheson, Crowley, Currie and Cox that he did not, 'consider that the dollar balances are yardsticks any more' so far as the amount of Lend-Lease aid for Britain was concerned. He added that 'I think we might just as well have this

Stage II Lend-Lease and the Quebec Conference

straight from the beginning'. He told the meeting that this was the spirit in which he had talked with Churchill and Anderson in London, and that this was 'certainly the spirit in which Roosevelt had talked at Quebec'. He said that their job was now to rehabilitate the British financially. White was not happy about this, and Cox doubted whether they could do what Morgenthau wanted through Lend-Lease. Crowley surprisingly seemed to accept what Morgenthau said, but he then revealed his true colours by talking about Britain re-paying her Lend-Lease debts after the war. Even Harry White was incredulous at this and spluttered that he did not think that anyone actually expected Lend-Lease to be paid for. But, the hostile spirit towards the intent of the Quebec agreement aside, the important aspect of this meeting was Morgenthau's abandonment of the policy of restricting Britain's dollar reserves, and in the following weeks he was still influential enough to ensure that that policy was not actively pursued within the US Administration even though it was not entirely given up[36].

While political pressures in Washington were building up to push the administration away from the Quebec Agreement on Lend-Lease, in London it was becoming more imperative than ever for the government to gain the kind of economic help that Morgenthau had promised, and for it to reassert Britain's independence of action in the economic sphere. Apart from having to face up to Britain's enormous economic problems, Anderson, Dalton and Keynes also had to take account of a political storm that was brewing over Britain's economic relations with the US. There was widespread scepticism among the imperialists, among senior elements in the Conservative Party, and in the Labour Party about the efficacy of the liberal economic policies advocated by the Americans. The Bretton Woods Agreement on the IMF was under attack from powerful figures such as Beaverbrook and Robert Boothby; and squabbles with the US over meat supplies from Argentina, over civil aviation and telecommunication rights, and over oil concessions were seen in just as serious a light in London as they were in Washington. Finally, an explosive head of steam was building up concerning British export policy. Churchill and his government now regarded freedom to export as a top priority. The business community was extremely restless and by mid-August Dalton and

Stage II Lend-Lease and the Quebec Conference

the Board of Trade were thoroughly exasperated by the FEA's policy on British exports[37].

Even after taking all the above factors into account Britain's aims in the Washington Stage II Talks seem overly ambitious and aggressive until one takes into account what had happened to the British economy during the war. In August 1944 Anderson estimated that Britain's sterling liabilities by the end of the war would exceed $3½ billion - a figure which dwarfed her quick assets; around 400,000 houses had been bombed-out, and no new ones had been built for four years; civilian consumption of petrol and of consumer goods were 1½ per cent and 32 per cent respectively of their pre-war level; food was strictly rationed and Britain was still more highly mobilised for the war than was the US[38].

The British had four aims in the negotiations about the implementation of the Quebec Agreement on Lend-Lease. Firstly, they wanted the Americans to abandon their policy of trying to restrict the level of Britain's dollar reserves, and as we have seen from what Morgenthau said on 6 October they succeeded, at least temporarily, and we need say no more about this for the time being. Secondly, they wanted the Americans to put back items onto Lend-Lease and to add some new ones to it, particularly relating to housing construction, to help Britain's reserves because her main source of dollars was drying up as GIs moved on from the UK to Europe. Thirdly, they wanted large quantities of Lend-Lease to help with reconverting their economy, and finally they wanted as much freedom to export as possible.

By mid-October the British had given the Aemricans the break-down of their needs in Stage II. At a meeting on the 18th, after reading chapter three of the British document which was the section dealing with 'additional help' for Britain's reserves, even Morgenthau's determination to assist Britain wavered somewhat. 'This thing just bows me down' he wearily said. White commented irritably that, 'They are throwing in everything'. Among other things the British were asking for dollar relief on sugar imports and on aircraft contracts which they resurrected from pre-Lend-Lease days. Over the following weeks the US Air Force opposed re-opening the aircraft contracts and the FEA refused to re-include sugar into Lend-Lease supplies. A few items, notably to do with housing, were added onto Lend-Lease to give Britain 'extra help' with her reserves, but the amount involved was

Stage II Lend-Lease and the Quebec Conference

nowhere near that which the British had asked for, and in any case the supply of much of it was to be at the discretion of the US and was not in the form of firm commitments[39].

Britain's third aim, of gaining substantial amounts of Lend-Lease to help with the reconversion of her economy, occasioned more protracted discussions; however, at their conclusion, they seemed to have borne more fruit. By the time Keynes and Sinclair got to Washington it was clear to them that the Americans would not accept the idea of Lend-Lease continuing in proportion to Britain's level of war mobilisation. They tried instead to get the Americans to commit themselves to specific amounts of Lend-Lease for a specified period of time (i.e. for one year after the defeat of Germany), in the same way that they supplied the Soviet Union under the Lend-Lease protocol agreements. The purpose behind this was to prevent a return to the marginal theory. The Americans, led by the War Department opposed this suggestion. On 19 October Patterson said that it was, 'unthinkable that commitments already assumed by our own forces and necessary supply of these forces should be subordinated to firm commitments to satisfy British requirements'. Stimson went even further; he told Hopkins that he 'would follow the principle that the present Lend-Lease appropriations were intended as war aid to allies who were actually fighting for us and not for rehabilitation'[40].

At the second meeting of the Combined US/UK Lend-Lease Committee on 20 October Morgenthau told Keynes that,

> there was no disposition to question or depart from the Quebec agreement [sic]. But they found it difficult to agree in advance in the translation of the Quebec understanding into terms of concrete proposals as they appeared in the British document.

It is important to comment here that Morgenthau was not reneging on the Quebec agreement. He was angry about the requests for 'additional help' for Britain's reserves, and he remarked to White on 24 October that, 'what the British are asking us to do is almost impossible if we take their figures at face value', but unlike his Cabinet colleagues he still wanted to carry out the substance of the

Stage II Lend-Lease and the Quebec Conference

Quebec commitments in the spirit in which they had been made[41].

Despite British disappointment at their failure to achieve a Soviet-type protocol agreement, over the next three weeks good progress was made in the talks and on 13 November Morgenthau was able to report to Roosevelt that of the British request for $3.7 billion of military Lend-Lease $2.7 billion had been agreed upon and that agreement was imminent on civilian Lend-Lease; they soon in fact agreed to a figure of $2.8 billion[42].

On the surface it looked like the British had successfully followed up the Quebec understanding on Lend-Lease. Morgenthau had acted in good faith and he regarded the new figures as commitments to help Britain recover her economic well-being; however, the failure to make the 'agreement' as firm as the Soviet Lend-Lease protocol agreements left matters vulnerable to prevailing political pressures in Washington. We shall see later in this chapter that they undermined the status of the figures the British and the Americans 'agreed' on for Lend-Lease in Stage II even before the talks were completed.

The fourth aim that Keynes pursued in Washington proved to be the most troublesome. Brand and officials at the Board of Trade identified two factors that could interfere with their goal of achieving a clear break with the export restrictions that had been applied by the FEA and the US Army procurement people in the past. The first threat came from the 'scarce supply' restriction, and even though few items now had that designation in the US, there was always the danger of the FEA using it as an excuse for screening and delaying the delivery of supplies. The second factor was Churchill's agreement at Quebec not to export items identical to those received on Lend-Lease. The British were prepared to pay for their export freedom so far as the 'identical criterion' applied to civilian supplies, but they were worried that the Americans would also apply it to the vast range of military Lend-Lease items which could provide them with grounds for extensive screening of and interference with British exports. The British decided that the best course of action was to try to persuade the Americans to exclude military Lend-Lease entirely from exporting considerations, but if this was rejected then as a last resort they would agree to pay for those articles which could be transferred to civilian end use[43].

Stage II Lend-Lease and the Quebec Conference

At meetings on 25 and 27 October it looked as if the Americans were going to be accommodating. On the 27th White said that they would accept most of the British proposals: the only alteration they made was to change the date for relaxation of the export restrictions from 1 December 1944 to 1 January 1945, and the only reservation they expressed concerned Keynes' request that military Lend-Lease should be excluded from the application of the 'identical criterion', though even here Currie said that he would reconsider things[44].

There now followed a lull in the discussions, partly caused by the presidential election, which lasted until mid-November. During this period there was a reaction in the FEA against relaxing the export restrictions, and pressures in Washington from the service departments, the military, the State Department and the FEA not to use Lend-Lease to help Britain with her reconversion and postwar economic problems continued to rise.

At an Executive Policy Committee meeting in the FEA on 15 November Crowley said that he would recommend no change in export policy, no publicity and no announcement until the President had considered things. The following day Cox pointed out to State Department and Treasury officials that there might be domestic political difficulties if British export restrictions were relaxed before the defeat of Germany. Morgenthau, unaware that this was the thin end of the wedge, said that the President would probably agree with Cox. It was then tentatively decided, despite a protest from Acheson, that VE-day should be the starting date for the new arrangements on exports. The decision was not final: the matter was debated further some days later, but no mention of this possible new starting date was made to the British[45].

Although the State Department supported export freedom for Britain there was much ill feeling there over other economic matters. There was general unhappiness in the department about Britain's refusal to enter talks under the auspices of article seven of the Mutual Aid Agreement, and also there were specific problems over both civil aviation rights and Britain's policy of entering long-term meat contracts with Argentina. The former issue involved American attempts to gain entry into the air routes of the British Empire, which the British were resisting for fear of an American postwar monopoly of civil aviation; and the latter involved America's desire to reduce Britain's economic

Stage II Lend-Lease and the Quebec Conference

eminence in Argentina and her tacit support for the anti-US regime there. At different times both Hull and Hickerson, the head of the State Department's British Commonwealth Division, suggested using Lend-Lease as a lever to get Britain to cooperate with the US over Argentina. These areas of Anglo-American dispute eventually affected Roosevelt's attitudes towards Britain, but the more immediate effect was a last attempt by the State Department to get an economic quid pro quo from the British for Lend-Lease in Stage II. The British were asked to liberalise the Sterling Area dollar pool but Keynes staunchly refused. On 15 November he told Currie that, 'he was not prepared to enter into any sort of bargain on this point as part of the present discussions' and he stuck to his guns. The British made no commitments on economic policy to the State Department during the Washington talks[46].

The day after Keynes told Currie that he would not consider modifying the dollar pool Anderson, Eden, Dalton and Llewellin, now Minister of Food, wrote to the British delegation in Washington complaining about the lack of progress on export policy. They told Keynes that a debate on the matter in the House of Commons could be put off to no later than 29 November. In response to this timetable pressure the pace of the talks accelerated, but much of the movement was contrary to British interests. On 17 November Currie told Keynes that although the FEA would waive consideration of many military items it was not willing to exclude them from the consideration of export policy. This was a disappointment because it meant that Keynes was not going to achieve the clear break with the existing policy of screening which he had hoped for. Nevertheless, the British were glad that things seemed to be moving: they were unaware of the possibility that the Americans were going to postpone the relaxation of export restrictions to VE-day, and they did not realise that a major shift in Roosevelt's attitude towards Lend-Lease in Stage II was taking place[47].

We have already noted the extensive opposition in the US Administration to the Quebec understanding on Lend-Lease: Morgenthau's report on 13 November to Roosevelt concerning agreement in the Washington talks on $5.5 billion of Lend-Lease assistance for Britain in the first year of Stage II sparked off renewed objections, which led to a series of conferences at the White House. One of the firmest

Stage II Lend-Lease and the Quebec Conference

and most influential of the voices in these conferences belonged to Admiral Leahy, who said that Congress would react violently to the amounts of Lend-Lease being suggested by Morgenthau and Keynes. With Crowley and Stimson also having expressed opposition in the Cabinet to using Lend-Lease to help Britain with her reconversion and postwar difficulties, and in the light of arguments from the State Department that the US needed leverage to push Britain into economic policies which were compatible with the interests of the US, Roosevelt decided to withdraw from the position that he had adopted at Quebec[48].

On 18 November Roosevelt told Leahy that he wanted Lend-Lease to Great Britain to be conducted as heretofore and that, 'additional commitments should not be made'. This statement coincided with disputes over Argentine meat contracts and over civil aviation rights with the British coming to a head. In a letter to Churchill the President expressed his concern and said that he thought it would be 'disastrous' if Britain entered new long-term meat contracts with Argentina. The letter originally ended by referring to the Stage II Lend-Lease talks which had the threatening implication that Churchill ought to do as he was bid if he wanted economic help, but it was deleted before the letter was sent. A few days later Roosevelt had no such compunction about wielding Lend-Lease as a weapon to try to get British compliance with American civil aviation policy then under discussion at an international conference at Chicago. 'We are doing our best to meet your lend-lease needs', he duplitiously wrote, and continued, 'We will face Congress on that subject in a few weeks and it will not be in a generous mood if it and the people feel that the United Kingdom has not agreed to a generally beneficial agreement.' The State Department, the dispute over Argentine meat contracts and the difficulties with Britain over civil aviation rights, all helped to convince Roosevelt of the need for economic leverage to help to persuade the British to fall in line with America's foreign economic policy[49].

After a meeting at the White House on 21 November, in which Leahy successfully recommended to Roosevelt that no formal commitments whatsoever should be given to the British, Morgenthau reported to the American Steering Committee on the Stage II talks that the President,

Stage II Lend-Lease and the Quebec Conference

> doesn't want to give anything to the British, he doesn't want any publicity, he wants to be able to tell the newspapers that there was no agreement; and simply that this [i.e. the outcome of the Keynes/Morgenthau talks] was a recommendation to him, and he can take it into consideration. But he wants to be able to say there was no agreement.[50]

On the following day Stettinius, Crowley and Morgenthau agreed that there should be no formal agreement with the British. This meant that the status of the $5.5 billion figure for Lend-Lease for Britain in the first year of Stage II could now be whatever the Americans decided it should be which, given the prevailing view in Washington, did not augur well for Britain's reconversion plans. Pitted against the State Department, the FEA, the military, the service departments, and now Roosevelt, Morgenthau could not hope to sustain the spirit of Quebec.

At the same meeting on 22 November, after they had agreed that there would be no formal agreement with the British, Stettinius raised the question of export policy. Both he and Acheson still wanted to be more forthcoming than Crowley about the British request for export freedom. As we have seen they were angry that Britain had not entered economic planning talks with them and they still feared that she might continue with economic restrictions after the war. However, if they could persuade her to adopt liberal economic policies - and they were more determined than ever to do so - it would be to no purpose if Britain's economy was a total wreck. And so they pressed Crowley to ease the export restrictions; Stettinius introduced the issue by asking Crowley to explain the British position. He responded that they wanted to renew their export trade and to, 're-export in any form they liked' any items that they could, 'get from us for cash'. '"can't we agree to that?"' asked Stettinius. '"I don't see how we can"', replied Crowley stubbornly. By now Morgenthau was feeling distinctly uneasy about what his colleagues were doing to the Quebec accords and he read out the record of the conversation between Roosevelt and Churchill in which the President had agreed that no impediments should be placed in the way of the recovery of Britain's export trade. White asked him if he wanted to repeat that the President had also said

Stage II Lend-Lease and the Quebec Conference

that, 'he thought he had gone too far' at Quebec. Morgenthau said that he was simply going back to the record to which White responded that there was no problem because Churchill had been referring to Stage II and that that was when they were going to ease the export restrictions. Stettinius commented that this was probably the 'only way to salvage themselves'. He obviously thought that the spirit of the Quebec Talks was being contravened because at the time Churchill and Roosevelt thought that VE-day was not far away whereas the subsequent stiffening of German resistance now made VE-day look more distant, but that did not alter the fact that Britain needed immediate relief from her export restrictions which was what the two leaders had intended to do at Quebec. Crowley unctuously observed that both the US and the UK would begin to expand their commercial exports at the same time, that was to say VE-day, and 'So it puts us all on an even basis'. If it were not for a lack of sensitivity on the part of Crowley to what had happened to the British economy in the previous six years this would sound like a piece of calcualted black humour[51].

This was basically the end of the matter. Later that day Keynes was told about what had been decided by the Americans on export policy: he was angry. He said that,

> The suggestion that such arrangements should not come into effect until V.E.-day - a suggestion which the UK group had heard for the first time - would come as a surprise for ministers in London.

Nevertheless, the British had no option but to accept the American decision. Crowley made a cosmetic concession, offering to give the British some administrative relief on export restrictions between then and VE-day (on past experience the British could expect little from this), but more importantly the State Department persuaded him to give the British the option - which they promptly exercised - of paying for raw materials and manufactured items as of 1 January 1945, which they had previously received on Lend-Lease. This released a large number of items from export restrictions, but what remained were to continue under existing controls until VE-day[52].

On 30 November simultaneous announcements about the Stage II discussions were made in London and

Stage II Lend-Lease and the Quebec Conference

Washington. There was considerable controversy at the last minute over the announcement that the British were proposing to make. Cox and Crowley, despite the way they had modified the substance and the spirit of the Quebec Talks, were still worried that the British were going to emphasise their intention to renew exporting too much. In the end their statement was toned down, and Crowley's press release about the talks made it clear just how conditional the resulting recommendation was on Lend-Lease for Stage II.

> The amounts and types of supplies required continue to be subject, as always to adjustments from time to time in accordance with the changing conditions of the war.

It was as if the Quebec conversations had never been[53].

NOTES

1. Anderson to Halifax, 10 June 1944, T160/1418/F17660/072/5.
2. Note of a meeting between Anderson and Morgenthau, 11 Aug. 1944, UE765/5/71, FO371/41014.
3. See: FO to Washington, 13 Aug. 1944, T160/1418/F17660/072/5.
4. H.M. Diary, 765, pp.107-108, conversation between Morgenthau and Brand, 24 Aug. 1944; Morgenthau to Roosevelt, 19 Aug. 1944, Roosevelt OF, box 5577.
5. See: FO to Washington, 13 Aug. 1944 and the reply on 15 Aug., T160/1418/F17660/072/5.
6. Winant to Hull, 15 July 1944, 840.50/7-1544.
7. Memo.'s by Orchard, 15 July, 9 and 15 Aug. 1944, H. S. Truman Library, Clayton Papers: Reading Folder.
8. See: Hull to Winant, 15 Sept. 1944, 840.50/8-1144; and memo. by Hull, 8 Sept. 1944, Roosevelt PSF, box 94, folder: Hull.
9. Lubin to Hopkins, 4 Aug. 1944, Hopkins Papers, box 335, folder: England and Lend-Lease in Phase II.
10. See: British memo. 14 Aug. 1944; and memo. of conversation between Hopkins and Roosevelt, 18 Aug. 1944, ibid.

Stage II Lend-Lease and the Quebec Conference

11. Hopkins to Churchill, 19 Aug. 1944, ibid; Hull to Churchill and Anderson, 20 Aug. 1944, UE823/5/71, F0371/41014.
12. See: Churchill to Hopkins and his reply both dated 23 Aug. 1944, Hopkins Papers, box 332, folder: Second Quebec Conference; and editorial comment in W. F. Kimball, Churchill and Roosevelt: The Complete Correspondence 3 Vols. (Princeton University Press, New Jersey, 1984), Vol. III, p.316.
13. Churchill to Hopkins, 26 Aug. 1944, Hopkins Papers, box 332, folder: Second Quebec Conference; Churchill to Roosevelt, 12 Sept. 1944, Roosevelt PSF, box 176.
14. See: Hopkins to Roosevelt, 8 Sept. 1944, Hopkins Papers, box 332, folder: Second Quebec Conference; and memo. 'Lend-Lease Supplies for Britain in Stage II: Note for the President of the United States of America' from Churchill via Hopkins, 4 Sept. 1944, ibid.
15. See: memo. by Somervell, 'Lend-Lease Policy After the Defeat of Germany', 7 Sept. 1944, Hopkins Papers, box 335, folder: England and Lend-Lease in Phase II; and Hopkins to Leahy, 7 Sept. 1944, ibid.
16. See R. M. Hathaway, Ambiguous Partnership: Britain and America 1944-47 (Columbia University Press, New York, 1981), p.61, footnote 15. King was also notoriously anti-British.
17. Stimson Diary, 31 July, 5 Sept. H.S. Truman Library, Stimson Diary Microfilm.
18. See: Wickard Diary, entry 5 to 7 Sept. 1944, Wickard Papers; H.M. Diary, 771, pp.43-44, 25 Aug. 1944; W. Millis (Ed.), The Forrestal Diaries (Viking Press, New York, 1951), p.10.
19. Wickard Diary, entry 5 to 7 Sept.1944, Wickard Papers; H.M. Diary, 771, pp.43-44, 25 Aug. 1944; Stimson Diary, 24 Aug. and 5 Sept. 1944.
20. See: Stimson Diary, 6, 9 and 20 Sept. 1944.
21. See H.M. Diary, 773, p.5, minutes of a meeting in Hull's office 20 Sept. 1944.
22. Churchill to Attlee, Anderson and War Cabinet, 15 Sept. 1944, T160/1418/F17660/072/5; W. S. Churchill, Triumph and Tragedy (Cassell, London 1953), pp.138-139.
23. Stimson Diary, 20 Sept. 1944.
24. Ibid; and H.M. Diary, 773, p.4, minutes of meeting in Hull's office 20 Sept. 1944.
25. See: H.M. Diary, 783, pp.36-39, 18 Oct. 1944; D. Rees, Harry Dexter White: A Study In Paradox (Macmillan, London, 1973), pp.269-274; Hathaway, Ambiguous Partnership, pp.62-66; C. Thorne, Allies of a Kind: The United States, Britain

Stage II Lend-Lease and the Quebec Conference

and the War Against Japan 1941-45 (Hamish Hamilton, London, 1978), pp.388-390; R. Dalleck, Franklin Roosevelt and American Foreign Policy 1932-1945 (Oxford University Press, New York, 1979), pp.474-477.

26. 'Agreed Record of Conversation Between the Prime Minister and the President', 14 Sept. 1944, CAB 78.
27. H.M. Diary, 773, p.5, minutes of meeting in Hull's office, 20 Sept. 1944.
28. 'Agreed Record of Conversation Between the Prime Minister and the President', 14 Sept. 1944.
29. H.M. Diary, 773, p.6, minutes of meeting in Hull's office, 20 Sept. 1944.
30. See ibid, pp.2-3 and p.40; ibid. 772, pp.208-210, 'Report On Quebec Conference', for Treasury officials, 19 Sept. 1944; Stimson Diary, 20 Sept. 1944, notes by McCloy on the Second Quebec Conference; Breckinridge Long Desk Diary, 26 and 29 Sept. and 18 Oct. 1944, Long Papers, box 5.
31. See: Sinclair to Weeks, 18 Sept. 1944, Anderson to Cherwell, 19 and 25 Sept. 1944, T160/1418/F17660/072/5; Lee to Harmer, 6 Dec. 1944, T160/1375/F17942/010/6.
32. Stimson Diary, 3 Oct. 1944, and 29 March 1945.
33. See: Orchard to Stettinius, 26 and 30 Sept. and 7 Oct. 1944, Clayton Papers, Reading Folder; Stettinius Calendar Notes, 21 Sept. 1944, University of Virginia, Stettinius Papers; memo. of meeting in Hull's office, 22 Sept. 1944, Clayton Papers, box 5, folder: Phase II Lend-Lease Agreements between US and GB; Hull memo. for Roosevelt, 30 Sept. 1944, Roosevelt PSF, box 94, folder: Hull.
34. See Hull to Roosevelt, 2 Oct. 1944, ibid; H.M. Diary, 778, p.32, Crowley to Morgenthau, 2 Oct. 1944.
35. See: Stimson Diary, 9 and 13 Oct. 1944; and Stettinius to Acheson, 27 Oct. 1944, Stettinius Papers, US File.
36. H.M.Diary, 780, pp.1-13, 6 Oct. 1944.
37. See: A. J. P. Taylor, Beaverbrook (Hamish Hamilton, London, 1972), pp.556-563; The Earl of Birkenhead, The Prof. in Two Worlds - The Official Life of F. A. Lindemann Viscount Cherwell (Collins, London, 1961), pp.266-267; M. B. Stoff, Oil, War, and American Security: The Search for a National Policy on Foreign Oil, 1941-47 (Yale University Press, New Haven, 1980), Chapter 5; J. A. De Novo, 'The Culbertson Economic Mission and Anglo-American Tension in the Middle East 1944-45', Journal of

Stage II Lend-Lease and the Quebec Conference

American History, 63, 4 (1977) pp.913-936; A. P. Dobson, The Other Air Battle: The American Pursuit of Post-War Civil Aviation Rights, The Historical Journal, 28, 2 (1985) pp.429-439; and Board of Trade to Washington, 19 Aug. 1944, UE714/5/71, F0371/41014.

38. H.M. Diary, 773, pp.53-73, 20 Sept. 1944.

39. See: ibid, 783, pp.23-26, 18 Oct. 1944, 795, pp.244-267, 16 Nov. 1944; and 'Report on Deliberations of Joint Committee', 2 Feb. 1944, WP(45)77, CAB 66.

40. See: Patterson memo. 19 Oct. 1944, Clayton Papers: Office Files Assistant Secretary of State and Undersecretary of State for Economic Affairs, folder: Phase II Lend-Lease agreement US/GB; Stimson Diary, 19 Oct. 1944.

41. Minutes of Combined Committee, 20 Oct.1944; and H.M. Diary, 785, pp.139-140, 24 Oct. 1944.

42. H.M. Diary, 794, pp.79-80, 'Report to the President', 13 Nov. 1944.

43. Note by Helmore, 'Points of Interpretation on the Quebec Conversations Relating to Exports', and Brand to Self, 30 Sept. 1944, UE1554/5/71, F0371/41016.

44. Minutes of Combined Sub-Committee on Mutual Lend-Lease Aid Between US and UK, 25 and 27 Oct. 1944, CAB 78.

45. See: minutes of EPC meeting 15 Nov. 1944, Paul Papers, box 1, folder: FEA, EPC meetings; H.M. Diary, 795, pp.218-223, 16 Nov. 1943; and State Department memo. of conversation, 16 Nov. 1944, 841.24/10-1644.

46. See: Hull memo. for Roosevelt, 30 Sept. 1944, Roosevelt PSF, box 94, folder: Hull; memo. by Hickerson, 2 Nov. 1944, 841.24/11-244; and minutes of Combined Sub-Committee 15 and 17 Nov. 1944, CAB 78.

47. See: Dalton, Anderson, Eden and Llewellin to Keynes, 16 Nov. 1944, UE2186/5/71; and minutes of Combined Sub-Committee, 17 Nov. 1944, CAB 78.

48. W. D. Leahy, I Was There (Victor Gollanz, London, 1950), p.328.

49. Ibid. pp.328-329; Kimball, Correspondence, Vol.III, pp.397 and 407, Roosevelt to Churchill, 18 and 24 Nov. 1944.

50. See: Leahy, I Was There, p.328; H.M. Diary, 797, pp.166-207, 21 Nov. 1944; and Stettinius Calendar Notes, 21 Nov. 1944, Stettinius Papers.

51. H.M. Diary, 798, pp.24-49, 22 Nov. 1944.

Stage II Lend-Lease and the Quebec Conference

52. See: ibid; minutes of Combined Committee, 22 Nov. 1944, CAB 78; and 'Report on Deliberations of Joint Committee', 2 Feb. 1944, CAB 66.
53. See Cox to Hopkins, 27 Nov. 1944; and the press release signed by Crowley, Stettinius and Morgenthau, 30 Nov. 1944, both at Cox Papers, box 150, Diary.

Chapter Eight

CONCLUSION

Keynes' account of the talks about Stage II and the subsequent report of Anderson and Lyttleton to the War Cabinet about them were both quite optimistic and self-satisfied in tone. On the face of things the British had done well: the Americans seemed to have abandoned their policy of restricting the size of Britain's dollar reserves; some extra items were to be included in Lend-Lease supplies; a considerable amount of freedom to export had been won though Crowley 'had worsted' Keynes in the battle over its starting date; and the handsome figure of $5.5 billion had been agreed upon for Britain's Lend-Lease needs in the first year of Stage II. Keynes mentioned in his report some of the difficulties his team had experienced, particularly with Crowley whom he described as having his ear, 'so near the ground that he was out of range of persons speaking from an erect position', but he thought the talks had gone well, and that they had got more than they could reasonably have expected[1].

Frank Lee was more cautious than Keynes in his assessment of the talks, and he was rather bitter about the way the FEA had obstructed the British aim of achieving a clean break with existing export controls; he commented in connection with this that Cox, 'has again shown that he is willing to subordinate any question of principle to political expediency'. Lee was also worried about the format that the outcome of the talks had taken and he thought that while Crowley and Currie were in charge of the FEA that there would always be the possibility of problems arising from the implementation of the 'understanding' on Stage II[2].

Conclusion

Neither Keynes nor Lee, however, were aware of Roosevelt's crucial change of intention during November, and even Lee's caution did not therefore begin to do justice to the dangers which now confronted the British.

At Quebec an understanding had been reached, in accordance with British desires, that Britain should receive sufficient Lend-Lease in Stage II to help her with her reconversion problems. Morgenthau had explained to Treasury, State Department and FEA officials on his return to Washington that the job in hand was to rehabilitate Britain financially; the policy of limiting her reserves was to be abandoned, and the factors for assessing her Lend-Lease requirements were to include what she needed to begin reconverting her economy to peacetime production and rebuilding her export trade, as well as her contribution to the war against Japan. By the end of November everyone concerned in the US Cabinet, with the exception of Morgenthau, had rejected that understanding. As a result there was no formal agreement at the end of the discussions between Keynes and Morgenthau, and, although the figure of $5.5 billion was notionally agreed upon, if Keynes had been aware of how things were regarded by Roosevelt, Leahy, the FEA and the military side of Lend-Lease he would have realised just how tentative and conditional that figure was, and he would presumably have been less fulsome in praise of his achievements to Anderson.

The pattern for the remaining months of the operation of Lend-Lease was set by the beginning of December 1944, and the rest of this story is mainly to do with the way that that pattern manifested itself in denying Britain the help for her reconversion plans which she had been led to expect in the talks at Quebec.

The US Chiefs of Staff, the military side of Lend-Lease under Somervell and their political spokesmen Leahy and Stimson, took the lead in restricting Lend-Lease supplies to Britain. The army was particularly assertive and parsimonious. In September 1944 US Army representatives in London had even suggested that the British should maintain their then existing level of war production for the war against Japan at a time when a forty per cent reduction in US military production was being announced; and while this was one of the army's more extreme views, we have seen from looking at Somvervell's ideas about Stage II that it was not all that untypical[3]. The inclination to be

Conclusion

miserly with military Lend-Lease was given a boost by the German offensive in the Ardennes from 16 December 1944 to 5 January 1945. On 3 March Stimson recorded in notes for a conference with the President that the War Department faced, 'a complete revision of our procurement and production problem which brought about a situation almost like that which confronted us at the beginning of the war in its complexity and difficulty'[4]. There were problems but they were conveniently exaggerated to explain and to justify why Britain had not received the amount of military supplies that she had been led to expect. The Ardennes Offensive also had the effect of prolonging the war in Europe, thus delaying for Britain the clean break with export controls, and it also of course reduced the period of Stage II - though not as much, or as dramatically, as the atom-bomb was to do afterwards.

On the civilian side of Lend-Lease Crowley and the FEA moved with deliberation and caution: there was no evidence of 'the spirit of Quebec' existing there.

In the State Department William Clayton, recently arrived from the Department of Commerce, became Undersecretary of State in charge of foreign economic policy. He was a conservative, a Texas businessman, and an Anglophile, and also a worthy successor to Hull for carrying the banner of free-trade. In late 1944 Harry Hawkins had been sent to London to resuscitate economic planning talks with the British and he had had some measure of success. Clayton was immediately interested by this and soon his position on Anglo-American economic relations was virtually identical to the one that Hull had had. Clayton wanted to help Britain to the extent of enabling her to enter a free postwar international economy. He did not want to go to the extent of fulfilling the Quebec commitments because he wanted to strike a balance, much as Hull had wanted to do, between keeping the British economy viable for development and for entry into a liberal economic system and preventing her from becoming economically strong enough to defy American wishes. He adopted a sort of mid-way position on Lend-Lease between Morgenthau and the hard-liners.

The death of Roosevelt on 12 April is seen by some as a turning point in the story of America's failure to live up to its commitements on Lend-Lease in Stage II, but it was only a factor which accelerated a well established trend. The new

Conclusion

president Harry Truman was closely attuned to Congress: earlier in the war as a senator he had led an investigation into the financial conduct of the war, and just before succeeding to the presidency he had cast a deciding vote as chairman of the Senate on a bill which prohibited the use of Lend-Lease for rehabilitation purposes. His natural inclination therefore was to use Lend-Lease only for war purposes, and the fact that Roosevelt was dead made it easier for the personal agreement he had made with Churchill at Quebec, concerning its use for reconversion purposes, to be put aside. This was, however, a continuation of existing policy, though it was reinforced both by advisers who had been influential with Roosevelt such as Leahy, who soon became a key adviser to Truman, and by men that Truman himself chose to work closely with, such as James Byrnes the Director of War Mobilisation, who took over from Stettinius as Secretary of State on 1 July, and with Crowley, at least in the early days of his presidency. Fred Vinson of the Office of War Mobilisation also worked closely with Truman and took over the US Treasury after Morgenthau's resignation on 5 July. He sided with Clayton in taking a more generous attitude on Lend-Lease, but the hard-liners' attitude was more influential and more in tune with Truman's own disposition.

In April with victory in Europe in sight Crowley and the US Army began to reduce Lend-Lease supplies to Britain. Truman fully approved of such steps; he told the Director of the Budget Harold Smith, who was pressing for tighter controls over government spending, that the use of Lend-Lease for postwar rehabilitation purposes would expose them to the possibility of a lot of trouble with Congress. The following day Lyttleton handed an aide memoire to Harry Hopkins which disclosed what the British thought of America's present policy on Lend-Lease; it stated that they, 'were very disturbed about the present working of the Combined Munitions Assignment Board' which was denying British requests for military supplies. After VE-day, 8 May, there was a further sharp cut-back in Lend-Lease and protests were made by Brand and British Army officials to Fred Vinson and Morgenthau. They claimed that they were being denied munitions which they were entitled to under the accord which had been worked out at Quebec and in the subsequent talks in Washington[5]. Finally matters were regarded so seriously in London that Churchill wrote personally to Truman on 28 May.

Conclusion

'I am distressed to have to bother you with this', he wrote, but,

> I now hear that your War Department has told our people in Washington that they are expecting so large a cut in their forthcoming appropriations for United States Air Corps that supplies to us must be drastically curtailed below schedule of our requirements as agreed last Autumn...I hope your people can be told that principles your predecessor and I agreed at Quebec still stand and in particular that appropriations given your War Department will be enough to provide for our needs as finally worked out between us.[6]

Unfortunately for Churchill it was becoming increasingly unlikely that these requests would be met, though Morgenthau made one last attempt.

He was angry about the way the British were being treated and wrote to Truman explaining that they had queried the American interpretation of the understanding on Lend-Lease for Stage II on several occasions, but that there was no authoritative body in Washington to which they could appeal: he wanted to revive the Lend-Lease Committee that he had chaired in the talks during November 1944 to sort things out. A State Department memorandum recorded that, 'He feels strongly that this matter is being handled badly,...Mr. Morgenthau feels that we are going back on firm commitments made at Quebec'. The memorandum continued that he had told the President this, but that he would now take no further action unless the President approached him or took a firm decision on Lend-Lease. Relations between Truman and Morgenthau were less than cordial[7].

Clayton also had some sympathy for the British in their protests about Lend-Lease, and he drafted a reply to Churchill for Truman which reaffirmed the US commitment to supplying Britain, 'in accordance with the schedules...worked out...in October and November 1944'; but, although he wanted to be more generous with Lend-Lease than others we shall consider in a moment, he re-opened the question of the size of the British dollar balances, and suggested Britain should reduce them by undertaking to pay dollars for various items and services she received under Lend-Lease. In April Clayton had received a paper from Lauchlin Currie, who was in

Conclusion

London taking part in economic talks, which reported optimistically on Britain's balance of payment problem and on her employment prospects, and as Clayton did not want Britain to gain too much economic strength he was not prepared to carry out America's commitments to her on Lend-Lease Stage II to the extent that Morgenthau was. His draft letter was ratified by everybody in Washington concerned with Lend-Lease, with the notable exception of Morgenthau; however, it was not sent because of opposition from Leahy who wanted to restrict Lend-Lease to the direct prosecution of the war against Japan[8].

Crowley also supported this restrictive use of Lend-Lease. In a memorandum of 28 May E. D. Mckin, the Chief Administrative Assistant to the President, reporting on Morgenthau's wish to revive the November 1944 Lend-Lease Committee stated that Crowley opposed this because he thought these matters now to be the concern of the FEA and the army side of Lend-Lease supply. He went on to report that Crowley said that the British were, 'running to Morganthau [sic] to get things which he and the War Department had denied them'[9]. In the following weeks, although Morgenthau remained in the background, the moderates on Lend-Lease such as Clayton and Fred Vinson were involved in lengthy and occasionally heated arguments with the hard-liners - on one occasion Leahy walked out of a meeting after Vinson had had the temerity to suggest that he had no business advising the President about Lend-Lease - and in the meantime Lend-Lease continued to decrease and the British had to wait in exasperation and in impatience for the outcome.

At a meeting of his EPC on 7 June Crowley said that he wanted Lend-Lease to remain fluid and at the agency's administrative discretion. He told those present that there had never been any firm commitments given to the British about specific amounts of Lend-Lease and that they should be careful that the British did not build up their dollar balances too much: Crowley still adhered to the marginal theory[10].

On 16 June US Major General Crain of the London Munitions Assignment Board wrote to Somervell about talks he had had with the British about Stage II Lend-Lease, and he more or less gave the green light for further reductions of supplies for Britain by saying that, 'The British desire above all else continuance of friendship between the United States and the British Empire and will accept

Conclusion

philosophically the decision of the President as to the extent lend-lease will be given in the future'[11].

On 5 July the debate on Lend-Lease in Washington ended in victory for Leahy and Crowley. Truman issued a directive stating that Lend-Lease was to be restricted to that, 'which is to be used in the war against Japan, and it will not be used for any other purpose'. Stimson drily observed that this could be construed by the British as a breach of the commitments the US had made to Britain on Lend-Lease[12]. Rather fittingly Morgenthau had chosen 5 July to submit his resignation: he was an honourable man and he felt that the agreements that he and Roosevelt had made with the British at Quebec had been broken; it was not solely because of this that he resigned - he did not get on with Truman and he was unhappy about his views on Germany - but it was a major factor.

Two weeks later Churchill, Truman and Stalin met at Potsdam. At the conference Churchill tried to get Truman to alter his directive of 5 July so as to give Britain more Lend-Lease, but Truman was evasive. He raised the matter of the increase in Britain's dollar reserves which Clayton had indicated in his draft of a reply to Churchill's letter of 28 May, and he mentioned the legal and congressional difficulties involved in using Lend-Lease in the way Churchill wanted. On 25 July Truman did promise to help Britain and to give a more liberal construction to his directive of 5 July, but after Attlee had replaced Churchill at Potsdam, having defeated him in the general election, he discovered that the new directive prepared by Clayton and McCloy gave only small amounts of extra Lend-Lease help to Britain[13]. The British were intensely angry at the abandonment of the understanding that had been reached at Quebec and which, so they thought at the time, had been successfully built upon during the November talks in Washington. To make matters worse the fickleness of fate was about to match that of the Americans.

While the meeting at Potsdam had been in session Truman received news of the successful exploding of the atom-bomb. Stage II, envisaged at Quebec as lasting between fifteen months to two years, was about to be abruptly curtailed.

On 6 and 9 August Hiroshima and Nagasaki were devastated in turn by atom-bombs and on 14 August the Japanese Empire surrendered. Provisions for cutting off Lend-Lease were well in hand, and

Conclusion

Crowley intended to do it as quickly and as cleanly as possible. Roger Tubby one of Crowley's assistants originally drew up an announcement in which he, 'recalled the tremendous job that Lend-Lease had done during the war and indicated that there would probably be some follow-up measures taken to carry on the general thrust of Lend-Lease'. Crowley told him that, 'This isn't what I want at all. I just want a short brief statement indicating that Lend-Lease is to be terminated forthwith'. And initially, that is precisely what happened[14].

Subsequently the order terminating Lend-Lease was slightly modified, largely through the efforts of Clayton, to allow delivery of goods in the pipe-line providing recipients agreed to pay for them. Even then, however, Crowley tried to railroad the British into accepting terms for these supplies. On 1 September Attlee protested to Truman;

> You are aware that in the immediate future the maintenance of the physical flow of supplies from the United States, both of food and of certain essential raw materials is necessary for the maintenance of the living conditions of this country...
> It is impossible for our Government to give an answer to the proposals of the Foreign Economic Administration within a matter of a few hours, and you will not misunderstand me if I say that the preparation of a suitable answer would not be made easier for me by knowledge that instructions had been given to suspend the loading of supplies from the United States.

On 6 September Truman replied to Attlee that pipeline supplies would continue for a month simultaneously with the negotiation of terms. This gave Britain some relief but it was a saddening end to what Churchill had originally described as a 'most unsordid act'[15].

. . .

In March 1941 the British economy had been unable to provide the means to withstand the armed threat from Germany and Italy, and she had insufficient dollars to buy what she required from the US. In September 1945 Britain's economy was

Conclusion

unable to meet her civilian needs, and she had insufficient dollars to buy what she required from the US. In 1941 she had been vulnerable to armed attack because of her economic weakness; in 1945 she was vulnerable to unpalatable economic demands from the Americans for the same reason.

Lend-Lease helped Britain to hold the line against the Axis in North Africa and on the English Channel, and while she never had to pay cash for it, she still incurred costs. The consideration in article seven of the Mutual Aid Agreement commitided Britain to economic cooperation with the US and to the pursuit of a freer world economy. Those payments, which had been studiously avoided for most of the war (at least so the Americans thought), were now to be collected. Unfortunately, some of the consequences of Lend-Lease made those payments burdensome, difficult and dangerous for the British.

Lend-Lease had enabled the British economy to achieve a higher degree of conversion to war production than any other country with the possible exception of the Soviet Union. This helped to save Britain and benefited the Allies in general, but it also stored up enormous reconversion problems for the future and helped to shift Britain away from the market-economy which the Americans so dearly wanted Britain to re-embrace at the end of the war. Britain's export markets were largely abandoned for the sake of war production and to prevent unfair competition with the US through the use of Lend-Lease in connection with her overseas trade. Her reserves, depleted because of war expenditures, were inhibited from growing too much, once they began to recover in 1942, through a deliberate policy of the US Government which was motivated by the letter of the Lend-Lease Act and by broad economic considerations, including postwar policies.

Both countries suspected each others' motives and manoeuvred to safeguard their economic interests. The British broke the spirit and the substance of the Mutual Aid Agreement by not proceeding to a cooperative venture in postwar economic planning, except for the IMF, and by having no intention of abandoning Imperial Preference. They broke the export restrictions of September 1941 repeatedly from the end of 1942 onwards and staunchly resisted American demands in the Wheat Talks and over civil aviation rights. They did their best to keep the US out of the Middle East and out of oil concessions there. They stood by Imperial Preference and their sterling arrangements.

Conclusion

The sterling liabilities that the British accumulated were not accepted solely out of a sense of a moral duty not to impose war costs on countries, such as India, which were poor and under-developed; there were also thoughts that imperial and sterling ties could provide a position to bargain from with the US or that, as a final resort, they might provide an alternative to cooperation with the US if her economic policies and demands proved to be unacceptable.

The US was equally suspicious of the postwar intentions of the UK, and as a consequence, the treatment she received under Lend-Lease was very different to that experienced by the Soviet Union and China. They were not subjected to the demands made of and the conditions imposed upon the British mainly because, as Knollenberg pointed out in 1943, neither was a major economic competitor of the US, and also in an ironic way neither were close enough nor friendly enough to be treated as Britain was by the Americans. Lend-Lease was an act of generosity unsurpassed in its magnitude, but the US was determined to get a payment from Britain in terms of commitments to economic policies which were conducive to American interests. This was not entirely selfish, for there was also an element of altruism involved in the sense that many American officials believed that freer trade would be universally beneficial: it was a happy coincidence that the US would be the major benefactor. Thus when Britain showed her reluctance to commit herself to economic policies of a kind desired by the Americans they took steps to ensure that pressures could be brought to bear to change her mind. This kind of thinking was in evidence in the US Treasury, in the OLLA/FEA, and in the State Department from 1942 onwards, and it was one of the motives behind the violent reaction in the FEA and the State Department to the agreement at Quebec which, as Hull said, gave the bait away. The understanding reached there had the potential for strengthening Britain to an extent that would have enabled her to resist the kind of economic policies which members of the State Department and others wanted her to adopt.

By September 1945, partly because the Americans reneged on the Quebec Understanding and partly because both the Ardennes Offensive and the atom-bomb brought about a truncated period for Stage II, the Americans got the bait back again, and this time Clayton was determined that the British should not avoid the hook. As early as 25 June 1945 he

Conclusion

wrote to Vinson that, 'It would be quite unwise...to consider making Britain an outright gift of the required several billion dollars,...It would be unwise even to supply the funds as a credit without laying down conditions that would insure a sound advance towards our post-war objectives'[16].

America's failure to carry out the understanding reached at Quebec, the swift shut-off of Lend-Lease, and the unexpectedly short duration of Stage II left Britain with a current shortfall of $5 billion on her international account and with enormous pressures on sterling because of the accumulation of massive debts to the members of the Sterling Bloc. With reconversion and the re-establishment of her export trade having only just begun, and with a bleak international financial prospect before her Britain could do nothing but appeal to the US for help. During October, November and the early days of December 1945 a team led by Keynes negotiated a dollar loan of $3.75 billion from the Americans in the form of a line of credit that could be drawn on by the British as and when required. The Americans, with Clayton and Vinson working in harmony in a way Hull and Morgenthau had never achieved, insisted on a comprehensive economic, financial and monetary arrangement. It was to be an integrated package in which the Americans were to succeed in achieving most of the economic goals they had sought during the war: the mistakes of Quebec were not to be repeated.

At one point in the talks the Attlee Government was so split over the conditions the Americans were demanding that Dalton, now the Chancellor of the Exchequer, began to think of a speech to announce the breakdown of the talks with the Americans. In the end though, as Attlee later recorded, 'We weren't in a position to bargain' and Britain had more or less to take the loan on whatever conditions the Americans insisted upon[17].

Britain had to agree to ratify the Bretton Woods Agreement and enter the IMF; she had to agree to enter further commercial talks with the US with a view to reducing trade barriers and eliminating Imperial Preference; she had to commit herself to making sterling convertible in 1947, and she had to give up dollar discrimination against the US earlier than was demanded by the IMF[18].

Lend-Lease helped Britain resist Germany, Italy and later Japan, but it made Britain vulnerable to economic demands and interference in her economy by her closest ally which compromised her sovereignty.

Conclusion

In many ways Lend-Lease provides a salutory story of how close friends and relations can argue bitterly without falling out. During the years following the Second World War Anglo-American friendship became important in resisting a new threat to Western Democracy and economic matters were once again subordinated to political and military considerations, as they had been in the war, and many of the conditions of the Anglo-American Financial Agreement were either waived or else simply forgotten: but that, as they say, is another story.

NOTES

1. Report by Keynes and Sinclair, 9 Jan. 1945, WP(45)24; and memo. by Anderson and Lyttleton, 'The Washington Negotiations on Lend-Lease in the First Year of Lend-Lease in Stage II', 2 Feb. 1945, CAB 66.
2. Lee to Harmer, 6 Dec. 1944, T160/1375/F17942/010/6.
3. Reed to Crowley, Currie, Cox and Acheson, 22 Sept. 1944, Hopkins Papers, box 335, folder: England and Lend-Lease Phase II.
4. Stimson Diary, 3 March 1945.
5. See: W. D. Leahy, _I Was There_ (Victor Gollanz, London, 1950), p.435 and 439-41; Series of Articles in Milwaukee Journal based on interviews with Crowley, H. S. Truman Library, Vertical File, folder: Crowley; minutes of conference between Truman and Smith, 26 April 1945, H. S. Truman Library, Smith Papers, box 15, and Smith to Truman 29 June 1945, Truman OF, 356; R. M. Hathaway, _Ambiguous Partnership: Britain and America, 1944-1947_ (Columbia University Press, New York, 1981), p.147; memo. handed by Lyttleton to Hopkins, 27 April, 1945, Hopkins Papers, box 335, folder: England and Lend-Lease Phase II; and telephone conversation between R. B. Reams of the State Department and Morgenthau, 24 May 1945, 841.24/5-2445.
6. Churchill to Truman, 28 May 1945, 841.24/5-2945.
7. Memo. of conversation between Reams and Morgenthau for Matthews, 8 June 1945, 841.24/6-8 45.
8. See: draft letter by Clayton, 29 May 1945, 841.24/5-2945; and Vinson to Byrnes, 13 July 1945, 841.24/7-1345.
9. E. D. Mckin memo. for Truman, 28 May 1945, Truman CF, box 23.

Conclusion

10. Notes on EPC meeting 7 June 1945, Paul Papers, box 2, folder: FEA EPC meetings.
11. Crain to Somervell, 16 June 1945, Hopkins Papers, box 335, folder: England and Lend-Lease Phase II.
12. Truman to Joint Chiefs of Staff, 5 July 1945, Truman CF, box 23; Stimson to Byrnes, 11 July 1945 in *Foreign Relations of the United States 1945, Potsdam Conference Vol.I* (State Department, Washington), p.819.
13. See: conversation between Truman and Churchill 24 July 1945; Truman to Churchill 25 July 1945; Truman to Joint Chiefs of Staff (revised directive) 29 July 1945, all in *Foreign Relations Potsdam Vol. II*, pp.340-42 and 1183.
14. H. S. Truman Library, Oral History, Roger Tubby interviewed by J. N. Hess, Feb. 1970, pp. 8 and 9.
15. See: Clayton to Byrnes, 18 Aug. 1945, in E. F. Dobney, *Selected papers of Will Clayton* (John Hopkins Press, Baltimore, 1971), pp.150-152; Attlee to Truman and his reply 1 and 6 Sept. 1945, 841.24/9-145; and Attlee's thanks forwarded via Acheson to Truman 11 Sept. 1945, 841.24/9-1245.
16. Clayton to Vinson, 25 June 1945, in Dobney, *Selected Papers*, pp.147-149.
17. See: 'Overseas Assets and Liabilities of the UK' prepared by Keynes, 12 Sept. 1945, GEN89/1, UE4260/1094/53, F0371/45699; H. Dalton, *High Tide and After: Memoirs 1945-60* (Frederick Muller, London, 1962), p.84; and F. Williams, *A Prime Minister Remembers* (Heineman, London, 1961), p.134.
18. Cmd.6708, 'Financial Agreement between the Governments of the United States and the United Kingdom', signed in Washington 6 Dec. 1945.

SOURCES

Public Record Office London:
Foreign Office general diplomatic correspondence, F0371.
Treasury records: T160/1418, T160/1375, T160/1105, T160/1243, T160/1244, T160/F17660, and T177/58.
Board of Trade records: BT11/1733, BT11/1734, and BT11/2345.
Cabinet records: CABS 65, 66, 78, 87, and 92.

Command Papers
Cmd.5882, 'Anglo-American Trade Agreement', 1938.
Cmd.6311, 'The Export White Paper', 10 Sept. 1941.
Cmd.6391, 'Principles Applying to Mutual Aid', 23 Feb. 1942.
Cmd.6389, 'Reciprocal Aid Agreement', 3 Sept. 1942.
Cmd.6483, 'Report on Mutual Aid', 11 Nov. 1943.
Cmd.6708, 'Financial Agreement between the Governments of the United States and the United Kingdom', signed in Washington, 6 Dec. 1945.

US National Archives

State Department, Washington, files: 841.24, 840.50, 841.51, 841.5151, 561.311, 611.4131, 740,0011.
OLLA and FEA files, Suitland, Maryland: RG169.

US Library of Congress

B. Long Papers.
W. D. Leahy Papers.

Franklin D. Roosevelt Library

F.D.R. Official File (OF).
F.D.R. President's Secretary's File (PSF).
H. Morgenthau Diary.

Sources

Papers of: A. A. Berle,
          H. H. Hopkins,
          C. Wickard,
          O. Cox,
  and   H. Wallace.

H. S. Truman Library

H.S.T. Official File (OF).
H.S.T. Confidential File (CF).
H.S.T. President's Secretary's File (PSF).
Vertical File.
Papers of: W. L. Clayton,
          H. Stimson,
          S. J. Spingarn,
          A. Paul,
          F. Vinson,
  and   Roger Tubby, oral history.

University of Virginia

E. Stettinius Papers.

Published Primary Sources

House of Commons Debates, *Hansard*.
Congressional Record of the United States.
A Decade of American Foreign Policy, Basic Documents (US Government Printing Office, Washington, 1950).
Foreign Relations of the United States, selected diplomatic documents published by the US State Department; volumes 1939 through to 1946.
B. B. Berle and T. B. Jacobs, *Navigating the Rapids 1918-71, From the Papers of Adolf A. Berle* (Harcourt Brace Jovanovich, New York, 1973).
J. M. Blum, *From the Morgenthau Diaries: Years of War 1941-45* (Houghton Mifflin, Boston, 1967), and, *Roosevelt and Morgenthau: A Revision and Condensation of 'From the Morgenthau Diaries'* (Houghton Mifflin, Boston, 1970).
Sir A. Cairncross, *Anglo-American Economic Collaboration in War and Peace 1942-49: The Papers of Sir Richard Clarke* (Oxford University Press, Oxford, 1982).
D. Dilks, *The Diaries of Sir Alexander Cadogan* (Putnam's, New York, 1972).
E. F. Dobney, *Selected Papers of Will Clayton* (John Hopkins Press, Baltimore 1971).
G. C. Herring and T. M. Campbell, *The Diaries of Edward Stettinius Jr. 1943-46* (Franklin Watts, New York 1975).

Sources

W. F. Kimball, Churchill and Roosevelt: The Complete Correspondence, 3 Vols. (Princeton University Press, New Jersey, 1984).
W. Millis, The Forrestal Diaries (Viking Press, New York, 1951).
H. G. Nicholas, Washington Dispatches 1941-45 (Weidenfeld and Nicolson, London, 1981).
I. S. Rosenman, The Public Papers and Addresses of Franklin D. Roosevelt, 13 Vols. (Harper Row, New York, 1938-50).
A. H. Vandenberg Jr. and J. A. Morris, The Private Papers of Senator Vandenberg (Houghton Mifflin, Boston, 1952).

Secondary Sources

A complete list of secondary sources used in this account may be compiled from the notes at the end of every chapter; however some comments on the most important texts follow:

E. R. Stettinius Lend-Lease: Weapon for Victory (Macmillan, New York, 1944). This tells a rather factual story of aid to Britain from 'cash and carry' up to the autumn of 1943 when Stettinius became Undersecretary of State. It has a definite propaganda purpose and omits virtually any reference to Anglo-US disagreements.
The British Official History of the Second World War, Civil Series: E. L. Hargreaves and M. M. Gowing, Civil Industry and Trade; W. K. Hancock and M. M. Gowing, British War Economy; R. S. Sayers, Financial Policy 1939-45; H. Duncan Hall, North American Supply; R. J. Hammond, Food Vol. I; and J. Hurstfield, The Control of Raw Materials (Longman Green and HMSO, London, 1949-56). On the whole these are excellent accounts though a little compartmentalised at times, and of course they were written without any American sources.
R. N. Gardner, Sterling Dollar Diplomacy in Current Perspective: The Origins and the Prospects of Our International Economic Order (Columbia University Press, New York, 1980). This was first published by OUP in 1956, and was thus written before government documents became available for research. The 1980 re-issue contains no new significant historical sources. It is an able book, nevertheless, and covers quite a lot of the ground to do with Lend-Lease as well as the IMF and the ITO and the US/UK Loan Agreement of 1945/46.

Sources

J. J. Dougherty, *The Politics of Wartime Aid: American Economic Assistance to France and French Northwest Africa 1940-46* (Greenwood Press, 1978). This is an interesting account of Lend-Lease Aid to France during the war and includes much useful information about both how OLLA/FEA field operations and the central organisations worked.

W. F. Kimball, *The Most Unsordid Act: Lend-Lease 1939-41* (John Hopkins Press, Baltimore, 1969); 'Lend-Lease and the Open Door: the Temptation of British Opulence, 1937-42', *Political Science Quarterly* 1971, Vol.86, pp.232-259; 'Beggar My Neighbor: America and the British Interim Finance Crisis 1940-41', *Journal of Economic History* 1969, Vol.29, pp.758-772. Kimball provides a good account of the circumstances, origins and passage of the Lend-Lease Act.

G. Herring, 'Lend-Lease to Russia and the Origin of the Cold War 1944-45', *Journal of American History*, 1969, Vol.56, pp.93-114; 'Experiment in Foreign Aid: Lend-Lease 1941-45', unpublished Ph.D. thesis, University of Virginia. The latter is a useful account of Lend-Lease based upon the F.R.U.S. series and the Stettinius Papers.

R. M. Hathaway, *Ambiguous Partnership: Britain and America 1944-47* (Columbia University Press, New York, 1981). This is good on the Quebec II Conference and the later stages of the war.

D. Reynolds, *The Creation of the Anglo-American Alliance 1937-41* (Europa, London, 1981). This has useful information about both the 'interim finance crisis' and the early days of Lend-Lease.

R. G. D. Allen, 'Mutual Aid Between the US and the British Empire', *Journal of the Royal Statistical Society* 1946, Vol.109, pp.243-271. This contains a statistical breakdown of Lend-Lease and Reciprocal Aid.

C. Thorne, *Allies of a Kind: The United States, Britain and the War Against Japan 1941-45* (Hamish Hamilton, London, 1978). This has interesting sections on Lend-Lease policy as it was affected by Britain's role in the Far East.

L. Martel, *Lend-Lease Loans, and the Coming of the Cold War* (Westview Press, Colorado, 1979).

W. H. McNeill, *Survey of International Affairs, 1939-46: America, Britain and Russia - Their Co-operation and Conflict 1941-46* (OUP, London, 1953).

R. H. Dawson, *The Decision To Aid Russia 1941* (Chapel Hill, North Carolina, 1959).

Sources

G. Kolko, *The Politics of War: The World and United States Foreign Policy 1943-45* (Vintage Books, New York, 1968).
L. Gardner, *Economic Aspects of New Deal Diplomacy* (Beacon Press, Boston, 1964). These last two books provided my introduction to the politics of economic policy-making when I was an undergraduate, and, while they are written from a fairly obvious political stance, they are nevertheless good reading.

There are other books and articles that deal with Lend-Lease to Britain in one guise or another but this is, I think, an adequate introductory reading list. Some readers, however, may wish to consult some of my articles which appeared before this book and which go into more detail on specific issues. A. P. Dobson, 'Economic Diplomacy At The Atlantic Conference', *Review of International Studies*, 1984, Vol.10, pp.143-165; 'The Other Air Battle: The American Pursuit of Post-war Civil Aviation Rights', *The Historical Journal*, 1985, Vol.28, pp.429-439; 'A Mess of Pottage for Your Economic Birthright? The 1941-42 Wheat Negotiations and Anglo-American Economic Diplomacy', *ibid* pp.739-750; 'The Export White Paper, 10 September 1941, *Economic History Review*, February 1986.

INDEX

Acheson,D. 7,22,149; consideration 43,45,47, 49,51-6,62,66,94-101, 103-4,108,112-7; exports 150-2,206,209; Reciprocal Aid and reserves 134-6,139, 142,144,147,148, 150-2,161-3,166,168, 170,172,186,201
agricultural policy 4,9, 17,78-80,173,174,188
Amery,L. 3,6,8,9,37-38, 47,84,85,87,111,113, 173
Anderson,J. 8-9,174, 177-9,185,203; exports 198,207; Reciprocal Aid and reserves 152,164, 170-1,203; Stage II 185-186,198,202,207, 216-7
Anglo-American Committee on Stage II: see Lend-Lease Stage II
Anglo-American Economic Commission 46-48,53, 94
Anglo-American Financial Agreement 226-7
Appleby,P. 81-2,84,100
appropriations: see Congress
Arcadia Conference 104, 107-8,111-2,132

Ardennes Offensive 218, 225
Argentina 80,170,173,188, 202,206-8
article seven: see consideration
Athlone,Lord 22
Atlantic Charter 57, 69-77,87,98,109,114, 119; point four 64, 70-78,84-6,93,96; point five 73-4,86
Atlantic Conference 54, 62-75,84,93
atom bomb 189,199,218, 222,225
Attlee,C. 73-4,84,176, 222,226; letter to Truman 223
Australia 80,100,160
aviation 40,170,173,188, 202,206,208,224
Axis 2,64,224

balance of payments 10, 24-5,51,75,78-9,102, 186,226
Beale,S. 138,175
Beaverbrook,M. 9,26-7, 173,202
Belgian Government 127
Bell,D. 6,44,45,139,161, 170
Berle,A. 6,41-3,53,62, 66,96
Bernstein,E. 6,147

234

Index

Beveridge Report 174
Board of Economic
 Warfare 139
Board of Trade 8,18-19,
 36-7,39,67,86,95,
 101,137-8,143,203,
 205
Boothby,R. 202
Borah,Senator 15
Brand,R. 177,179,186-7,
 192,205,219
Bretton Woods 12,176,
 202,226; see also
 IMF
Britain,British Empire
 and British Govern-
 ment 1-12,17,22-3,
 41,54,56,79,82,85,
 97,101,115,127,139,
 142,145,161-2,165,
 177,179,185,194,
 198,206,208-9,211,
 216-9,221-3,226;
 see also Cabinet,
 under government
 departments and
 ministers' names,
 Dominions
Bruce,Australian High
 Commissioner 107
Burns,J. 41; letters
 131
Byrnes,J. 219

Cabinet: UK 8,27,70,
 73-5,77,81,84,94,
 97,108,110,113-6,
 146,152,173,177,
 188,216; US 21,
 24,56,112,133,163,
 169,194,201,204,
 208,217; US Dollar
 Committee 139,140,
 161
Cadogan,A. 68-9,71-3,
 93,113
Cairo Conference 166,
 169-71
Campbell,R. 79,179,
 187,189

Canada 80
capitalism 3,5-8
cash and carry 15,16,24,
 30-1
Catto,Lord 86
Chalkley,O. 133
Chamberlain,N. 20,65
Cherwell,Lord 8,68,95,
 165-6,190,194-6,199
Chesterfield,Lord 99,106
China 150,225
Churchill,W. 20,23,35,
 47,85,94-5,102,104,
 106,113,119,152,173-4,
 177-80,188,222-3;
 Atlantic Conference
 57,62-77; consider-
 ation 52,84-5,87,
 107-8,111-2,115-8,
 188; German pacific-
 ation 194-5; letters
 to Roosevelt 14,20-1,
 25,27,80,83,100,115,
 118,128,171-2,174,
 190; letters to
 Truman 219-20; Quebec
 Conference 190-7;
 Reciprocal Aid and
 reserves 128,141,153,
 165-7,169-71; Stage
 II 190,194,196-8,202,
 205,209-10,219-20,222
Clayton,W. 218-23,225
Cochran,M. 128
Cohen,B. 22
Colonial Office 86
Combined Exporting and
 Marketing Committee
 133,137
Combined Munitions
 Assignment Board 188,
 219,221
Combined Production and
 Resources Board 133,
 188
Combined US/UK Lend-
 Lease Committee: see
 Lend-Lease Stage II
Committee on Postwar
 External Economic

Index

Policy and Anglo-American Cooperation 78,82
Commonwealth 11
Congress 4,11,14-5, 22,24-5,29-30,35, 43,47,76,98-9, 101,112,128,130, 136,139,141,147-9,152-3,161-4, 170,178,200-1, 204,208,219,222
Conservative Party 9, 77-8,93,116,202
consideration 11, 35-6,39-57,73-8, 81,84-8,93-120, 132,174,209; Churchill 52, 84-5,87,107-8, 111-2,115,118; Roosevelt 46-9, 52-4,95,97,111, 114-5,117-9; State Department 41-4,46,55,66,73, 88,94,97,104,174, 189,206; UK Treasury 47-50,57, 87,99-100,102-5, 108-9; US Treasury 40,44-6
Cooper,D. 67
Corn Laws 2,78
Cox,O. 6,29,40,46, 130-1,136,139,141, 147,149-50,161-2, 164-5,178,201-2, 206,211,216
Cranborne,Lord 9,38, 84-5,111,113
Crain,General 221
Crowley,L. 7,11,149-50, 163,178,219; end of Lend-Lease 222-3; Reciprocal Aid and reserves 159-61, 164-72,174,201; Stage II 187,201-2, 206,208-9,211,216, 218-9,221-2

Currie,L. 159,161-2,164, 201,207,216,220

Daish,T. 86
Dalton,H. 9,84,143,146, 152-3,159,174-6,202, 207,226
D-day 11
D'Arcy Cooper 18
Dawes Plan 5
Debt Default Act 5,17,24
Democratic Party 76,163, 178
Denby,C. 7,141-2,147, 150,161,178-80
Department of Agriculture 79-82,101
Department of Commerce 149,218
Destroyers Deal 20-24
discrimination 3,16,43, 45,55-6,68-9,73-4, 77,85,87,93-6,98-9, 102,107-9,116-7,119, 226; see also Imperial Preference, sterling
dollar 6,15-6,20,224, 134; balances: see reserves; liabilities 48,129,178,185; loans 24,28,134,185,188,226
Dominions 37-8,50,70-1, 77,97,103,107,110, 113,115-6,134,146,153
Duncan,A. 51,74,84,131
Dunkirk 19

Eady,W. 176
Eastern Hemisphere concession 132-3, 137-8,143,145
Economic Section of War Cabinet Secretariat 8,67,95,120
Eden,A. 37-8,47-8,51, 64-5,75,77,83-4,113-5, 146,174
elections 9,18-9,24,148, 177,180,190,199,206, 222

Index

Evans,R. 82
Executive Committee on Commercial Policy 17-19
Executive Policy Committee: see FEA
Export White Paper: see exports
exports 11,16-7,20, 31,36,126-7,130-2, 136-8,143-4,146, 151,159,173,175-8, 187,191,197-8,200, 202,224,226; Export White Paper 10,130-133,137-8,143-6, 149,151,153,162, 169,174-5,205,210, 216,224; Stage II 177,197,203,205-7, 209-10,216,225; supersession of Export White Paper 143,160,174-8

Feis,H. 17,94,96-7,116, 144
five senators 150
Foley,E. 6,29,41,44-5
Foreign Economic Administration 7,11,149, 151,170,225; exports 153,175-7,187,206-7, 210,216; Reciprocal Aid and reserves 150, 152-4,159-60,162-3, 165-9,172,174,185, 187; Stage II 187, 189,191,198,201,203, 205-7,210,217-18, 221
Foreign Office 56,82, 86-7,95,103-4,108-9, 113,140; North American Department 67,95,100; see also Eden,Law,Ronald
Forrestal,J. 191,193, 201
France 14-5,19-21,24-6, 161,171,179,192-3,195

Free French 140
free trade 2-4,7-8,11,41, 43,56,67,70,81,106, 166,167,173,178,180, 188,193,200,202,209, 224-5

Garner,J. 15
Germany 10,14-5,17,19, 20-1,62-3,115,179,185, 204,206,218,222-3, 226; Committee 193-4, 197; pacification 186-7,190-1,193-6, 199,201; see also Second Quebec Conference
GI pay 136,141,169
Grady,H. 17-8
Great War 5,15,24
Greenwood,A. 9,38,75,78, 81,84-5,87,93,103-5, 108,110-11,113
Greenwood Committee: see Greenwood

Halifax,Lord 37-9,47-9, 51,53,54,56,65,68, 93-5,103,106-8,110-3, 116,148,164,168, 170-2,176,178,185
Hall,N. 108
Harriman,A. 68,137,143
Hawkins,H. 18,36-7,50-1, 53-4,56,62,94-6,101, 114,218
Hawley-Smoot Act 3
Hickerson,J. 94,108,207
Hiroshima 222
Hitler,A. 20,21,25,63, 189
Hopkins,H. 40,42,46,62-3, 66,117,128,130,141, 150,153,161,166,180, 193-4; Atlantic Conference 68,70,71; Stage II 174,177,179, 187,189-92,204,219
Hopkins,R. 49,86
House of Commons: see Parliament

237

Index

Hudson,R. 9,78,81,105, 173
Hull,C. 3-5,7,11,19, 29,35,39,75-7,79, 81,85,97,100,106, 119-20,160,178, 192,207; consideration 42,45,51,54, 93,95,103-4,107, 112,114,116,188; criticisms of UK 16,18; economic faith 16-7,37-8, 43,64,106,191, 193; exports 145; Germany Committee 193-4,197; Reciprocal Aid and reserves 139,163, 166-7,177; Stage II 187-9,192,198, 201-1,225

Ickes,H. 21
Imperial Preference 2-4,9,36,44-5,48, 51-2,55,67-8,70-1, 75-7,86,95-6,98-9, 103,108-18,173-4, 178,188,224,226
imperialists 3,9, 26-7,37-8,47,84-6, 93-5,98-9,202
India 127-8,135,146, 160,225
interim finance crisis 28-9,128
International Clearing Union 110
International Monetary Fund 1,8,12,142, 170,173-4,176,202, 224,226
inter-war 2-7,42
isolationism 15,17,19, 22-4,161
Italy 21,223,226

Jackson,R. 32
Japan 14,21,43,63,75, 97,102,118,179,188, 190,192,197,201,217, 221-2,226
Johnson,H. 5
Jones,J. 28,127,149

Kennedy,J. 20
Keynes,J. 38,50-1,65,95, 109-10,149,226; consideration 42,44,49-50,52-7,66,74,81, 85-6,94; IMF 8,142, 173,176; Reciprocal Aid and reserves 128-9,152,161,168-9; Stage II 187,201-2, 204-8,210,216,217
King, Admiral 192
King,M. 22
Knollenberg,B. 7,141, 149-50,225
Knox,F. 19,21

Labour Party 9,85,93, 173,202
laissez faire 3-4,75,106
Landis: see marginal theory
Latin America 16,24,96, 130,132,139; see also Argentina
Law,R. 8,95,104,108-9, 152-3,177; Mission 152,173-4
Leahy,W. 191-3,201,208, 217,221-2
Lee,F. 40,179-80,216-7
Lend-Lease 1-2,10,12,23, 25,28-9,31,35-6,40-1, 43,86,96,101,111-3, 115,119-20,126-31, 134-8,142-50,153,159, 161-4,169,171-2,175, 177-80,186,192,203, 207,224,227; end 222-3,226; OLLA 97, 130-1,137-8,141-6, 149,225; pre-Lend-Lease contracts 30, 118,128-9,135,139, 203; reductions 136, 140,149-50,152,154,

Index

160,164-9,171,176, 219,222; Stage II 174,176-8,185-93, 195-211,216-22; White Paper Committee 138,143; see also consideration, Crowley, Export White Paper, FEA, marginal theory, Second Quebec Conference, Stettinius
Leith-Ross,F. 8,81-2, 84,105
Lenin,V. 16
Liberals 93
liberal world economy: see free trade, postwar economic policy
Llewellin,J. 145,151, 207
London Economic Conference 5-6
Long,B. 82-3,93,112, 133,198
Lord President's Committee 176
Lothian,Lord 21-2,24, 37
Lubin,I. 189
Lyttleton,O. 18,190, 216,219
marginal theory 147, 159-60,169,174, 176-7,191,198
McCloy,J. 194,198,201, 222
McKin,E. 221
Middle East 135,188, 224
Morgenthau,H. 6,7,11, 18,24-6,28-30,35, 40-6,114-5,129, 136,163,178,191; plan for Germany 186,193-9,201; Reciprocal Aid and reserves 128, 139-42,146-8,152, 159,161-2,164-74,177, 201,203; Stage II 174, 177,186-7,189-90,192, 196,198,200-1,203, 205,207-8,217,219-21
most favoured nation principle 65
Moyne,Lord 38,84
Murphy,R. 140
Mutual Aid Agreement 10-11,66-9,93-100, 106-120,152,166,174, 188,206,224

Nagasaki 222
Neutrality Law 5,14-5,97, 129
New Deal 41,63,76,79,139, 148,163
Nicolson,H. 67
non-discrimination 64, 70-2,75,207,226; see also consideration, Imperial Preference
North Africa 62,140,161, 174-5,224

oil 170,173,188,202,224
Opie,R. 52-3,93-5,144, 147,177
Orchard,J. 188,199
Organisation for Economic Warfare 149
Ottawa Conference and Agreements 2-3; see also Imperial Preference

Parliament 115,119,146, 168,174,207
Pasvolsky,L. 64-5,106, 109-10
Patterson,R. 201,204
Penrose,E. 105
Phillips,F. 18,24,28,39, 51,108,128,133,140, 142,144-5,147,150
pooling resources 11,103, 111,132-3,144,145,147, 149,160,162,166,168
postwar economy 3,7,36-7,

39,41-9,55,62,64,
75,101,115,119,
127,143-4,152,
164,167,173,178,
180,188,218,224,
226; see also
consideration,
exports, Stage II
Potsdam Conference 222
pragmatists 3,8
protectionism 3-5,70;
see also Imperial
Preference, tariffs
Purvis,A. 128,130,132

Quebec: see Second
Quebec Conference

Reciprocal Aid 1,49,
127,130,133-8,
140-3,146-53,
159-61,176
Reciprocal Trade
Agreements Act 4
Reconstruction Finance
Corporation 28-9,
127,129
reconversion 11,126,
152,177-9,185-7,
189,191-2,201,
203-4,206,208,217,
219,224,226
Republican Party 19,37
reserves: British 7,11,
31,45,126-9,134,136,
138-54,160-73,185-6,
224; Stage II 201-4,
216-7,220,222
Reverse Lend-Lease: see
Reciprocal Aid
revisionist historians
5
Robbins,L. 120
Ronald,N. 8,44,82-3,86,
93,96,104,106,118,
169
Roosevelt,E. 66
Roosevelt,F. 14-5,17-20,
23,25-6,28-9,40-3,
45-6,65,79,104,107,
127,129-30,136,143,
148,150,163,172,
178-80,186,207,218;
Atlantic Conference
57,62-76; British
exports 197; consider-
ation 46-9,52-4,95,
97,108,111-2,114-5,
117-9,188; German
pacification 193-5,
199; letters to
Churchill 22,66,100,
114,117-8,170-2,174,
208; Quebec Confer-
ence 190-7; Recip-
rocal Aid and
reserves 140-1,153,
161-7,169-71; Stage
II 179,187,190,192,
194,196-8,202,205-10,
217-9,222
Roosevelt,K. 166-7
Rublee,G. 22
Ruhr 194

Salter,A. 100-1,105
'S' Branch 8, 95
Schacht,H. 66
Scheuer,S. 175
Second Quebec Conference
179-80,185-202,225-6;
Germany 186,193-6;
Stage II 185-202,
217-22
Second World War 1,17,
227
secret agreements 63-6
Senate Committee to
Investigate the
National Defense
Program 162
Shackle,R. 37
Sherwood,R. 25,117
Shirer-Hyde Report 138
Sinclair,A. 113
Sinclair,R. 201,204
Smith,B. 168
Smith,H. 30,128,219
Somervell,General 191-2,
201,217,221

Index

South African gold 26-7, 127
Soviet Union 17,63,83, 100,102,105,133,150, 162,166,171,193, 204-5,224-5
Spingarn,S. 29
Stalin,J. 222
Stanley,O. 16-7
State Department 3-4, 6-7,17-8,28,41-4, 46,53-5,62,65-7,73, 78,82,88,94,97,102, 104-6,111,114,116-7, 119-20,132,140,143-4, 173-4,180,187,191, 199,225; exports 143-5,151,160,187, 206; Reciprocal Aid and reserves 129, 134,142,146-7,149. 151-3,159,162-3, 165-7,172; Stage II 187-91,198-201, 206-8,217,220
Steere,L. 81-2
sterling 4-6,16,31,126, 224,226; Area 119, 134,136,139,141,146, 169,186,207,226; debts and liabilities 127,135-6,140,146, 163,166,203,225
Stettinius,E. 7,19, 149-50,178,185,219; exports 132,138,143, 145,175,177,209-10; Reciprocal Aid and reserves 137,139, 141-2,144,146-8, 152-3,161,163-7, 170,177,186; Stage II 174,176-7,185, 200,209-10
Stevens,R. 143; Committee 143,145,149
Stimson,H. 19,21,139, 194-8,201,204,208, 218
Stirling,J. 36-7,39,51, 175

Supplementary Trade Talks, 18,31,35-9,43,47,50-2, 54,73,79,95
supply 14-31; see also Lend-Lease

tariffs 3-4,36,38,51,57, 71,77,95,98-9,107, 109,119,174; see also Imperial Preference
Teheran Conference 166
Thatcher,T. 22
Truman,H. 142,162,219; letter to Attlee 223; Stage II 219-22
Tubby,R. 223

U-boats 14,20-1,31,78
UK Treasury 24-5,39, 47-50,57,78-9,86-7, 99-100,102-5,108-9, 131,179,185,198; exports 175; Reciprocal Aid and reserves 128,135,142,164; see also Anderson, Keynes, Wood
US and US Government 1-12,17,19,23,31,38,54, 103,112,115,138,141, 160,186,202,207,216, 222,224,226; see also Cabinet, under departments and secretaries
US Army 209,217,219,221
US Chiefs of Staff 68, 192,217
US service departments 30,99,185,190,192, 201,206
US Treasury 6-7,11,25-6, 35,40-6,129,151,172, 193,219,225; exports 143,206; Reciprocal Aid and reserves 126, 128,134-5,140,146-8, 150,152-4,159,161-3, 165-8; Stage II 191, 217; see also Morgenthau, Vinson, White

Index

US War Department 129, 144,201,218,220-1

Vandenberg,A. 15,178
VE-day 133,178,189, 206-7,210,219
Versailles Settlement 5,65
Viner,J. 44-5,126
Vinson,F. 219,221,226
Viscose Corporation 29, 31

Wadsworth,Representative 178
Waley,D. 49,149,161,164, 170-1
Wallace,H. 4,7,79-80,114, 139
war production 11,19-20, 30-1,126,185,217,224; see also reconversion
Welles,S. 47,53,94,114, 116-7,149; Atlantic Conference 62,64,66, 68-74
wheat 7,9,75,78-9,101; Talks 80-5,97,100-6, 224
White,H. 6,28,44-5,194, 196,203,210; Dollar Committee 139-40; Reciprocal Aid and reserves 130,134-6, 142-4,147,150,161-2, 164-5
Whitehead,T. 101
Whitney,H. 7,138,143, 145-6,153,174-5,177
Wilson,W. 5,15,42
Wickard,C. 4,7,80,193
Winant,J. 67,77,81,83-5, 93-4,97,102-7,111, 114,116,130-1,188
Wood,K. 8-9,38,51,74,81, 107,130-1,152; consideration 47-50, 52,57,75,77,84,94, 100,103-5,111,113, 114; Reciprocal Aid and reserves 128,140, 146,148

Young,P. 149
Young Plan 5
Yugoslavia 65

For Product Safety Concerns and Information please contact our EU representative GPSR@taylorandfrancis.com
Taylor & Francis Verlag GmbH, Kaufingerstraße 24, 80331 München, Germany

www.ingramcontent.com/pod-product-compliance
Lightning Source LLC
Chambersburg PA
CBHW070600300426
44113CB00010B/1338